SECRETS OF THE
GREAT GOLF COURSE
ARCHITECTS

SECRETS OF THE
GREAT GOLF COURSE ARCHITECTS

*The Creation of the WORLD'S GREATEST GOLF COURSES
in the Words and Images of History's Master Designers*

MICHAEL PATRICK SHIELS

and the American Society of Golf Course Architects

SKYHORSE PUBLISHING, INC.

Skyhorse Publishing books may be purchased in bulk at special discounts for sales promotion, corporate gifts, fund-raising, or educational purposes. Special editions can also be created to specifications. For details, contact the Special Sales Department, Skyhorse Publishing, 307 West 36th Street, 11th Floor, New York, NY 10018 or info@skyhorsepublishing.com.

Skyhorse® and Skyhorse Publishing® are registered trademarks of Skyhorse Publishing, Inc.®, a Delaware corporation.

Visit our website at www.skyhorsepublishing.com.

10 9 8 7 6 5 4 3 2 1

Library of Congress Cataloging-in-Publication Data is available on file.

Cover photo credit ASGCA

Print ISBN: 978-1-62914-468-9

Printed in China

This book is dedicated to the memory of Bruce Borland, *ASGCA*—our friend and colleague whose career was cut much too short while on a golf course site exploration mission with golfer Payne Stewart in October, 1999.

CONTENTS

INTRODUCTION

As an author, I have the good fortune to venture vicariously through the lives of my varied subjects and shadow my compelling collaborators. I get to see the world though their eyes, endure their failures, and experience their triumphs through their words and memories.

Chronicling the recollections of golf's greatest architects to write this book has taken me on a virtual journey through the mountains and valleys; beaches, lakes, and streams; pine forests and pine barrens; meadows and plains; and landscapes and landfills that would become beloved and beguiling golf courses in lands far and near.

The architects have dressed me in Wellington boots, put me on 'dozers, allowed me to peek at their drawing tables, let me sit in on client meetings in their boardrooms, and, most blessedly of all, put a golf club in my hands—indeed, put golf clubs in all of our hands!

You can come along too in these pages … architect after architect … course after course … secret after secret.

—Michael Patrick Shiels

The architects have dressed me in Wellington boots, put me on 'dozers, allowed me to peek at their drawing tables, let me sit in on client meetings in their boardrooms, and, most blessedly of all, put a golf club in my hands.

Located in the southwest of Ireland, Ron Kirby's magnificent Old Head Golf Links
is a seamless example of the perfect marriage between golf and nature.

WELCOME

"Ah, the glamorous life of a golf course architect!"

That's a line that I have shared with my colleagues in instances when we are fighting our way through a sea of cobwebs and biting flies in a virgin forest, or up to our knees in heavy, sticky mud on a rain-drenched construction site. The life of a golf course architect is one that can vary greatly from day to day.

Some days are glamorous—like getting to ride in the gold-trimmed helicopter formerly owned by the son of the Sultan of Brunei.

Some days are mundane—like driving four hours from Toledo to Pittsburgh to meet for two hours to discuss the placement of a few trees and then driving the four hours back home.

Some days are scary—like being robbed of everything in your possession, including your passport, outside Budapest, Hungary.

The day in Budapest was the adventure that was the inspiration for this book. It was a day to remember. After I told the story to others, they would usually tell me that I should write a book about the experience. I reasoned that others in our profession must have equally enthralling stories that they tell to their families and friends. I wondered what had been the most incredible days in their architectural careers. Those were stories that needed to be told.

Please enjoy this collection of tales from our members. Golf course architecture is a most rewarding profession. It has its demands, but the benefits are pretty amazing sometimes. It's true that there are scary, mundane, and glamorous days, but it's the rewarding ones that we remember most—like when members praise a design at a grand opening or professionals battle it out on a finishing stretch of holes in an important tournament. Whatever kind of day they're having, golf course architects are trying to create beautiful playing fields on which people can get away from the pressures of everyday life and enjoy the great game of golf.

—Steve Forrest, ASGCA
2007-2008 President,
American Society of Golf Course Architects

Jason Straka's 3rd hole at Georgian Bay in Ontario, Canada

CHAPTER 1
HORSES FOR COURSES

PAUL ALBANESE

#18 Lawsonia
William Langford Original

Albanese has redesigned classic William Langford holes.

Paul Albanese captained the Cornell University golf team before earning a master's in landscape architecture at Harvard. During his tenure at Harvard, Paul received a prestigious Penny White grant for travel to Scotland to study classic precedents in golf architecture, as well as how the golf landscapes of Scotland function as vital components of its society. Paul is also the director of Golf Course Architecture at the Edinburgh College of Art in Scotland. After working with Michigan golf architect Jerry Matthews, he partnered with Chris Lutzke, a Pete Dye disciple, to found Albanese & Lutzke. He's worked on the following golf course designs: Timberstone Golf Course in Iron Mountain, Michigan; Mill Creek Golf Club in Rochester, New York; Quail Ridge Golf Course in Ada, Michigan; the Traditions Golf Club in Edmond, Oklahoma; Cana Hills Golf Club in the Dominican Republic; and the Equestrian Club in Marrakech, Morocco.

I was excited to work on the restoration of the bunkers at Christiana Creek Country Club in Elkhart, Indiana. This was a Golden Age William Langford design, and our goal was to authentically restore the bunkers in his style.

During the process, the construction managers, shapers, and I were discussing the forms of the bunkers.

"Back in the day," I explained, "the original bunkers were built using horses."

My construction manager quipped, "If we want to be authentic, that's how we should do it!"

The room was full of chuckles.

"No, really," he maintained. "I can find some horses to do the work."

"Let's do it," I agreed.

And we did.

Even though the idea was tongue-in-cheek, the actual process of constructing a couple of bunkers with horses was an eye-opening experience. It truly gave me an appreciation for how the old architects from the Golden Age were able to create the unique and interesting forms of that era.

This was a Golden Age William Langford design, and our goal was to authentically restore the bunkers in his style.

CHAPTER 2
BULL FIGHTING

BILL AMICK

Traditional courses send players out and bring them back in as displayed by holes 10 and 18.

Bill Amick earned his degree in turfgrass management under a USGA Green Section Grant before he entered the U.S. Air Force, where he supervised the maintenance and operation of the base golf course. Amick opened his own practice in 1959. He was elected president of the American Society of Golf Course Architects in 1977, and has since been named a fellow in the ASGCA. Amick now specializes in smaller, less expensive golf courses such as nine-hole, executive, and par-3 courses, which appeal to developers because of the reduced land requirements, water usage, and environmental impact. These courses also appeal to juniors, beginners, people with disabilities, and those who appreciate faster play. Some of his works include Halifax Plantation Golf Club in Ormond Beach, Florida; Vineyards Country Club's south course in Naples, Florida; Sky Meadow Country Club in Nashua, New Hampshire; and Gut Heckenhof Golf and Country Club in Germany.

Early in my career, I was designing a new course near Tallahassee, Florida, and I went on a walking tour of the property with the housing and course developer and several other men. The property had massive live oak trees scattered across rolling hills, which provided an ideal setting for laying out an attractive golf course. The eventual result would be three interchangeable nine-hole loops radiating from and returning to a clubhouse atop a prominent hill near the center of the property.

As we ambled along, we spotted a large bull in the far corner of the field. When we got closer, the animal began snorting and pawing the ground vigorously. It was obvious that we'd bothered him by invading his territory.

"Don't worry, everyone. That bull is all show," the developer assured the group.

Since I had been raised on a farm, I was a bit wary, so I stayed at the far end of the group of walkers. I rationalized that at least the raging bull would have to gore seven or eight others before it could get to me!

Fortunately, no one was attacked that day, but we did learn later that a week after our walk, that same bull seriously injured a farmhand. I still contend that being a coward is not a bad thing entirely for a golf course architect!

Since then, Killearn Country Club has hosted twenty-one PGA Tour Tallahassee Opens and four LPGA Tour events. The developer sold all the houses surrounding that course at a nice profit, and a lot of golfers have enjoyed their rounds on that course.

And that's no bull.

I still contend that being a coward is not a bad thing entirely for a golf course architect!

CHAPTER 3
THE BEAR NECESSITIES

IAN ANDREW

Ian Andrew of Golf Design Inc. is a golf course architect based in Brantford, Ontario, Canada. Andrew is a graduate of the landscape architecture program at Guelph University and began his golf course architecture career with fellow Canadian Doug Carrick. His design portfolio includes Ontario layouts at Ballantrae Golf & Country Club in Aurora, Copper Creek Golf Club in Klienburg, Osprey Valley (Hoot and Toot Courses) in Alton and a nine-hole addition at Nobleton Oaks in Nobleton.

My final project with Carrick Design was Muskoka Bay. The golf course was carved out of 250 acres of bush and rock with the holes strung out over eleven kilometers. The surveyor laid in centerlines for the holes by clearing a five-meter-wide opening from tee to green. The opening revealed something unexpected: a bear.

The next stage was for Doug Carrick and me to go out and flag out the trees destined for removal and the trees to be preserved. The tree cutters established paths between holes for access, and once again our new friend, the bear, was sighted on one of the paths.

After a while the bear found the lunch coolers kept by the tree cutters and enjoyed a delicious meal. In response, the crew tied their coolers in the trees, so after a while the frustrated bear approached the cutters looking for food. We now had a serious problem.

One of the site supervisors had had enough and took to carrying a shotgun to scare the bear away from the site. The skidder team and cutters worked closer together since the bear didn't like the skidders—food or no food—but there was concern for the individuals walking the trails on the site.

The joke on the site was that it was best to walk in pairs with someone you could outrun—or, if you were the slow one, the trick was to trip the other guy first and then run away.

I carried a shotgun with me for nearly a year—particularly during the times that I was out there by myself. There was nothing more nerve-wracking than the couple of times that I could clearly smell the bear nearby. Imagine your heart beating a hundred beats a minute, while you're unable to get reception on your mobile phone! I began wondering why I chose this line of work.

It would be a perfect ending to say I now sit in front of my fireplace with my feet resting on a bearskin rug, but the truth is that someone else ended up having to kill our bear after it began venturing into town looking for easy food.

CHAPTER 4
THAT DAMNED YANKEE

BRIAN AULT

Brian Ault, ASGCA past president, has been recognized on numerous occasions by *Golf Digest* magazine for outstanding courses, including Wyncote Golf Club in Oxford, Pennsylvania, which was voted third-best new public course in America in 1993. Some of his other projects include the River Creek Club in Leesburg, Virginia; and Rehoboth Beach Country Club in Wilmington, Delaware. He currently serves as co-president of Ault, Clark & Associates, Ltd. in Kensington, Maryland.

Eighteen years ago, I was working on a very complicated course just outside of Dallas, Texas. The site was in Irving, just down the street from Cowboy Stadium. Since I was from Maryland, I was quite the oddity in Dallas. With my northern accent, I couldn't even pronounce the word "pecan" correctly.

Pecans are what really got me into trouble.

The complicated course was on a river, with two or three easements for underground oil pipelines and two sets of overhead electrical power lines. Some of the site was a floodplain and some was landfill. It was a mess. The Corps of Engineers discovered that some of the landfill had been filled too high and had to be lowered by readjusting the garbage.

We started redeveloping the site by creating a plan that showed how we could adjust the garbage and make the ground ready for golf holes. Most people have seen an active landfill, with bulldozers pushing trash into a ravine and cover-ing it up. But, can you imagine what it was like when we basically had to dig all of that garbage back up? The bulldozer operators, and anyone else who got within a quarter mile of the site, had to wear gas masks. It wasn't a pretty sight—or smell—but we got it done.

Then, during the initial walkthrough of the proposed holes, when we reached the area for the proposed eighteenth hole, we found a grove of pecan trees.

"We're going to cut all of these trees down to make way for the eighteenth hole," I told the assistant director of parks, Bill Thompson, with certainty.

I didn't realize my Yankee mistake until I saw the look on Thompson's face.

Not only had I mispronounced the word "pecan," but I also failed to realize that the pecan tree is the official Texas state tree!

Needless to say, I had to come up with a new plan that saved the trees.

CHAPTER 5
CLIENT CAPERS

RICHARD BARIL

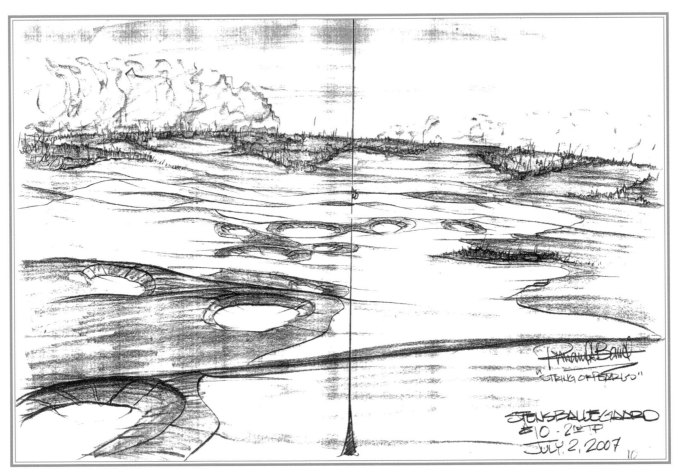

Hole 10 at Stensballegaard Golf Club in Denmark.

Richard Baril is a senior partner with von Hagge, Smelek, & Baril, the Texas-based firm he joined in 1982. When von Hagge, Smelek & Baril ventured into the European market, Rick was designated project architect for that theater. As such he has been instrumental in the design of world-renowned golf courses in France, Spain, Italy, Denmark, and Morocco. His works include Red Tail Golf Club in Avon, Ohio; Houston National in Houston, Texas; El Tigre in Paradise Village Country Club, Puerto Vallarta, Mexico; White Witch in Montego Bay; Rose Hall, Jamaica; and Real Sociedad Hípica Española Club de Campo in Madrid, Spain.

The planting season was drawing to a close and we needed to make any necessary improvements to our golf course project quickly. We needed to get the grass planted.

It was a typical client visit, with the shaper, construction superintendent, and assorted interested parties in tow. As architect, I was guiding the delegation in search of unwelcome incongruities before providing planting approval.

As we made our way to the twelfth green, I was giving the shaper instructions to ensure a good pin location near the water. This dangerous pin location would require finesse.

Midway through my instructions to the shaper, the client, apparently annoyed by all the changes, impatiently inserted himself into the discussion.

"Why is this place in the green so important?" he asked.

"Well, this will truly be an excellent pin location that will provide great challenge. It will be a difficult pin placement."

"But the pin is way over there," the client answered, pointing to the stake in the center of the green. "How could this area over here possibly be important? Besides, we need to get this hole planted."

"Yes," I answered, "but this front right pin location will provide a particularly delicate challenge when we put the flag here."

The client just stared at me.

At this point, I began to fear there was something seriously wrong. By this time in the project, the client and I had spent two years having detailed discussions about golf, design philosophy, construction issues, permitting, agronomy, and more.

"You do understand," I asked tentatively, "that the hole is regularly moved to different locations on the green? We discussed this on more than one occasion."

"The hole is in the center of the green," the client said.

"Yes, the hole can be in the center of the green, but it will be moved to different locations," I said.

He looked me quizzically, and then asked, "You mean the hole moves around the green?"

And this is the question that continues to echo in my mind still today—"You mean the hole moves around the green?"

13th Green at Stensballegaard Golf Club in Denmark.

CHAPTER 6
CASHING OUT IN KOREA

MICHAEL BEEBE

Palm Coast, Florida–based Beebe & Associates was founded by Michael Beebe, who has helped create Hidden Cypress Golf Club in Bluffton, South Carolina; Greystone Golf Club in Dickson, Tennessee; Osprey Cove Golf Course in St. Mary's, Georgia; Edmund Petroleum Golf and Country Club in Edmonton, Alberta, Canada; and the Tournament Players Club at Heron Bay, in Coral Springs, Florida.

I was working for Mark McCumber's design firm in the early 1990s when I got the opportunity to be involved with my first international course. We'd secured a design project in South Korea for a gentleman fondly known as Chicken Papa because he owned one of the largest poultry businesses in the country.

Prior to starting design work, we made plans to visit South Korea to discuss the project, meet the rest of the team, and visit the site. We were also supposed to collect the initial deposit on our design contract so that we could begin work when we returned to the states.

Stan Norton, one of our project superintendents who oversaw much of the company's construction work, accompanied me on the trip. Neither Norton nor I had ever been to South Korea and neither of us spoke the language, so we spent several days struggling to communicate with the locals.

Our trip included a visit to the site, which was so mountainous we couldn't walk certain areas, and we had discussions with engineers and contractors during which we had no idea what they were describing.

After five days it was time to return to America, but we were disappointed because we still didn't have the check for our initial contract deposit and reimbursement for our travel expenses, and we were having trouble communicating that need.

Norton and I sat in Chicken Papa's office just before we were to catch our cab to the airport when Papa appeared with a brown paper bag, which he handed to me. He politely bowed to thank us and then escorted us out of his office.

As Norton and I took the elevator down to the lobby, I opened the bag, expecting a jar of kimchi or some other Korean delicacy. Instead, I found our deposit … all in brand new hundred-dollar bills! Stan and I were rookie international travelers, but we knew for certain this was substantially more than what we would be allowed to bring through customs.

We feared the security officials would assume we had completed a drug deal and might throw us in jail, so we knew we couldn't simply declare the money on the customs form.

On the cab ride to the airport, we crafted a plan to get the money back to the United States. We agreed there was no way we were going to let the money leave our possession, which ruled out trying to put some of it in our luggage, so we decided to split it up and stuff it in every pocket, shoe, waistband, or other discreet area on our body. We went to the airport restroom and started stuffing stacks of hundred-dollar bills in every conceivable place we could.

Norton and I decided to split up and then reconnect once we'd (hopefully) cleared customs. The next thirty minutes were the most nerve-wracking time of my life.

Norton and I each survived security screening and reconvened in the Korean Airlines pre-boarding lounge. We discreetly began removing the money from our hiding places and secured it in our brief-cases for the rest of the flight home.

We didn't sleep much on that flight!

Sixteen hours later we arrived back in Florida with the brown paper bag safely in our possession. We went straight to the McCumber office, where we were greeted with cheers as we emptied the bag onto the conference room table and told our smuggling tale.

We went to the airport restroom and started stuffing stacks of hundred-dollar bills in every conceivable place we could.

CHAPTER 7
PERSISTENCE PAYS OFF!
EDWARD BEIDEL

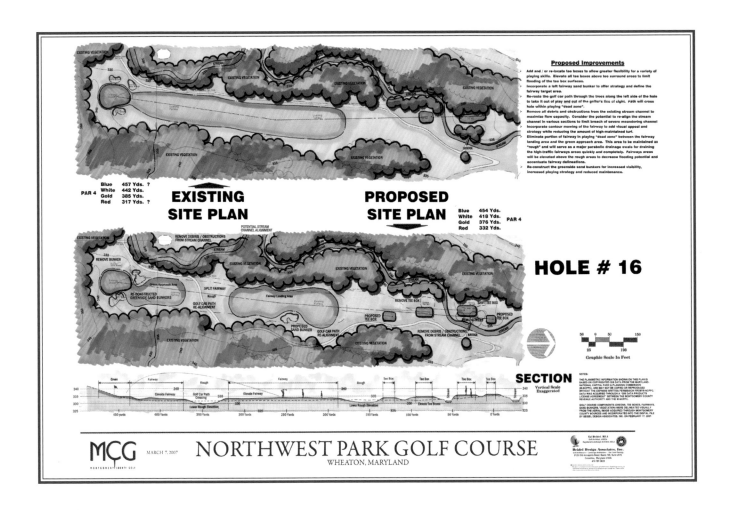

Orlando, Florida–based Edward Beidel graduated from Pennsylvania University with a BS in landscape architecture. He has designed such Pennsylvania courses as Turtle Creek Golf Course in Limerick; Groff's Farm Golf Club in Mt. Joy; Five Ponds Golf Club in Warminster; and Ebensburg Country Club in Ebensburg. Beidel also remodeled Riddell's Bay Golf and Country Club in Bermuda; Pinecrest Country Club in Lansdale, Pennsylvania; and the U.S. Naval Academy Golf Club in Annapolis, Maryland.

Who could have ever guessed that opening a phone book would end up changing my life?

It was 1976, and I, with my degree in landscape architecture from Penn State University, was unable to find a job. Times were lean for landscape design jobs and I had interviewed, unsuccessfully, at nearly every landscape architecture firm in western Pennsylvania, eastern Ohio, and West Virginia. There were simply no jobs to be had. I had been advised by the firms to head to Arizona, where recent college graduates could find work.

But I was born and raised a Pittsburgh boy. After my numerous interviews, all resulting in fingers pointing West, I was still hesitant to take their advice. I decided to check the yellow pages.

I found something in the phone book that was both surprising and exciting to me: three listings of people who were "golf course architects" in the Pittsburgh area. Golf course architects! I was shocked. I never knew golf course architecture was a full-time profession. I had to learn more. After all, I had been playing golf since I was nine years old. Caddying in Pittsburgh over the summers had paid for my college education.

I had no car, so I walked three miles from my house to Mr. Denison Hassenplug's office in Pittsburgh the very next day. I knocked on his door and explained that I had found him in the yellow pages.

"I would like to know what it's like to be a golf course architect, and I'd like to become one as well," I pronounced.

Mr. Hassenplug saw my enthusiasm, and even though I was just a kid walking in off the street, he graciously invited me to lunch, where he spent two hours telling me everything about his profession.

I walked back to his office every day for the next week, bringing technical projects I had worked on during college, and spending three hours each day discussing different facets of golf course architecture.

I also told him repeatedly I wanted to work with him and have him teach me the craft. His firm did not have the workload to support hiring another architect, but Mr. Hassenplug saw how passionate I was about the profession. He hired me the next week, and I worked with him for the next fifteen years.

Golf architecture and design—part science and part art.

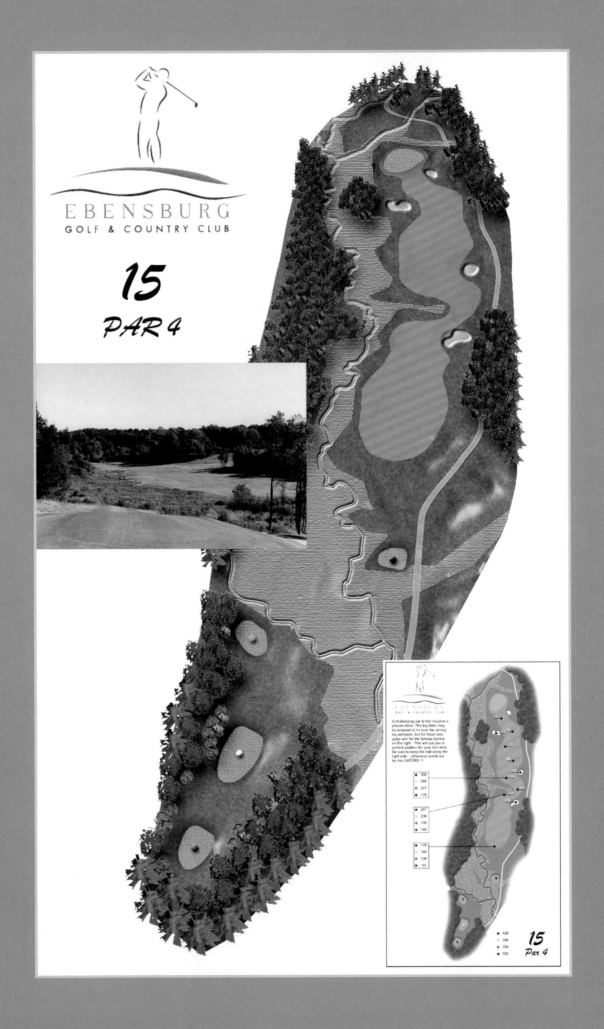

EBENSBURG
GOLF & COUNTRY CLUB

15
PAR 4

CHAPTER 8
TIMING AND DESTINY LED ME TO FAZIO
JAN BELJAN

Jan Beljan is a lead golf course architect for Tom Fazio Course Architecture in Jupiter, Florida, and has been with the company for more than twenty years. She helped create such Florida courses as Gateway Golf Club in Fort Myers; Pelican's Nest in Bonita Springs; Windstar on Naples Bay; the Champions Club at Summerfield in Stuart; and the Bayou Club in Key Largo.

After college, I was working in my hometown of Pittsburgh, Pennsylvania as a sales representative and technician in the lawn care division of the Davey Tree Expert Company with a degree in landscape architecture and a background as an assistant golf course superintendent. My job included corporate mass marketing and direct sales, as well as driving a split-shift, 1,200-gallon tanker truck to the sites of my sales and applying, from that tank, the prescribed fertilizer, herbicide, and pesticide for the clients' lawns. My assigned territory was the northeast side of the city, including Fox Chapel and Oakmont.

I had just finished the application on a business lawn in Fox Chapel, had reeled in the hose, and was already in my truck when the owner's assistant hailed me.

"Jan," he called out. "The owner would like to speak with you!"

I don't remember the date, but that day, the world as I knew it changed.

It was Davey company policy to leave a business card at the site before departing so that clients knew the service had been completed. I saw the surprise on the face of the owner, Jack Mahaffey Jr. when I walked into his office. He had played many rounds of golf with two of my professional golfing uncles, Carl Beljan and Willie Beljan, and had played at their respective clubs in various amateur events. He had expected "Jan" to be a nephew, not a niece!

Mahaffey was a renowned western Pennsylvania amateur golfer and a longstanding member at famed Oakmont Country Club. In fact, when I visited with him that day, in the spring of 1978, he was the president of Oakmont and chairman of the 1978 PGA Championship, which was being staged at Oakmont later that summer. Mahaffey enjoyed winter golf as a member at the highly regarded George Fazio/Tom Fazio–designed Jupiter Hills Club in Jupiter, Florida.

"What do you have in mind for the rest of your career?" Mahaffey asked me.

I told him of five opportunities I was weighing.

"Have you ever heard the name Fazio?" he asked me.

I had heard my father and uncles discuss golf since I was a toddler, so I told him I had heard the name.

"Well, I happen to know that Tom Fazio is looking for someone to work on the paper side of the design work," said Mahaffey. "Would you like to meet him?"

My first interview with Tom Fazio was on the clubhouse porch, overlooking the double green at Oakmont Country Club, on the Friday of the 1978 PGA Championship. After a little conversation, Tom asked me to send a portfolio and resume to the Jupiter office for his review.

Several weeks later, I was on my very first airplane trip for a second interview.

When the interview ended, Fazio asked me, "How soon can you begin?"

I thought I knew then, but now I believe: so much of life is destiny.

CHAPTER 9
FROM DOODLES TO DESTINY

MICHAEL BENKUSKY

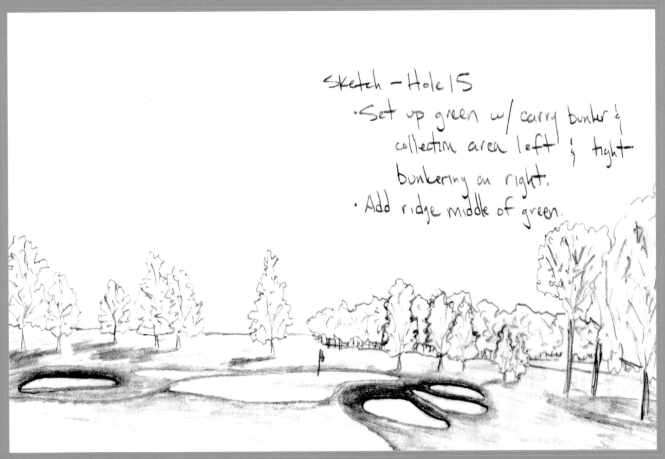

Imagination with specific direction results in thoughtful beauty.

ichael Benkusky began his study of golf course architecture early and firsthand by working on and playing the Donald Ross–designed Cedar Rapids Country Club. In 1983 he studied landscape architecture at Iowa State University, focusing on golf design. Benkusky played on the varsity golf team, where he was introduced to another of the game's giants, architect Perry Maxwell, who designed Veenker Memorial Golf Course. Benkusky then joined Lohmann Golf Designs, authoring more than fifteen original designs and directing hundreds of renovations, including classic originals by Maxwell and others. In January 2005, Benkusky started his own design firm, Michael J. Benkusky, Inc. in Lake in the Hills, Illinois. Some of the courses he created at Lohmann Golf Designs include Canyata in Marshall, Illinois; Twin Bridges Golf Club in Danville, Illinois; Eagle Valley Golf Course in Evansville, Indiana; and Hunters Ridge Golf Course in Marion, Iowa.

I grew up in suburban Cedar Rapids, Iowa, and had a dad who enjoyed the game of golf.

I began the game at age five and must have enjoyed it because I immediately took lessons from my dad and the golf professional. I wasn't allowed on the course except at certain times with my parents, though, so my dad got a couple cups and flags from the club and we put them in the backyard so I could practice. I developed golf holes and layouts to make the practice more interesting. I imagined golf holes that went around a tree or over the house, with any concrete acting as a water hazard. The neighbor kids would come over to test my links.

By age ten I was able to get on the course Friday mornings without an adult, so I played as much as I could. That summer, my parents drove into Chicago to see the 1975 U.S. Open played at Medinah Country Club. I was just starting to understand professional golf because most of the touring professionals would play at the Amana VIP Tournament in Iowa City. My parents came back from the U.S. Open with a championship program and I studied it completely. Then I began to copy the routing and holes on blank paper—my first doodle of a golf course.

I started to doodle more golf courses from scorecards we had or from layouts in golf magazines. After a while I began conjuring up my own layouts, and at one time went down to the city hall and got a copy of our club's topography and surrounding farmland. That is when I really got serious and would fantasize about remodeling our existing course.

By the time I started junior high, I began to think about golf design as a living. I took drafting classes during high school, and I began to consider landscape architecture programs for college. Luckily, my older sister attended Iowa State University, where they had a program.

I attended Iowa State and worked two summers at Cedar Rapids Country Club, a Donald Ross design. I played on the golf team as a freshman at Veenker Memorial Golf Course, a Perry Maxwell design. These two designers led me to study more about the history of golf course architecture and earlier architects.

During my second summer at Cedar Rapids Country Club, architect Bob Lohmann was hired to complete a master plan. I met Bob at the golf course and explained to him my desire to become an architect, and he hired me as an intern following my junior year. After two summers of internships, he hired me on full time in 1988. I worked at Bob's company for seventeen years learning the craft and business before starting my own firm in 2005.

> **After a while I began conjuring up my own layouts, and at one time went down to the city hall and got a copy of our club's topography and surrounding farmland.**

CHAPTER 10
BIG DIG ... BIG BANG

JIM BLAUKOVITCH

Quakertown, Pennsylvania–based Jim Blaukovitch Associates Golf Course and Irrigation Design created Keystone State courses such as Old Homestead Golf Club in New Tripoli; Island Green Country Club in Philadelphia; Honeybrook Golf Club in Honey Brook; and Stone Hedge Country Club in Tunkhannonck. Blaukovitch also designed Deerwood Country Club in Westhampton, New Jersey. Early in his career, while working with Killian & Nugent, Blaukovitch assisted in the construction of Kemper Lakes Golf Course near Chicago, the site of the 1989 PGA Championship.

While doing some preliminary site investigation for a new project, the golf course superintendent and I decided to dig some test holes. We started to dig in the area of a proposed pond to test for the presence of rock that might impede construction. As we were digging, someone from a neighboring property started waving his hands and signaling for us to stop.

"What's wrong with that guy?" we asked each other.

We motioned back that we were on our own property and kept digging. But the neighbor was relentless and kept yelling to us to stop.

"We're on our own property," we yelled to him.

This time he came running over towards us. We braced ourselves for a confrontation.

When he got close enough, however, we understood his urgency. Turns out, we'd been digging on top of a high-pressure gas transmission line!

When he got close enough, however, we understood his urgency. Turns out, we'd been digging on top of a high-pressure gas transmission line!

CHAPTER 11
HE HAD ALREADY KILLED A MAN
JEFF BLUME

Jeff Blume, a graduate of Texas A&M University, designed Grand Pries Golf Club at Brentwater in Montgomery, Texas; and, also in Texas, Elkins Lake (Ravines Course), in Huntsville; La Paloma Golf Club in Amarillo; a renovation of Hide-A-Way Lake Club (West and Center Courses) in Hide-A-Way, Texas; and the Sunset Golf Course in Fort Bliss. He also designed the Farm Golf Club in Lafayette, Louisiana.

APPROACH SHOT

2ND
T.P.
13+00

10/19/07

More than one way to skin a cat!

Many years ago I was working on Pelican Marsh Golf Club, in Naples, Florida. I was in my mid-twenties and was working for Robert von Hagge's firm. Mr. von Hagge was a celebrity. He had been on television and was very charismatic. It was always interesting to see how the clients and others acted because he was so well known.

Golf course architects end up working with a lot of different people: company personnel, the golf course management team, and, of course, the construction companies. There were plenty of characters around to keep things interesting.

One such character, a shaper named Robert, was a pretty intimidating guy. The rumor around the course was that he had spent time in jail for killing someone. We were unable to confirm this, but we were cautious around Robert regardless.

One day I was walking around the course with the construction superintendent when we saw an ambulance driving down the course. Then the superintendent's cell phone rang.

"This can't be good," he said.

Robert had just beaten the hell out of a laborer with a shovel.

It turns out Robert asked one of the laborers to help with something, and the laborer, for whatever reason, refused to do it.

The ambulance was on its way to pick up the laborer and take him to the hospital. Robert spent some more time in prison for that one.

The last I heard of Robert, he was preaching in Egypt.

As far as working with different people, it's always best to be careful and courteous, so that no ambulances are necessary!

Robert had just beaten the hell out of a laborer with a shovel.

CHAPTER 12
A MEMORABLE SEPTEMBER DAY

GLENN BOORMAN

Glenn Boorman is with Denis Griffiths and Associates, based in Braselton, Georgia, and is responsible for such Peach State courses as River Pines in Alpharetta; St. Marlo Country Club in Duluth; Chestatee Golf Club in Dawsonville; and the Georgia Club in Statham. Boorman also worked on President's Reserve at Hermitage in Nashville, Tennessee, and the second Shiron Golf Club in Niigata, Japan.

One of the many great things about golf course design is that we have the opportunity to develop friendships and build lasting relationships with our clients and those associated with each project. There are also those rare occasions when we share an experience or event that will forever stay with us.

I experienced such an occasion on a visit to Colorado on Tuesday, September 11, 2001.

The day started earlier than most because I had to make the hour-long journey to the airport for an early flight from Atlanta to Denver. Rental cars that morning in the Mile High City were scarce, so I was scheduled to be picked up at Denver's Stapleton Airport around 8 a.m. by Mark Krick, the golf course superintendent. We planned to meet the contractor and to do a final walk-through at the Homestead at Fox Follow in Lakewood.

The flight was normal except for the fact that I noticed the co-pilot make several trips to the back of the plane just before we started the descent. We were somewhere over Kansas with less than an hour to go before reaching Denver. I later pieced together that this was just about the time the first tower of the World Trade Center was hit, and air traffic control was directing planes to land at the nearest airport. I was very fortunate that Denver was the nearest airport.

Oblivious to any of the dreadful events in New York, I phoned my wife upon landing.

"Glenn," she asked, "have you heard what's happened?"

As my wife was telling me what she knew, I saw a television in the terminal that was showing footage of the first plane hitting the tower. Then came an announcement on the public address system: "All flights in and out of Denver International Airport have been suspended. All passengers are asked to please proceed directly to the main terminal."

I phoned Krick, who was waiting in his truck at the pickup area. We were both in shock during the forty-five-minute drive to Lakewood.

We arrived at the maintenance building to find the entire maintenance staff and construction personnel in the break room watching the television coverage. Everyone was stunned. We all spent the rest of the morning there watching the television and discussing the situation.

We did eventually make our way out to the course in the afternoon, but it was clear that our thoughts were elsewhere.

Since no flights were happening anywhere in the United States, I was stranded in Lakewood until Saturday. Needless to say, I had not packed or prepared for this length of trip, but the client gave me a maintenance pickup truck to drive to my hotel and to get around in while there. I spent my time playing golf, going to the City of Lakewood employee picnic, and having dinner with Bill Jewel, the regional parks and golf manager, at his home.

This was a defining moment in American history and one which made evident that the playing and design of golf courses is fairly insignificant in the grand scheme of things.

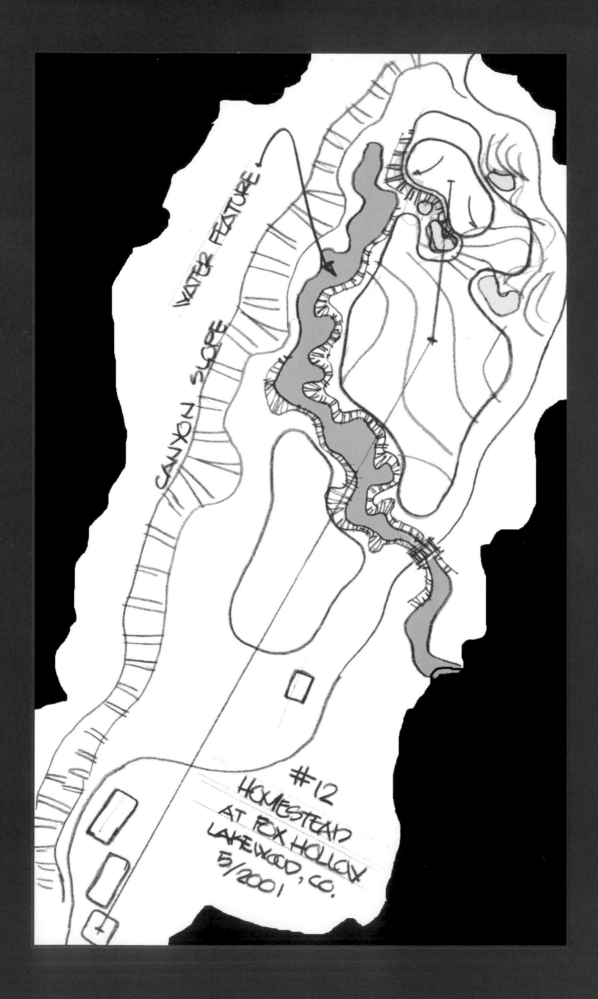

WATER FEATURE

CANYON SLOPE

#12
HOMESTEAD
AT FOX HOLLOW
LAKEWOOD, CO.
5/2001

CHAPTER 13
LEARNING FROM ROBERT TRENT JONES
WILLIAM F. BOSWELL

William F. Boswell, of Evans, Georgia, designed Blackthorn Golf Course in South Bend, Indiana; Lassing Pointe Golf Course in Boone County, Kentucky; Valley Brook Golf Club in River Vale, New Jersey; and, in Europe, Marbella Golf & Country Club in Marbella, Spain and Campo de Golfe da Madeira in Portugal.

I was one of the last architects to work as an assistant for the legendary Robert Trent Jones Sr. I worked in his office in Fuengirola, Spain, from 1985 until 1992, when the Gulf War, combined with Jones's age and poor health condition, forced us to close down.

About a year after I joined the European office, Robert Trent Jones was still very active, even though he was in his early eighties. The first time I personally drove him around, I had picked him up at the Nice airport and was driving him to our Grand Motte project near Montpellier, France.

"Mr. Jones," I said at some point in the four-hour drive, "we are close to finishing construction of the twenty-seven-hole project you will see today. Practically everything is shaped out. The irrigation is almost complete, and we are getting ready to start grassing the holes."

Jones said nothing, but I could see he was familiarizing himself with the plan. Then, after a careful study, Jones started scrutinizing some of the holes on the plan. He was clearly unhappy.

"The plan has too much water. The course will prove to be too difficult for the novice French golfers to play," Jones stated.

As we got closer to the site, Mr. Jones got more upset—almost irate—about the plan.

"This par-five, with water on the right and out-of-bounds on the left, is impossible," he proclaimed, before attacking the other eight holes of the side.

Now, it was normal for Jones to make changes in the field—he might change some shaping, add bunkers, or move some tees. That was to be expected. But this criticism was something much

more monumental. Jones was critical of an entire nine-hole routing! We were getting paid to shape the golf course, too, so Jones himself was financially responsible for some of the construction.

After we'd arrived at the site, during our lunch meeting with our contractor, Jones concluded that it would be best if we converted the erroneous nine into a par-three course.

"But Mr. Jones, we already have a six-hole practice course," I informed him.

"We've got to fix this or I'm sending you back to the States," he exclaimed.

He was mad, and blaming me! I was getting worried.

I expressed concern about admitting to the clients that we screwed up our design and now, when construction was almost finished, we wanted to change it.

"Let me handle it—don't say a word," Jones advised me.

We met with the clients and Robert Trent Jones Sr. worked his magic. Not only did Jones convince the clients to convert the proposed nine holes to an eighteen-hole par-three, he managed to charge them for the changes in design, and charge them for shaping nine new greens and tees. I couldn't believe it! The clients were actually happy because, as far as they were concerned, they were getting nine more holes!

Jones was proud of the new deal he made. Before he left, he lectured me on making sure new designs are not too punishing.

"And always get paid for your work," Jones added with a wink. "That's the most important part."

When I worked with Jones, our operation was almost entirely in continental Europe. It was said that two things didn't cross the English Channel: golf to continental Europe and good food to England. So, not surprisingly, our clients often didn't know much about golf courses or, for that matter, golf and the socially proper way to play. Many of our clients just knew a golf course would make them money.

Our typical meeting would be with a group of owners or investors that wanted us to design a golf course. Their advisors for the project would be present.

After reviewing one particularly good site, we returned to our office and found that the land would easily support twenty-seven holes. We included that plan along with the standard eighteen-hole course routing. After presenting the twenty-seven-hole option to the client, we sensed one member of his entourage was a bit upset. We weren't fluent in the language, so all we could do was catch the odd word or so. This angry fellow dominated the discussion between the investors to the point we were worried that we were losing the deal.

We jumped in and explained to the client that he could adapt the third nine even if he decided not to build it until later. But the objector remained adamant that it couldn't work.

It was clear the client was confused. He didn't know whether to side with Robert Trent Jones—the world's most famous golf course architect—or to trust the objections of his animated advisor.

After a tense bit of silence, with everyone standing around the plans laid out on the table, the client finally, in broken English, blurted out, "It is too much golf—everyone would be too tired." He then gave gestures imitating and indicating an exhausted person.

We quickly realized that we had to educate our new clients about the basics of golf.

We had many laborers working on the job in Madeira. Most laborers were poor and were from the nearby town of Santo da Serra. Some of the laborers walked over a mile to the site each day. They were hardworking people who did not know anything about building golf courses. Only a few had ever been off the island.

During construction of the fourth hole—the signature, long, par-three over the deepest cliff edge—I carried my golf clubs out to give it a try. I was a three handicap. The workers who stopped to watch me swing the club seemed impressed with my shots.

I offered to let some of the workers grab a club and give it a try. One of the laborers reluctantly took the fairway wood and gripped the club cross-handed. I corrected his grip and he promptly dribbled the ball barely off the tee. Everyone laughed.

Another worker looked curiously into my bag and pulled out a three-iron for the 220-yard shot, and like the first man who grabbed a club, he gripped the club cross-handed, but would not let me correct his grip. He motioned for me to keep away. His swing, taken off loose dirt in tennis shoes, was as full and flowing as that of the great Spanish golfer Severiano Ballesteros. The ball soared up in the air, hung for a second or two, and fell squarely on the green! I was shocked beyond belief. The workers grinned and laughed, knowing he had showed me up!

Several others took turns and most played cross-handed. I was flabbergasted. I had to find out where these islanders learned to play, since I was building was the only golf course on the island!

My curiosity revealed that part of our site was a defunct nine-hole golf course built in the 1930s. It wasn't even noticeable even to me, but during the time that the course had been active, the boys from Santo da Serra were hired as caddies and naturally took up the game. The town's best player used to play cross-handed, so all the kids learned from him. Even after the course became inactive, the grassy plain allowed the development of generations of cross-handed players just waiting for a golf course.

Once I'd finished the course, I loved to take the workers out and watch them play. They never commented on the fairness, shot values, or other fluff used to describe courses. They simply enjoyed the challenge.

CHAPTER 14
LEARNING FROM THE PROS
AND HANDLING CRITICISM

JEFFREY BRAUER

Jeff Brauer, a past president of the American Society of Golf Course Architects, began his career in Chicago and, in 1984, formed Jeffrey D. Bauer/GolfScapes in Arlington, Texas, which has designed more than fifty new courses, including Minnesota courses The Quarry at Giant's Ridge in Biwabik and The Wilderness at Fortune Bay in Tower. He also designed Wild Wing Plantation's Avocet Course in Myrtle Beach, South Carolina; Colbert Hills Golf Course in Manhattan, Kansas; and Cowboys Golf Club in Grapevine, Texas.

My first rounds of golf as a boy were secret Monday outings on the closed country club courses. The woods and solitude of an empty course impressed me, particularly the championship No. 3 course at Medinah Country Club in Chicago.

My parents were less impressed when I presented them with a $140 guest fee bill. The club pro had unexpectedly come to work one Monday and spotted me.

Years later, I'd see famous PGA Tour players compete at the U.S. Opens and PGA Championships staged at Medinah, and I've even collaborated with some of those stars. I've worked with PGA Tour players Fuzzy Zoeller, Jim Colbert, Larry Nelson, Steve Elkington, Lanny Wadkins, and Fred Couples.

By far the biggest contributor to our design philosophy has been Colbert, who is both dogmatic in his architectural ideas and eloquent in expressing them in terms I can understand. Some of the others having trouble articulating the detail necessary to make a difference. All of the players have given me general ideas about how they play, and those tidbits have worked their way into their designs.

Colbert was adamant about certain things since, in many cases, he was the owner of the project as well. But he was the type of player who was a grinder, so he tried to create shots that maximized his chances

for success, unlike some of the players who always played the same shot—a draw, for instance—out of convenience. Colbert taught me bunkering, contouring, how to punish a miss hit, and how to design a hole to encourage a particular type of shot.

He told me, "Pardner, there are smarter guys than me, but if the ground slopes to the left, the green angles to the left, and the prevailing wind blows to the left, I think the ball is going left no matter what I try to do, so I'm going to hit a draw!

"You wouldn't know what to do if you came to an intersection, and it had both a stop sign and a green light. Golf shots are the same—all the signals should be saying the same thing!"

I think of golf design like a bunch of little comedy bits strung together in a routine. Others architects use a song analogy. I tend to find inspiration and satisfaction in little things, like an irregularity in the land or shaping that is just plain different.

On my first solo job—a remodel of Desert Rose for Jim Colbert—I got upset with a shaper who wasn't using enough depth on the course. Then I left for another green site. I came back and didn't see his bulldozer anywhere. I thought maybe he'd gotten mad at my criticism and had left the job. But as I approached the green, I saw the dozer popping out of the deepest grass bunker I had ever seen! Since it was deep enough to hide a bulldozer, I was going to have him fill it partially back in, but Colbert liked it, so it stayed.

I get the most press from my Giant's Footprint bunker at Giant's Ridge Golf Club in Minnesota. I needed a long, skinny bunker on the third hole, and was aware of the legend of a giant roaming the area, so I added toes to the bunker. The client insisted I take out the Giant's Footprint bunker, but I prevailed. The client did convince me not to go forward with my plan to create three similar bunkers, which would have appeared to be the footprints left by a giant walking across the course.

The footprint bunker has become the signature of the course and created millions of dollars in shirt sales!

Later I created a cat paw bunker at Kansas State University as an ode to their team mascot, the Wildcats.

Unusual and different features can give each course a sense of place, but can also draw criticism. Golf architects, despite what they say, all live and die by reviews. Good reviews please us and bad ones infuriate us. Very few reviews are totally negative, though, because reviewers have ways to subtly pan a course with double entendres, including:

- "You'll be lucky to enjoy this course" (it would depend on something besides design).
- "I would like to enthusiastically recommend this course to you" (but I can't).
- "Best of its kind" (the bad kind).
- "Never seen anything like it" (and hope not to again).
- "He designed a course like he's never designed before." (How do you mean that?)
- "Now, that's a golf course." (What kind?)
- "I had a hard time believing what I saw."
- "It redefines the meaning of 'a place to play golf.'"
- "It had it all" (tee markers, flags, ball washers, the works).
- "I don't usually write about clubhouses, but this one is the club's focal point."
- "It's always interesting to see a designer take chances."
- "I would like to recommend this as a must-play course" (but I just can't).
- "It proves you can build a golf course just about anywhere."
- "Years from now, golf course architecture students will visit this course just to study it."

One review affected my general design theory: Tangle Ridge in Grand Prairie, Texas, which got favorable press, but one reviewer noted that all of the par-threes were of medium length. I purposely designed them that way because public players like such holes. But that criticism made me think about creating par-three holes of different lengths for variety. In newer designs, like my current renovation of Indian Creek in Carrolton, Texas, a similar public course, I have par-three holes of 130, 180, 205, and 270 yards, which provides great variety. The full-driver, 270-yard hole and the partial-wedge, 130-yard hole, with a deep swale in the green, are memorable and different! Since these two holes sit just two holes apart on the back nine, I doubt any golfer will forget them when they review their round.

So I will live with reviews—good and bad—and use them as one source to further my personal education in golf course design.

I love the old-style courses, but our designs encompass philosophies inherited from the past with a realistic look at the needs of golf in the future. I don't think new courses should look substantially like old ones because golf and life have changed. With more recreational activities available, golf must retain its charm and strength: being in a beautiful environment playing a game you can't master, while gradually changing to appeal to younger generations that expect more visual excitement, instant gratification, and entertainment than previous generations. Courses need visual excitement, which, given how far we are getting away from nature, need not be truly natural. And life is easier, so most courses need to be easier, balancing the need for beginner's achievable success by dumbing down courses with the risk of failing to hold long-term interest if they are too easy.

I love the old-style courses, but our designs encompass philosophies inherited from the past with a realistic look at the needs of golf in the future.

CHAPTER 15

WHY DID IT HAVE TO BE SNAKES?

STEVE BURNS

Steve Burns is owner and principal of Chicago, Illinois–based Burns Golf Design, which he founded in 1988, and vice president of TD&A. After graduating from Ohio State University, Burns served as a design and construction associate for Fazio Golf Course Designers. He's designed Club de Golf Malinalco in San Sebastian de Amola, Mexico; Laura Walker Golf Course in Waycross, Georgia; Cobblestone Golf Club in Kendallville, Indiana; and, in Ohio, the Country Club of Fox Meadow in Medina and Hawks Nest Golf Club in Wooster.

Back in the early eighties, when I got my start with Tom Fazio, I worked on lot of projects in the southeastern states. Before I started working in the field, I'd heard stories from other architects about snake encounters during land clearing operations. Having heard those tales, I went to my first field project properly prepared with tall, snake-proof boots and a .357 pistol loaded with snake shot.

On that first project, I didn't see one snake.

With my flat feet, the boots quickly wore out on me. I wasn't quite confident about snakes just yet, so I bought a pair of snake-proof chaps for the next project. I wore the chaps while traipsing through the brush to flag trees, and then removed them once things opened up. I found the chaps to be very handy for hiking through palmettos and other dense vegetation that would otherwise have cut my legs. Of course, on the second project, I again had no close snake encounters until I almost stepped on a water moccasin—sans chaps—when the clearing was nearly done.

Then we started clearing operations at Amelia Island in November. On my first morning, I forgot my gun and chaps, but the terrain mostly consisted of tree-covered dunes.

I walked over a dune onto the first hole and saw a rattlesnake coiled up, about five feet in front of me. I shook that one off, and started flagging trees. I was shinnying backwards under a low tree limb later

that morning when I looked toward my outstretched rear leg and saw another rattlesnake. The serpent was slithering silently away from where my foot was. There was no rattling warning sound, which surprised me.

Needless to say, I got my chaps and gun at lunchtime.

A fairly bright young man was assigned to help me that afternoon. When we almost stepped on another rattlesnake, he went after it with a machete. He swung and missed three times before the snake finally rattled at him. Apparently the rattlesnakes had otherwise been silent because it was getting cold and they were going into hibernation.

The clearing foreman and the owner's rep arrived on site the next day. Of course, they made fun of me, despite my descriptions of my earlier encounters. The following day, the contractor and I were walking one fairway that seemed like a series of islands in knee-deep water, due to recent heavy rains and the undulating terrain of the dunes. We walked onto one island with an eighteen-foot pine on it. The foreman walked around the tree while I stopped just short of it and pointed at something off in the distance. Just then, out of the corner of my eye, I spotted a rattlesnake, coiled about six inches away from my feet. I backed off, drew my gun, and shot it. The snake was just over six feet long—not a record, but big enough for us!

CHAPTER 16
PUTTING THE PUZZLE TOGETHER
TY BUTLER

Ty Butler is currently the vice president and senior project architect of the Robert Trent Jones Jr. design company, based in Charlotte, North Carolina. He worked on the Kaluhyat Course at Turning Stone Casino Resort in Verona, New York; Rock Barn Golf and Spa in Conover, North Carolina; and Charter Oak Country Club in Hudson, Massachusetts. Butler also designed the Reef Course at Our Lucaya Resort in Freeport, Grand Bahama Island, and Margarita Golf Club in Margarita Island, Venezuela.

I began playing golf when I was eight years old, and to be honest, I absolutely hated the game. However, my mother insisted that I join the junior golf program at my parents' club in Arkansas City, Kansas. I was part of the "three holers" group that first summer, and I beat it around in the blazing heat with the rest of the kids. I averaged a respectable ten to twelve strokes per hole—not bad for a "three holer." By the second summer, I was hooked on the game for good.

I remember sitting around the house during all those frozen Kansas winters, while the courses were covered by a blanket of snow, drawing imaginary golf courses. To me, it was a lot like putting a puzzle together: fitting in all the pieces until it was perfect, based only on my limited knowledge of what a golf course looked like from my then short golfing career. I remember thinking it would be great if this actually existed as a job and I could do it when I grew up.

A short time later my mother encouraged me again by giving me a copy of *Golf's Magnificent Challenge*, by the renowned golf course architect Robert Trent Jones Sr. It was the most interesting book I had ever read, because it was about the very profession that I thought only existed in my imagination. The stories about Jones's life as a golf course architect and the various projects he had designed around the world convinced me, at the age of twelve, that I wanted to spend my life creating golf courses. But I had

no idea how to go about reaching my newfound goal.

I met Dick Metz when I was fifteen years old, working my summer job on the grounds crew at Arkansas City Country Club. Dick had been a professional golfer in the 1920s and played in the inaugural Masters Tournament in 1934. I was riding on a tractor, pulling a seven gang reel mower down the thirteenth fairway. Metz played the course every morning. This particular morning he came strolling down the fairway I happened to be mowing, so I paused to let him play on. As he passed, he stopped to talk. As we made small talk, we discovered that my grandfather was one of his childhood friends. At that moment Dick Metz became my very good friend and mentor. He educated me about the world of golf and golf course design by telling me fascinating stories from his playing career.

Dick had played many of the great courses around the country and had wonderful insight into golf course design. He is credited with the design of the front nine at Arkansas City Country Club, which was added to the original nine designed by the great Perry Maxwell. Metz was kind enough to obtain an old set of plans from a George Fazio course for me to study!

As I look back, I realize that my mother's persistence got me started, and Dick Metz then steered me in the right direction toward the career path I am now traveling. I have them both to thank!

CHAPTER 17
A ROYAL FLUSH AND A ROYAL HONOR

DOUG CARRICK

Architect meets royalty—Carrick with HRH Princess Anne.

Based in Toronto, Doug Carrick has served on the American Society of Golf Course Architect's Board of Governors as membership chairman and secretary. He began his career in golf course architecture in 1981 when the late C. E. Robinson schooled Carrick in design principles passed on to him by Stanley Thompson. Carrick founded his own design firm four years later, and it's become one of Canada's leading golf course architecture firms. His first solo design, King Valley Golf Club, was voted Canada's second-best new course by *Golf Digest* in 1991, and in 1995 his Angus Glen Golf Club earned the top honors from the same magazine. He's also designed The Carrick at Loch Lomond, Scotland; Fontana Golf Club in Oberwaltersdorf, Austria; and, in Canada, Bigwin Island Golf Club in Lake of Bays, Ontario; Greywolf Golf Course at Panorama Resort; and Osprey Valley's Resort Course.

When I was young and naive, I met a developer who was planning to develop a golf resort on a small island in the Bahamas called Whale Key.

We met in Toronto, and he arrived in a nice Mercedes 450 SL wearing a diamond-studded Rolex watch. He couldn't have been much more than thirty years old. I remember being impressed, but I also wondered how a guy that young became so wealthy at such a young age. But I didn't worry, because this was a very exciting opportunity for me: to design my first international course in the Bahamas.

Plans were made to visit the property. The client arranged for us to fly down to Miami with his own pilot, where we would pick up his twin-engine Cessna and fly from Miami to Whale Key.

As we approached the island of Whale Key, the pilot made a pass over the island to make sure that the coral landing strip was clear. As we made our final approach, I noticed debris strewn along both sides of the landing strip; that debris turned out to be from a series of airplane wrecks. The landing was a little tense.

Upon taxiing over to the terminal, which was a wooden shack on the side of the landing strip, we were greeted by the client's father, who arrived in a beat-up old Ford flatbed truck. I arrived at the old mansion house a little shaken, but in one piece.

We spent the next two days exploring the island through its thick underbrush, trying to determine the best routing for fairways. After all of that dirty work, at the end of the day we were treated to a fine dinner of salami, which was also the meal of choice for breakfast and lunch.

When Sunday arrived, after two exciting days on the island of Whale Key, I was looking forward to flying home to a nice meal of pasta, pork chops, or anything other than salami, but when I arrived at the lobby of the mansion house with my packed suitcase, the client informed me that we weren't leaving until Monday.

"But I told my wife that I would be returning home today," I explained to him. "I need to call and tell her that I won't be home until Monday."

"No problem," he said, "but there is no phone on the entire island of Whale Key."

I must have looked frustrated.

"Not to worry," he continued. "My pilot can fly you over to the closest island at Chubb Key. There is a pay phone in town. It will allow him to pick up some more salami—supplies are running low."

So off we went, just the pilot and myself, on our adventure to Chubb Key. The five-minute flight was uneventful. After checking in with the two local Bahamian customs officials brandishing rifles, we ventured into town in search of a phone and, of course, more salami.

Once I'd phoned my wife and we'd finished our business in town, we returned to the airstrip, where we found one of the local customs officials leaning back in his rickety chair, asleep with his rifle resting on his shoulder. We checked in with the official who was awake, and once the pilot filed his flight plan, we were off again into the wild blue yonder.

When the pilot lined up his approach to Whale Key, the setting sun blasted its rays into our eyes, making the runway virtually invisible. Somehow the pilot was able to put the aircraft down before crashing into the jungle at the end of the runway. Another joyful ride back to the mansion house on the three-tired pickup truck allowed us to arrive just in time for another salami dinner.

We dined quietly as the sun set into the Bahamian Sea.

In the middle of dinner, we heard a knock at the door. My client excused himself to answer it. He was greeted by two Bahamian customs officials from Chubb Key.

"Hello suh. We is customs officers from Chubb Key and we is lookin' for de two gentlemen dat was in Chubb Key earlier today," one of the officials said.

"What is this about?"

"We has been informed by some peoples in Nassau dat dey is dealin' drugs!"

"I'm sorry, but I think you must be mistaken. Those two men are here as my guests and I can tell you they are not drug dealers." The officials shook their heads.

"Our sources tell us dat dey is drug dealers and we has to take dem back to Chubb Key tonight for questioning."

My client asked the officials how they got to Whale Key.

"We comes here by boat. A nice little Boston Whaler."

"And you want to take these gentlemen back to Chubb Key tonight, in the dark, in your little Boston Whaler?"

"Yes, we has to take dem for questioning. Dey is drug dealers!"

"Look, they are not drug dealers. One gentleman is here to design a golf course for me on Whale Key, and the other is my pilot! They are not drug dealers and you are not taking them back to Chubb Key!"

This back-and-forth conversation went on for almost an hour, and eventually the client convinced the gun-toting customs officers that we were not drug dealers.

I was never so glad to arrive home after a business trip. I never did design a course for Whale Key and I haven't eaten salami since.

I did eventually get international design projects, particularly a very special one in Scotland. Designing a course in the homeland of golf has been the biggest thrill of my career so far.

My good friend Ken Siems, who is superintendent of the famed Loch Lomond Golf Club outside Glasgow, recommended me to a gentleman by the name of Mitch Higgens, who was planning to develop a golf resort on the shores of Loch Lomond, next door to Loch Lomond Golf Club. Fate was on my side. I happened to be planning a flight to visit a project we were working on in Spain when Mitch Higgens called one Friday afternoon. I would be flying through Heathrow the following Monday, and so he made arrangements for me to meet Mr. Higgens at Heathrow Airport three days later. The meeting went well.

I stayed in close touch with Mr. Higgens over a period of approximately eighteen months while he searched for a financial backer and partner for his Scotland project. Eventually De Vere Resorts, owners of the five-star Cameron House Hotel, located just two miles down the Loch Shore, came to the table to take over the project.

I made another trip to Scotland to meet with the director of De Vere Resort Ownership, Craig Mitchell. Mr. Mitchell and I seemed to hit it off right away and we both shared the same vision for the golf course. He green-lighted the golf course project with me as the designer.

After two years of planning and another two years of construction, the golf course, which they named The Carrick, was completed. Joe Longmuir, the general manager of Cameron House at the time, made arrangements for HRH Princess Anne to attend a formal opening ceremony for the golf course and the adjacent mansion house time-share development.

My wife Rosa and my two design associates, Cam Tyers and Steve Vanderploeg, made the long trip to Scotland to join in the opening festivities. It was pouring rain when Princess Anne arrived with her various staff members. The princess was to greet the long line of consultants, contractors, and representatives from De Vere inside. We'd all rehearsed our bows and royal greetings, hoping not to embarrass ourselves. Following a series of short and courteous conversations with the princess, we ventured out onto the eighteenth green in the pouring rain, where I handed Princess Anne a royal purple flagstick, which she set into the hole. It was a very special and proud moment.

A few photo opportunities ensued, and just when I was certain the princess had tired of the weather and the perfunctory visit, she surprised me and the others by leading me on a short, private stroll across the eighteenth green. She asked me many questions about the design of the course. The other onlookers were convinced that she was asking me for my phone number, but I'll never tell!

Designing a course in the homeland of golf has been the biggest thrill of my career so far.

CHAPTER 18

GOURMET DINING BY A MASTER CHEF?
OR FAST FOOD FROM A FRY COOK?

NAI CHUNG LEE CHANG

Nai Chung Lee Chang, based in Atlanta, Georgia, has created the Wood Stork Course at Wild Wing Plantation in Myrtle Beach; Port Royal in Hilton Head, South Carolina; Lions Paw Golf Links in Ocean Isle Beach, North Carolina; Southland Country Club in Atlanta; and Harborside Golf Club in Longboat Key, Florida.

Would you rather dine in a gourmet restaurant at a comfortable table with fine china and silverware, soft music in the background, roses on your table, and superior service ... or get your dinner in a paper bag tossed at you out of a window?

I believe walking, instead of riding in a motorized cart, enhances the experience a person has playing the game of golf.

Walking is not only part of the tradition of the game but also a physical exercise that can really help the players. If you don't allocate enough time to play a round of golf through walking, you will not get the true enjoyment and benefits from the game.

The appreciation and vantage point one gets by walking during a round is a bit like the experience of fine dining, where you're able to spend time enjoying the food, environment, and the entire dining occasion.

By not walking a course, one definitely misses an important component of the whole golf experience. Riding in a cart is comparable to the dining experience one has with drive-through fast food, or eating at a sports bar. Since no two golf holes or golf courses are alike, the best and truest way to experience the game and the course is by walking when you play.

I started my golf architect career while attending Georgia Tech, where I was pursuing my master's degree in city planning and architecture. While in school, I worked for Willard Byrd, an accomplished golf course architect. As a result of that apprenticeship, I got to drive over from Atlanta to Augusta to see the Masters Tournament. Walking the holes at that famed club was an important moment for me.

I began reading all of the golf books I could find. Alister MacKenzie created Augusta National, so I read his book *Golf Architecture*. The great English golf writer Bernard Darwin's book, *Golf Courses of the British Isles*, whetted my appetite for traditional golf, so as soon as I could I began taking trips overseas to play and study the Scottish golf courses.

Because of my academic training in conventional and practical city planning, and my experience playing very old courses in Scotland, I always strive to balance and maintain the equilibrium of the man-made and the natural environment when I lay out and design a golf course. I take into account the strategy of the game, the beauty of the environment, and the essence of the course maintenance to "design with nature."

The golf course should be part of the natural ecosystem, but also enjoyed by mankind.

And should be walked.

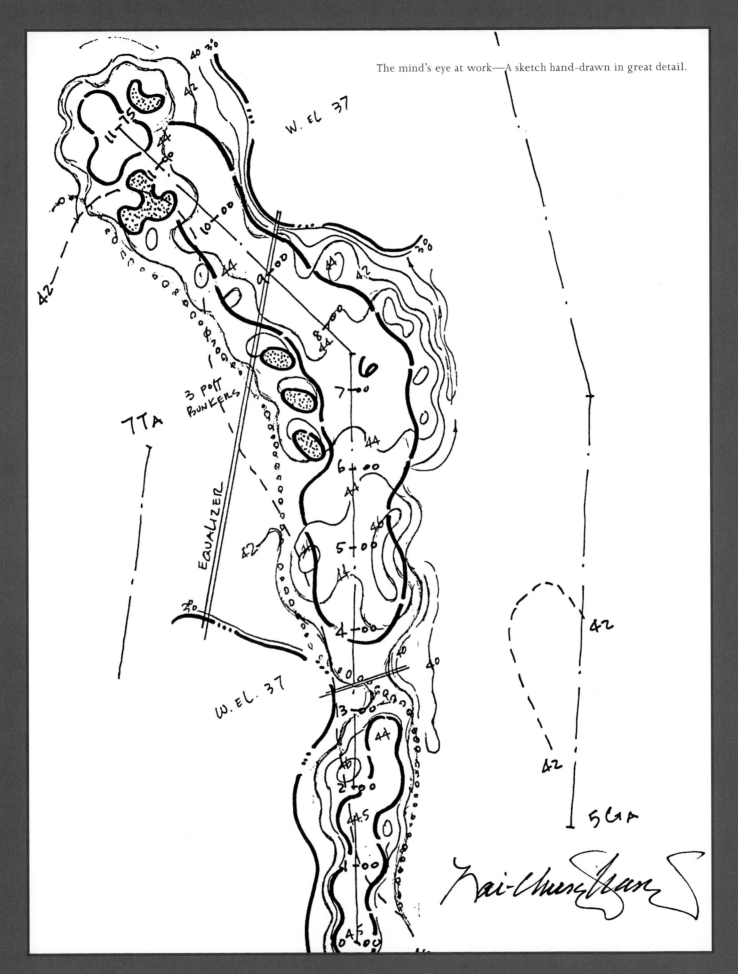

The mind's eye at work—A sketch hand-drawn in great detail.

CHAPTER 19
THE SWIMMING MOOSE
BRUCE CHARLTON

Hole 2 of the Bjaavann Golf Course in Norway.

Bruce Charlton, 2008-2009 president of the American Society of Golf Course Architects, grew up in Iowa and enjoyed a fine amateur golf career. Upon graduation from the University of Arizona, Bruce joined the design firm of Robert Trent Jones, Jr., where he has developed a number of outstanding designs, including Southern Highlands Golf Club in Las Vegas; Thunderhawk Golf Club in Lake County, Illinois; and The Bridges Golf Club in Rancho Santa Fe, California. Chambers Bay, the spectacular municipal links course located on the scenic lower Puget Sound in University Place, Washington, has been awarded the 2015 U.S. Open Championship.

Hole 17 at Bjaavann—playing along the fjord.

I was working on a course in southern Norway, and while the course was under construction, the construction chief, Darryl Moulder, and I climbed up on what would eventually become the second tee on an early morning in mid-June.

We were stopped in our tracks when, from the tee, we spotted a very large moose. The moose was sprawled out on the sand, sunning itself on what would become the putting surface of the second green!

Darryl and I, keeping our eyes on the moose, walked quietly around the green, which was perched on a rock outcropping along a fjord. We were about thirty yards from the green when, suddenly, the moose started to move. Again, we froze in our tracks, because the moose then stood up and looked at us. We were scared because it looked like the huge moose was going to charge us! Just when we were about to turn tail and run, the moose turned from

us, trotted off the end of the green, and jumped into the lake!

Man, that moose could swim! We watched in fascination as the moose pedaled about five hundred yards across the lake and hopped up on the bank behind the site for the seventeenth hole, walked up the hill, and laid down on what would someday be the green. I'd never seen anything like it.

About a year later, we staged the grand opening of the course with the customary round

of golf. After my foursome finished the sixteenth hole, I was the first to walk up to the seventeenth tee. During the moments I spent alone there waiting for my fellow players, I stared out at the green and thought about the moose. The memory was very vivid. I had lost my father in the year between seeing the moose and the grand opening of the course. For some reason, my emotions took over and I started to cry uncontrollably. My father's death finally hit me.

My fellow players finally arrived and, finding me in that condition, were concerned. I told them the story of the swimming moose, and in my heart, wondered if maybe, in some way, my dad and that swimming moose were somehow connected.

Hole 17 at Bjaavann—The orange line is where the moose swam across!

CHAPTER 20
SAM SNEAD AND CEREMONIAL GOLF COURSE OPENINGS GONE BAD

TOM CLARK

Tom Clark is a past president of the American Society of Golf Course Architects and a partner of Ault, Clark & Associates, Ltd., based in Marshall, Virginia. Over the course of his thirty-seven-year career, he has completed nearly 100 new courses as project architect and more than 250 remodeling projects. Projects have taken Tom throughout the United States and abroad to countries including Korea, Ireland, South Africa, Canada, and Mexico, and some of his highly ranked courses include the Tournament Players Club at Avenel in Potomac, Maryland; The Woods Course at Kingsmill Resort in Williamsburg, Virginia; Stonehaven at Glade Springs Resort in Daniels, West Virginia; and renovation work at Canada's Hamilton Country Club. His company has also been involved with courses on which PGA Tour, Nationwide Tour, Hooters Tour, and Futures Tour events have been staged.

Cooper Communities hired a new director of marketing in 1985. At the time I had designed and built ten very successful courses for the Cooper family. They were expanding their horizons out of Arkansas and had been granted the opportunity to develop over five thousand acres around Tellico Reservoir outside of Knoxville, Tennessee.

Toqua was to be the first of three courses, but the new marketing director thought that involving a big name professional golfer, preferably a senior player, would attract a more affluent real estate buyer to this somewhat isolated area. Knowing that such golf greats as Arnold Palmer and Jack Nicklaus had already started their own architectural shops, I recommended Sam Snead, who was still playing on the senior circuit and was arguably one of the greatest players and personalities of all time.

On a beautiful October morning I went to visit Sam with a friend of mine who happened to live in Bath County, Virginia. Since Sam lived directly below the Cascades Course at the Homestead Resort, we planned to take the opportunity to play a little golf after the meeting.

Sam and I talked for about half an hour on his porch, and then he suggested we retire to his trophy room for a cool drink and to share some nostalgic moments. I assumed that his trophy room would be full of awards from his illustrious golf career, but instead, the room was packed with the heads and feet of many of the big game animals he had bagged.

We spent the next three hours swapping stories of our hunting and fishing exploits. Never once did the words "golf" or "architecture" cross our lips. Sam did offer to play golf with us afterwards for "just a few bucks," but my friend was so intimidated, I declined.

Opening day at a new golf course is always a special affair. Media members, local officials, investors, and the local residents are invited to participate and meet the architect. Opening day at Toqua was a sultry July scorcher. The temperature soared to nearly 100 degrees. On that day, Snead, the "consulting architect," made his first-ever visit to the course. He delighted the crowd with his exhibition on the practice tee and told some raunchy stories on the microphone.

I was thrilled to learn that I would be paired with Sam for a ceremonial opening round—the two of us would simultaneously strike the first tee shots on the first hole! I was less thrilled when I heard Sam's voice belting over the loudspeakers. Sam still had the microphone he had used in the exhibition. His amplified voice was unmistakable:

Sam answered, "What hole-in-one?"

"Tommy, which way does this hole go?"

Snead's manager quickly pulled me aside.

"Sam is virtually blind in one eye and has trouble seeing distances," he said. "He has no depth perception. You'll have to give him yardages."

Since the course was brand new and had no yardages marked, giving Snead yardages would pose quite a problem.

Snead and I hit our simultaneous, ceremonial opening drives, and my drive stopped just a yard short of his. After that drive, Sam switched to a rock-hard, distance model Top-Flite golf ball he'd had in his back pocket. He wasn't about to be out-driven by a whippersnapper like me in front of a crowd.

Sam and I, followed by his large gallery, arrived at the fifth hole. We'd caught up with the group in front of us, which included my partner Brian Ault, so we watched their tee shots. Brian's six-iron shot on this slightly uphill par-three hole found the bottom of the hole for an ace! Since Sam's arrival had brought the entire gallery, a huge roar went up. The media members present asked Snead to comment on Brian's hole-in-one.

Sam answered, "What hole-in-one?" His attention had been focused on a cute blond woman he'd invited to sit next to him in his golf cart and ask any questions she dared!

Our opening day round was played under a four-man scramble format. I was amazed when looking at Snead's vintage Wilson Staff irons. The sweet spot was a completely worn and slightly concave surface. How many perfect shots had he struck with those irons?

Snead's laser accuracy with his irons, aided by my best guesses at the yardages and his unforgettable sidesaddle putting stroke, put us ten under par after nine holes. After a brief break for a beverage we proceeded to the tenth tee.

"You boys better pick it up," Snead admonished us. "I don't intend to lose this thing."

We finished the event at a record twenty-one under par, eight strokes ahead of our closest competitors, having carded four eagles, thirteen birdies and the one lonely bogie.

The day ended with an outdoor barbeque dinner and a few more off-color jokes from Sam. Cooper Communities got their high-profile media event with a golf star ... and I got an unforgettable memory with the legendary Sam Snead.

CHAPTER 21
IT'S ALL IN THE PRESENTATION

GEORGE M. CLIFTON

George Clifton, a second-generation golf course architect, designed Florida courses with CEC Golf Design Group, such as the Legends Course in Clermont, Stoneybrook Golf Club in East Orlando, Prestwick Golf Club in Ormond Beach, and the Grey Oaks Palms Course in Naples. CEC is also responsible for countless golf holes at The Villages in Ocala.

I had been selling fertilizer chemicals to golf courses when my buddy Kenny Ezell and I decided we were going to make a career change to golf course architecture. My father, Lloyd Clifton, was already working in the profession, so we assumed, with his help, we'd be able to make a smooth transition.

We quit our jobs when we found ourselves in the talks to create four possible golf course projects. We gave the best presentations rookies could give, albeit somewhat low-key.

Three of the jobs never happened.

Then Ken Ezell and my father were driving back from Ocala through Lady Lake when Ken said to Dad, "Why don't we pull in and see how the guys at The Villages are doing?"

My dad and I had designed a course in The Villages development a few years earlier. The timing was very good—it just so happened they were actually planning on building another course and asked if we would do it for them.

That was almost twenty years ago, and we're now up to 294 holes of championship golf and 279 holes of executive. At the end of the day we'll have 621 holes of golf in one development, the largest golf development in the world.

We've made a career's work at The Villages, where thousands of active, retired residents drive through the neighborhoods on golf carts and play golf daily.

We quit our jobs when we found ourselves in the talks to create four possible golf course projects.

CHAPTER 22
WE'RE IN THE POT

BILL COORE

Bill Coore began his professional design and construction career in 1972 with the firm of Pete Dye and Associates. Coore formed his own design company in 1982, completing Texas courses Rockport Country Club and Kings Crossing Golf and Country Club in Corpus Christi and Golf du Medoc in Bordeaux, France. Admiration and respect for the classic golf courses of the Golden Age of Architecture by MacKenzie, Macdonald, Maxwell, and Tillinghast inspired PGA Tour star Ben Crenshaw and Bill Coore to establish the firm of Coore and Crenshaw Inc. in 1986. Together, they created the Sand Hills Golf Club in Mullen, Nebraska; Cuscowilla Golf Club in Lake Oconee, Georgia; Friars Head Golf Club in Baiting Hollow, New York; and the Plantation Course at Kapalua.

One of the very few times I worked outside the country was a decidedly memorable experience.

In the middle 1990s, I traveled to Irian Jaya, Indonesia, to build Klub Golf Rimba Irian, a golf course for Freeport MacMoRan, which was an American mining company working on one of the largest gold, silver, and copper mines in the world. Irian Jaya, near the equator, was truly one of the most remote, isolated places in the world. Downed World War II–vintage aircraft, which had crashed due to heavy cloud cover, were still being discovered high on the glacier.

The mining company commissioned the course for political reasons. President Suharto, the dictator at the time, loved to play golf, as did many Indonesian government officers. The company had already created a village, with a mosque, church, theater, and schools, for its many employees.

Design associate Rod Whitman and I laughed about it at the time, but we'd been warned that the golf course site was so remote that there were still tribes in the jungle that practiced cannibalism.

"I wonder how they cook people?" Whitman joked.

One morning, after breakfast, Whitman and I went out on the site alone. We were clearing centerlines for the fairways when we were startled by four indigenous tribesmen who came out of the bushy growth right in front of us. They weren't wearing any clothes, but they had bows and arrows, blowguns, and spears.

We froze in our tracks.

The tribesmen looked at us. We looked at them. Nobody said a word until Whitman finally uttered, "Oh, man . . . we're in the pot!"

Much to our relief, the tribesmen turned and moved on.

CHAPTER 23
DANGEROUS LIAISONS

JOHN COPE

John Cope is a senior design associate with Nicklaus Design. He's worked on The Peninsula in Rehoboth Beach, Delaware; Cap Cana's Punta Espada Course in Punta Cana, Dominican Republic; and, in North Carolina, The Palisades in Charlotte and St. James Plantation—The Reserve in Southport, as well as a number of golf courses in Asia.

When I was working on a project in India, I was driven around by a fellow I took to calling Maverick due to his rather aggressive driving style. On one trip back to New Delhi from Chandigarh, I actually broke off the "hang on" handle above my head in a brand new Volkswagen Passat. Maverick had made a "shoot the gap" maneuver between a sacred cow and a ten-wheeler truck!

Hazardous driving in foreign countries is not the only danger I've faced as a golf course architect.

During a lunch break at Westlake Golf Club in Hangzhou, China, a thunderstorm moved in and unleashed a strong downpour of two inches of rain. I was eating with the contractor and decided to go back to the site to help remove the drain grates from the catch basins, which were plugged up with grass clippings.

The drainage foreman was on a golf hole on the other side of the lake from where the irrigation technician and I were working. He wanted to join us on our side of the lake, but rather than walking around the lake he decided to swim across the water at its narrowest distance—about thirty yards. Without taking off his jacket or boots, he jumped in and started swimming across, but quickly became waterlogged. He realized that he was not making much progress and started to panic.

After watching him for a couple of seconds, I realized he wasn't going to be able to swim the last five yards to make it to the bank. I cautiously worked my way into the lake to grab him while trying to keep a grip on the bank. My reach came up about a foot short of him so I had to let go of the bank to grab him. But the second I touched his arm, he stood up and we both realized that we were standing in only four feet of water!

CHAPTER 24
WORLD WAR II WORKS IN PROGRESS

GEOFFREY S. CORNISH

Geoffrey Cornish, a past president of the American Society of Golf Course Architects, began his career in 1935 and by 1980 had planned more courses in the New England states than any other architect in history. He is now a principal in Mungeam Cornish Golf Design, based in Uxbridge, Massachusetts. He's designed, among many others, International Golf Club in Bolton, Massachusetts; Center Valley Club in Center Valley, Pennsylvania; and the Quechee Club in Quechee, Vermont. Cornish also designed, in Canada, Summerlea Golf and Country Club in Montreal, Quebec; and the New Ashburn Golf Course in Halifax, Nova Scotia.

This story is typical of a period from the end of the Korean War in 1953 to around 1960. That period followed almost a quarter century of depression and war, starting with the stock market crash in 1929 and lasting until 1953.

I entered private practice in 1953 following seven years of working with renowned Canadian course architect Stanley Thompson and spending five years with the Canadian Army overseas, before five years of teaching at the University of Massachusetts.

By 1953 there were fewer golf courses in the United States than in 1929, while millions of servicemen and displaced persons had returned or were returning to their homelands. The world was in a state of flux. Nonetheless, intense interest in golf was apparent, but money to build new courses was inadequate.

An answer was "work in progress" layouts, which involved opening courses with many features, even important ones, missing—but with the intention of adding them when funds became available from memberships and greens fees. The method worked, perhaps because families that had been scattered around the globe, often in peril, were happy to be together again on a course, finished or unfinished.

Probably there is a bit of a pioneer in each of us that revels in creating something out of nothing. Members also contributed to actual construction, often in stone-picking parties. Those work parties were also surprisingly successful, except when the keg of beer was opened too early. Many work in progress layouts eventually became fabulous, if plans were followed. Yet problems abounded for the course architect, mostly when committees promoting the course neglected to tell members that the layout would open, but unfinished.

I look on the guys and gals that tolerated these conditions and eventually achieved greatness as giants on earth, as were the course superintendents who maintained and enhanced the courses with limited funds.

CHAPTER 25
NAKED MEETINGS, SNAKES, AND BUZZARDS

BRIAN COSTELLO

San Francisco native Brian Costello joined JMP in 1989 and became a principal of the firm in 1994. Among his most noteworthy designs are Whiskey Creek Golf Club near Washington, D.C.; Callippe Preserve Golf Club and Los Lagos Golf Club in California; Costa do Sauipe Golf Links and Fazenda da Grama Golf Club in Brazil; Belnatio Golf Club, Nasu Chifuriko Country Club, and Golden Palm Country Club in Japan; and Blackstone Exclusive Golf Club in Jeju, Korea.

While on a business trip to Japan, a client invited me and several of the project mangers to play golf over the weekend at his club. As is customary after a round of golf, we took a shower and a soothing soak in the indoor hot springs.

This particular club also had an adjacent outdoor hot springs pool fully enclosed by a beautiful garden and cascading waterfall. Eventually the group gathered at the outside pool and sat up to our necks in the hot water.

We had been discussing different styles of waterfalls for the clients' new eighteen-hole golf course, which was about halfway through construction. The hot springs' waterfall had some interesting features, and with the assistance of one of our English-speaking associates, I was pointing out some of the features we wanted to try to emulate. We got into a rather animated discussion, until the chairman stood up out of the water and walked, completely naked, over toward the waterfall to point out a particular feature.

In short order, all of us were standing buck naked in front of the waterfall, in water now at our knees, pointing in deliberate fashion and carefully waving our arms, so as to not produce any exaggerated movement in the nether regions! It must have been quite a sight for any other club members watching the four of us gather in front this waterscape, blocking their view with our naked bodies. I can only imagine they must have been thinking, "What the heck is so interesting?"

Working in the Far East has resulted in many colorful experiences. For several days we had been canvassing a site on Jeju Island, in South Korea. In addition to struggling to walk the centerlines through some very difficult forested and heavily vegetated terrain, we were also trying to identify the best location for the clubhouse. Our local guide, with machete in hand, was quite helpful when we needed to clear waist-high brush and vines. He also cautioned us about the occasional loose lava boulders we had to traverse.

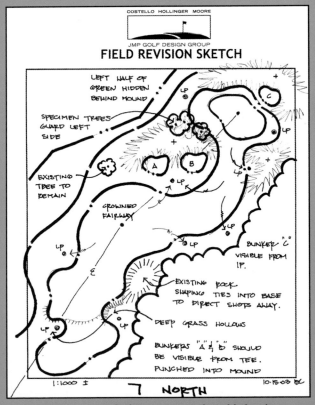

Black Stone 7 North Field sketch—some insight into the methods and purpose.

On the third day the client joined us to review our general findings and our recommendation for the location of the clubhouse. We retraced our steps across areas that we had previously cut our way through. As we were approaching the bluff where we had spent considerable time over the past few days, the guide went berserk. He waved his machete, ran up to the owner, and grabbed him to pull him backwards. The commotion caused everyone to pause and take notice.

"What is going on?" I asked the translator, who listened intently to the conversation. He then turned to me.

"He is warning the owner that there are several dens of very poisonous snakes right where he was going to step."

I asked for clarification.

"There are poisonous snakes all over here," he said. "These snakes are small, but they have enough poison to kill over twenty men!"

Traffic in São Paulo is miserable. With a population of over 19 million people, there seems to be a perpetual traffic jam into and out of the city. As a result, there is a considerable number of helicopters that crisscross the skies to move executives and the well-to-do.

We were working on a project, which, on a good day, was about an hour's drive from the edge of the city. The client used his helicopter to go back and forth to the site frequently. I was able to use the helicopter on occasion and had a few thrilling incidents—landing on top of a downtown skyscraper with firefighters in full gear waiting for us to land on the postage-stamp landing pad. I was told the firemen were a requirement in case something went wrong with the landing.

One day, during lunch at the site, the client explained that his helicopter pilot had died in a motorcycle accident and he would be flying with his new pilot for the first time that afternoon.

"I worry about the health of my pilots," he said in front of his new pilot, "because, even though I sit up front, if the pilot gets into trouble or has a heart attack, I don't know how to fly."

It was at that point the client informed me I'd be flying back to São Paulo with him in the chopper at the end of the day.

When it came time to fly, we strapped into our seatbelts. As I put on my headset, the client looked back at me and winked. I took a look at the pilot; he looked healthy.

We took off from the heliport in the sleek, brand-new craft and, after circling the site a few times to look at the shaping and the shadows being cast across the course, we turned toward São Paulo for the twenty-five-minute ride. We leveled off, and shortly after that, I heard the pilot responding to the air traffic controller over the headsets. The pilot then adjusted something on the dashboard and then pointed just off to our left side, and then suddenly took a hard dive to the right.

"Oh my God," I thought. "Is he having a seizure or heart attack?"

The pilot quickly regained control and explained that he had made the dramatic maneuver to avoid a flock of buzzards ahead of us.

"Hitting them would have been trouble," he said in broken English, illustrating his point by making a motion with his hand rolling off toward the ground.

The pilot then asked us to help him look ahead because there were a lot of buzzards flying around at that time of year. I don't think we blinked for the remainder of the trip!

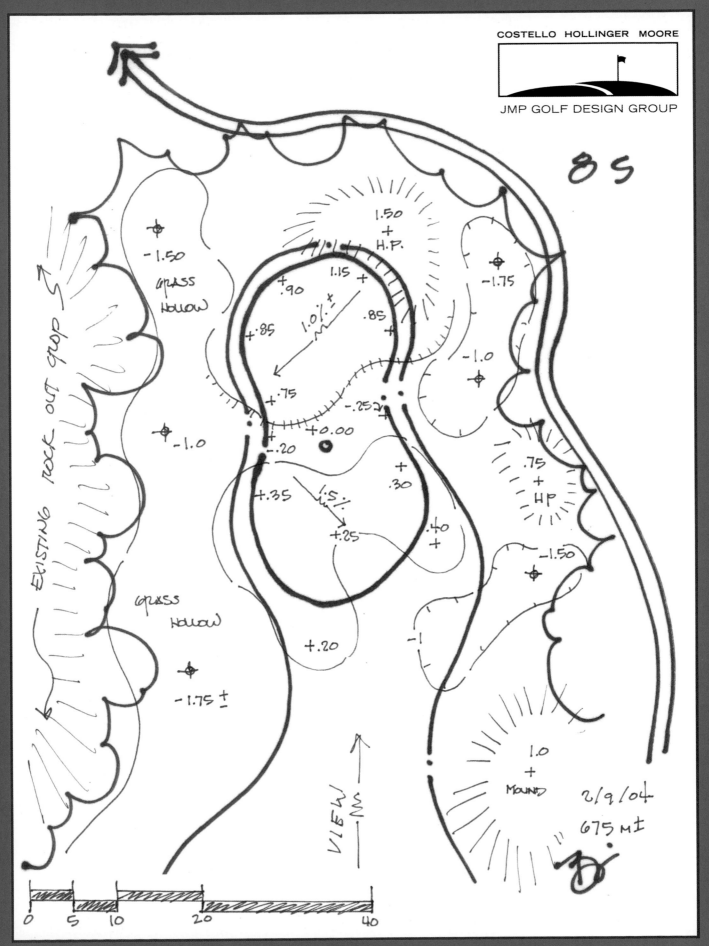

CHAPTER 26
FACING JUST ANOTHER EPIPHANY

BOB CUPP

Bob Cupp served as senior designer for Jack Nicklaus for fifteen years before forming Cupp Design, Inc. in 1984. He served on the board of directors of the American Society of Golf Course Architects. He also authored the acclaimed book, *The Edict: A Novel from the Beginnings of Golf*. His golf course design work includes Cloud 9 at Ghost Creek and Witch Hollow at Pumpkin Ridge Golf Club; Angel Park in Las Vegas; The Club at Savannah Harbor; Crosswater at Sunriver Resort; Old Waverly; Emerald Bay in Destin; Indianwood Country Club's New Course; the Plantation Course at Reynolds Plantation; Star Pass Resort in Tucson; and Shadow Wood Country Club in Bonita Springs.

It was one of those March days in south Florida when the wind gusted in unpredictable blasts up to thirty miles an hour, testing every player in an obscure PGA event conducted each month by the South Florida Section at one of the member clubs, which were always closed on Mondays. The players (local club pros, their assistants, and a few winter-time visitors) threw fifty dollars in the pot and competed for the prize. It was a time for newcomers to make their mark or for the old hands to prove they still could.

In 1967 I was still several years short of thirty, an assistant club pro as obscure as the event in which I placed my money; precious dollars in those days, but that particular fifty, it turned out, would buy me a glimpse of my future—or perhaps more accurately, an honest look at a spotted past that was about to come to a close.

Less than a year prior, I had held a relatively good position as an art director for an advertising agency into which I followed my education and stated goals for life. Unfortunately, I had hit a wall. A year and a half into my directorship, creativity had become my pariah. The evolving emotional upheaval was ostensibly an early mid-life crisis or, perhaps, just sheer boredom. As far back as memory served, creativity had always fueled my psyche. When I took that job after my military commitment was complete, I discovered that creativity-on-demand was no longer fun. The spontaneity, variety, and freedom

evaporated in the neckties, blazers, and starched shirts, and it was a crisis of the first order.

But I was still young enough to be bulletproof. Quite accidentally, I fell upon an opportunity to produce an advertising program for a man who owned a small golf course—a strange, diminutive character with a shifty glance that belied his otherwise honorable (I would later discover) character. The marketing "package" was primarily composed of a series of newspaper ads, which, for all intents and purposes, was the volume merchandising of golf equipment at discount prices. He asked my fee and I blithely responded, in my most professional manner, "One percent of the gross increase of business—and, since I really need to understand the golf industry, playing privileges." The latter, of course, was the hook, and I said it in dead earnest. All I wanted was free golf. We wrote a simple agreement.

I know he believed an ad might have a lot of value because he told me so many years later. He thought the sales would cover the cost of the ads plus a little. I knew exactly how every element of the ad would work, but was oblivious to its potential. It exploded, driving his inventory from less than $15,000 to over a quarter of a million in less than a year.

Within three months the owner told me he could not afford to pay me the gross percentage because I would be making more money than him, but that if I was interested, he would be happy to hire me to run his growing shop. The following Monday I walked calmly into the office of the senior partner of my firm and said good-bye. Welcome to the golf business.

I continued playing as an amateur with some success because suddenly there was plenty of time to practice—and I had rid myself of my demon. Within the year, a private club offered me a similar position and the new pro suggested I declare my status as a professional. He even allowed me to give a few lessons and put my name on the door below his. In my liberation from "art-on-demand," the creative urges came back and in the first few months in this exciting new environment I drew a number of adjustments to the course, some new tees, two fairway bunkers, and a new bunker at one of the greens, all of which the pro thought should be presented to the owner.

Now fade to the windy March day at Redlands Country Club, well south of Miami—forking over my hard-earned fifty.

For whatever reasons, the golf that day was easy. I was not distraught over a thirty-seven in the blow on the front nine because it could have been much better, but I was a rookie and nerves had undercut my confidence somewhat. But as we played on, it became obvious that I was doing much better than my two mates—one of the oldsters, a well-regarded club pro, and another assistant like me in his third year. I was becoming comfortable.

A birdie on a downwind par-five preceded a four-hole run of bogey-birdie that put me on the sixteenth tee at even par and feeling pretty good, though not bulletproof enough to stave off visions of doubles from there to the house.

But one long putt and two downwind holes enabled me to turn in a seventy-two, to the raised eyebrows of the scorekeeper, which felt especially good.

Little did I know at the time that this would be the apex of my professional playing career. What happened next would change my life.

From the scorer's table I turned toward the scoreboard. Two seventies met my eye right away, becoming the first twinges of reality. Then I saw a sixty-eight. "Good grief," I thought, "what kind of animal goes four under on a day like this?"

Then I saw it. There, the last score on the board at the bottom. A sixty-two.

I traced the numbers back to the left; a series of twos and threes, several fours, maybe a five, and the total was not a mistake. My eyes finally reached the name. "Gibby Gilbert! Who ever heard of Gibby Gilbert?" My mind disintegrated into disbelief.

But I would soon learn who Gibby was; within a few years he would win PGA Tour victories at Houston Champions, the Danny Thomas in Memphis, and the Walt Disney World National Team Championship. All in all, he would win ten events plus a record three Tennessee State Open Championships.

But there I was. Having just played what I thought was a great if not brilliant round, and I had been beaten by ten shots. Through the combined astonishment, disappointment, and anger, the forces of the real world settled on my soul. The truth was obvious. I was not good enough for this and could never win. My transformation had begun.

Looking back now, I realize that human resilience is amazing. About the time I accepted defeat, my remaining elements had formed into some sort of new alignment. The drawings of tees and bunkers came into focus. They were golf. I loved golf. I could draw. Maybe I couldn't beat the Gibby Gilberts of the world, but I could draw—so that's where I had to go. I think I turned away from that looming dark green structure a different person. The transformation was that fast. Just as suddenly, the confidence (or was it wishful thinking?) was coming back. I knew that as soon as it was possible to arrange a meeting with my new boss, I would present those changes to our course.

It was in fact the next day, and again, with the help and support of the head pro, I found myself sitting in an office with my drawings.

"Wow," said the boss, to my surprise. "These look really good. Go do it!"

When the stars actually do align, or if indeed there is a grand plan, I must have been in it. I found the help and did the work to the satisfaction of everyone, followed by a number of other repairs to the course. I received inquiries from other clubs for services, and collaborated with an engineer to do three holes for the Air Force base (then, ludicrously, the remaining six holes) and finally a new eighteen for another developer. I was on my third eighteen and had completed a number of other revisions when I had a call from Jack Nicklaus. He called me himself as I sat in my little construction building on the unfinished fourth fairway and I almost fell out of the shack onto the dirt. His voice was unmistakable. Nicklaus wanted to speak with me about his dream of his own independent design company. Over the years I would learn he, too, had a sudden, striking understanding about himself and his love of design. As it turned out, this phone call was about more beginnings; certainly for him and what

I know now to be a great source of satisfaction to him. But for me, it was the beginning of the rest of my life.

About thirty years later, when Gibby was inducted into the Tennessee Golf Hall of Fame, we fried him at the banquet with all the humor and honor we could muster. It was fun. I told him this story, up to the point of my epiphany, citing my decision to enter the design world at the instant I saw that sixty-two on the scoreboard—and Gibby's comment was a classic. "Bob," he said, "You made the right choice."

When the stars actually do align, or if indeed there is a grand plan, I must have been in it.

CHAPTER 27
FROM PEBBLE BEACH TO THE FAR EAST

BRIAN CURLEY

Seeing the hole through an architect's eyes.

Brian Curley, a principal with Scottsdale, Arizona–based Schmidt-Curley Design, Inc., was raised in Pebble Beach, California, where he played, caddied, and worked at area courses developing an appreciation of the game and its architecture. He began his career with Landmark Golf Company as a land planner and eventually focused largely on course design and construction, working later with Ron Fream on an extensive list of international projects. Schmidt-Curley has combined with twelve golfing legends to create Mission Hills, the world's largest golf resort, outside Hong Kong. Some of his other projects include California courses such as the Crosby National Golf Club in Rancho Santa Fe, the Faldo Course at Shadow Ridge in Palm Desert, and Talega in San Clemente. He also designed Royal Oaks Country Club in Houston, Texas; the Las Vegas Paiute Resort; Royal Dunes in Phoenix, Arizona; and Vidbynas in Stockholm, Sweden.

Hole 14 at Royal Dunes in Phoenix, Arizona.

I have been going to Asia once a month for twelve years, so my travel experiences have been varied, especially within mainland China. The main lesson I've learned is that when it comes to travel, you have zero control over some things, so there is no sense in getting upset. The key is to fly first class or business whenever possible—not so much for the seat but for the lounge and preferential treatment when there is an issue; the waits can extend for hours and hours.

I can't say I've had a "difficult" client, but we have certainly worked for some inexperienced developers: those who didn't know a par-three from a par-four or -five. I would hate to see what could have happened to them with a poorly qualified architect and no checks and balances.

Our company has probably worked with more PGA Tour players as golf course design consultants than any other—the list is long. The input of those players varies from none to slight with the occasional decent contribution. Although the input is often small, I never forget the notion that it is their name on the golf course and I need to honor their wishes and those of the client. Once the design process starts however, it keeps going. I tell the players and design consultants that we are like the bus driver: you can choose to get on or off, but the bus keeps moving!

I owe my career to my parents, especially my dad for moving the family to Pebble Beach when I was young. I may never have gotten into the business if my dad hadn't been a golfer himself. He taught me the game and, since he was very gregarious, showed me how to deal with people.

From the age of twelve, I knew I wanted a career in golf. I was a decent player but far from a threat to join the Tour, especially with the talented juniors around the area, including Bobby Clampett. Every golf professional I knew complained about his or her job, so I ruled out being a club professional. Very little if any attention was paid to the golf architect, even on the most highly regarded courses. Cypress Point, for instance, was never referred to as an Alister MacKenzie design—it was simply Cypress Point. The architect of Pebble Beach was similarly anonymous.

One day, while working as a cart boy at Spyglass Hill, I noticed that the course was designed by a guy named Robert Trent Jones. If he could make a living at it, so could I, I thought. The artistic end came naturally to me, as I could always draw, although Pete Dye later told me that the most important thing to be able to draw is a paycheck!

There is no question that both my partner Lee Schmidt and I consider Pete Dye our mentor. I was extremely fortunate to cut my teeth with Pete during a period of time when he was doing some of his most influential designs. Part genius and part knucklehead, he could not only come up with crazy ideas but convince a client to buy into them. Nobody in this business comes close to Pete in combining quality work and a unique personality. Nobody ever will.

There is no doubt that the architect's role is much more art than science, and becoming more so all the time. As the world of communication grows, imaging of courses becomes more prevalent and accessible. There was a time when a course's reputation was spread strictly through word of mouth or a photo or two shown to the privileged few. Now photos are easily obtained, shared, and promoted. Even the most private facility can be accessed by Google Earth. The result, in a world of instant gratification, is that a golf course gets judged largely on looks. This, in turn, places greater demand on a course to look good now, not years down the road. The architect, in turn, must keep pace with the visuals as well as the long list of other elements of design and construction.

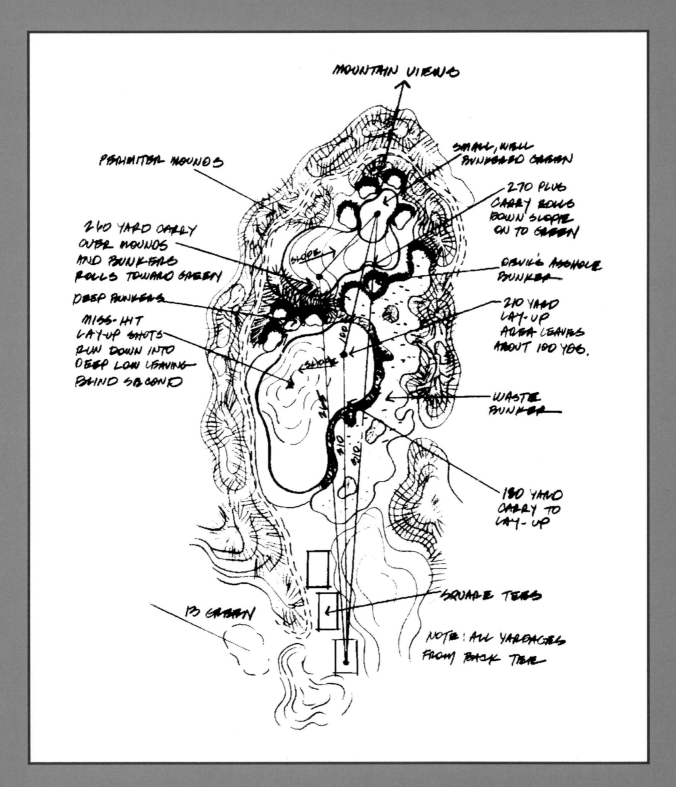

Royal Dunes 14th hole on paper.

CHAPTER 28
READING THE GRAIN IN
BERMUDA GRASS GREENS

MIKE DASHER

Mike Dasher has twenty-six years of experience in golf course architecture, having completed more than fifty new courses. The majority of Winter Park, Florida–based Dasher Golf Design's work is in the southeastern United States, although he has also completed projects in Texas, Pennsylvania, and Puerto Rico. A civil engineer by training, Dasher believes that great courses should be able to be maintained to a high standard of maintenance at minimal cost, and that good drainage is crucial to high quality maintenance. Dasher designed Florida courses such as Eagle Dunes Golf Club in Sorrento, Highlands Reserve Golf Club in Davenport, and North Shore Golf Club in Orlando, as well as Georgia layouts Bentwater Golf Club in Acworth and the Traditions of Braselton Golf Club.

A friend of mine, Tom Horan, hosted a live, call-in television show titled *Let's Talk Golf* on Orlando cable television in the 1990s. I made two guest appearances on the show.

The routine was to arrive thirty minutes early before airtime, have my makeup applied, get a microphone attached, and go through a sound check.

One of the stagehands, just before we were to go live, brought a handful of golf clubs up onto the stage and laid them to the side of my chair.

Computer imagery changed the golf architecture business.

"What are those for?" I asked her.

"Some of our guests will pick up one of the clubs in order to demonstrate a proper golf swing," she explained.

While Horan and I both had reasonable golf swings, I doubted any callers would, or should, be asking us for instructional demonstrations!

Instead, we took some viewer calls from listeners asking about a golf course we had just finished building about an hour west of Orlando. I showed some photos of the course on the air.

A caller named Herb then rang through.

"Tom, I just moved here from New Jersey," Herb told Horan, "and I'm having a heck of a time reading these Bermuda grass greens here in Florida. Ask that architect fellow if he could give me a few tips."

I thought for a second about discussing the principles of grain in the green and the ways golfers can determine which way the grain was going until I remembered there was an old putter in the stack of golf clubs next to my chair. I grabbed the putter and swung into action.

"If you want to know how to read the Bermuda grass greens in Florida," I told the caller, crouching low in front of the camera while closing one eye, "try this!"

CHAPTER 29
THE TRUE GRIT ABOUT GOLF
COURSE ARCHITECTURE

TRIPP DAVIS

Norman, Oklahoma–based Tripp Davis approaches golf architecture from the perspective of a player. He was an NCAA All-America selection while at the University of Oklahoma and is currently ranked as one of the top amateur golfers in the country. He plays a limited number of national amateur events each year. His Texas courses include the Tribute Golf Club in The Colony and Raven Nest Golf Club in Huntsville. He also designed Grand Elk Ranch and Club in Granby, Colorado; Coldwater Golf Links in Ames, Iowa; and Cherokee Hills Golf Club in Catoosa, Oklahoma.

While I wish I could say I get up at around 5 a.m. every Monday morning to head to the gym for a workout, it probably happens only a few times a month. I try to stay in shape because the travel schedule and long work hours are both a mental and physical challenge.

On most mornings I will set up my large light table with the drawings I need to work on that day. I have a four-foot by eight-foot light table that I love working on because I can get almost any size drawing on it and I can usually set up two or three different drawings for the day.

Depending on everyone else's schedule at Tripp Davis and Associates Golf Architecture that day, including Gary Brawley who works out of Peoria, Arizona, we try to get together around 10 to 10:30 for a Monday conference call to discuss each project, everyone's schedule, and objectives for the week.

Deciding on where to go to lunch, with all of the great restaurants in Norman, can be the toughest decision of the day. On most days, we all go together and everyone tries to leave their cell phones at the office. We rarely talk about work at lunch.

Right after lunch almost always seems to be my most productive drawing time. I am a big believer that anyone can get more done, and do their work at higher level, if they are focused on specifically what they are working on for relatively short chunks of time. If I try to spend more than an hour and a half to two hours on one single thing, it becomes hard to stay extremely focused.

After a short break, I will start drawing again at around 3 p.m., work for another hour and a half, and then get with Hattie, my assistant, to see what she has been working on, review her work, and go over what she needs to be focused on if I am going to be out of town for the next two or three days. By 5 p.m. I will get back to drawing, or attend to paperwork until I usually head for home around 6:30.

Now, let me be clear that this is an ideal day, that does not include conferences calls, putting out fires (they do happen), meeting a deadline, meeting a request (such as getting info to a client, consultant, or builder who has an immediate need in order to keep their work moving), and more. While there are a lot of things that can inhibit a typical day, it is vital to stay disciplined on two things—remaining focused, without interruption, on a task for at least forty-five minutes, and switching gears (attending to e-mail, phone calls, or something else) at least once every two hours.

For a travel day or a day on site, it is typical for me to get up around 5 a.m. Once I get to a site, I like to spend a few minutes with the builder's project superintendent to see how things are going. With almost every visit there are also meetings I have with the client or a client representative, or on occasion one of the engineers or planners.

I get the greatest satisfaction from seeing things being built and making those minor adjustments that will make the work that much better. I anticipate the opportunity to get out on the course the whole time I am on the way to a project, and I like to get out there as soon as possible.

I have the most fun working on features to make sure they work visually. I am a firm believer that what the player sees is most important. Even a subtle shift of a tee ten feet left or right, or the raising of a bunker lip just one foot, can have a dramatic impact on the feel the player has. I use the ability to create a certain feel to a shot as much or more than the plan view layout of features in the development of strategy. It is one of the ways in which I can make a hole look more challenging, especially to the better player, than it really should play—an important tool in making a golf course strategically interesting, yet not overly difficult physically for the average player.

I actually like the time during construction right before we are ready to grass. A golf hole that is prepped for grassing is about as beautiful to me, if not more so, than after it is grassed and ready for play.

I will try to spend at least a day and a half on each job site—or more if I might be gone for a couple of weeks before getting back. I really prefer to be around as things are built rather than coming in merely to comment on design and provide direction for something I hope to look at during my next visit. Being on site as things are built is more fun, it engages the guys on the job to work harder, and we can get more done and move on. I like to try and get a few of the guys on site together for dinner.

The day to day of being a golf course architect is not often as glamorous as it might seem to be, but at the end of the day, after a plan you worked hard to develop comes to life in the dirt, it is satisfying.

A golf hole that is prepped for grassing is about as beautiful to me, if not more so, than after it is grassed and ready for play.

CHAPTER 30
SPEAK TO YOUR CLIENTS
IN THEIR LANGUAGE

P. B. DYE

P.B. (Paul Burke) Dye is the youngest son of groundbreaking architects Pete and Alice Dye. Despite his lineage, Dye is known as a self-made, hardworking architect who has no office, staff, or overhead, preferring to live on job sites and build golf courses himself by hand. Dye also spends time between his Ohio and Florida homes and on the family compound in the Dominican Republic. His most notable courses include Loblolly Pines, The Honors in Chattanooga, Fisher Island, Palm Beach Polo Cypress Course, Debordieu, Punta Cana Resort's La Cana Course, and P. B. Dye Golf Club.

I've grown up understanding the necessary balance of golf and real estate. If you ask a real estate developer to build a golf development, you're going to have a poor golf course, since the course will be secondary to the home sites. If you ask a PGA Tour player who has won twenty majors to design a course, the home sites will be shortchanged. But ask a ditch digger and son of Pete Dye like me, and you'll find out that I know how to find the balance between the golf course and the real estate.

At Punta Cana Resort and Club, in the Dominican Republic, I was able to build the La Cana Golf Club, thanks to my friend Oscar de La Renta, the fashion designer, getting my foot in the door. Oscar lives in a very stylish oceanfront home at Punta Cana, and he designed the Tortuga Bay Suites for the resort. Oscar introduced me to Frank Rainieri, the chief executive officer of Punta Cana, and Rainieri hired me to design the course beside his beloved resort and residential development on land along the Caribbean Sea.

The coastline, where I designed the seventeenth hole, was fronted by a row of palm trees all along the beach. I wanted very much to take out those trees and open up the hole to the beach and ocean. But Mr. Rainieri loves trees—and I knew it. He is a creative and avowed environmentalist. His Punta Cana is a very "green-friendly" resort. He did not want

those trees removed under any circumstances. He is also a keen businessman, so I figured I could reason with him. I took him out to the site so he could see the potential for the hole and so I could explain to him why I wanted to take the trees out. But Rainieri, for all his vision and talent, was not a golfer. The more I pled my case about removing the trees, the higher I could sense Rainieri's blood pressure rising. But I was justifying my reasoning to him from a golfer's point of view, so I wasn't really connecting.

Frank was a pilot. In fact, that is how he discovered the land—and the investors—to develop Punta Cana Resort and Club. On the far eastern reaches of Hispaniola, the land was so thick with growth and vegetation it was inaccessible in any way other than by air. Young Frank, twenty at the time, was a crop-dusting pilot who, since he was very familiar with the terrain, had been hired to give some New York investors an aerial tour of the "wasteland" they'd just acquired. Since Frank was a local Dominican, the investors relied on his expertise, and his vision that resort cottages would be a good start. The rest is history—and those palm trees would be, too, if I could just find a way to convince him. We were both pilots, so I tried a fresh angle.

"Frank, imagine the seventeenth hole is a runway, and you're trying to land your airplane. You're at the controls," I said, grabbing the steering wheel for effect. "Your aircraft has a three-hundred-foot-wide wingspan, but your landing strip is only two hundred feet wide. That would frustrate you as a pilot just as much as that row of trees will drive golfers mad when they try to drive a golf ball down this fairway!"

Rainieri leaned toward me and listened intently. I had his attention, and I knew it was time to talk turkey and go for the close. I told him, "Those two golf holes on the ocean, if the trees are taken out, will be very photogenic. Pictures will appear in magazines all over the world. People will want to come to Punta Cana and the course will be very popular. And if the course is popular, it will continue to make money for your children and grandchildren long after you are gone, Frank."

The light bulb went on. I could virtually see it in Rainier's eyes. We agreed to remove the trees but then replant them three hundred feet inland in beach sand as part of some elaborate landscaping on a residential lot, which would dramatically increase the value of the home site.

Later, Robert Trent Jones Jr. told me he'd been trying to get Rainieri to remove trees for years! It only took me fifteen minutes to convince him … but I had to speak his language in order to help him see my vision.

I had his attention, and I knew it was time to talk turkey and go for the close.

CHAPTER 31
DIRTY JOBS

PERRY DYE

Perry Dye began his apprenticeship under his father, Pete Dye, at the age of twelve. Full-time work in golf course design and construction began in the 1980s, with Colorado courses Plum Creek Golf and Country Club in Castle Rock, Glenmoor Country Club in Cherry Hills Village, and Riverdale Golf–The Dunes Course in Brighton. Perry also designed Rancho Santa Fe Farms Golf Club in California, and he collaborated with his father on Big Island Country Club in Hawaii. Perry first took Dye Designs to Japan in 1986 and has since been involved in the design, construction, and maintenance of twenty-two courses there. Golf course projects in Taiwan, Thailand, Japan, Korea, Australia, Austria, Spain, Germany, Brazil, Mexico, Guatemala, Panama, Honduras, and the United States are keeping Dye Designs busy around the globe.

I'm very proud to be part of a strong golf family dedicated to the advancement of design.

Mind you, the job is not always glamorous.

Working for my father when I was thirteen, I was directed to clean out a wet well intake structure. Since I could fit into it, I had to crawl up inside the pipe and drag out the mud bucket by bucket.

Someone came along and asked my father why I was cleaning out the pipe.

"It might be dangerous, and Perry can't sue me 'cause he's my son," my father answered.

Obviously, I was lucky my father introduced me to golf at a young age. He was convinced that the motorized golf cart would mean the end of golf. He felt that the absence of caddies would result in the deterioration of the game because young people, who served as caddies, wouldn't get an introduction to the game.

But the golf cart has allowed people to continue playing into old age, which has benefited the game greatly. In addition, the golf cart has allowed us to put golf courses on land that we could not have used without carts. What the walkers say is true, but they should walk while others should ride.

CHAPTER 32
DUBIOUS DYE DEBUT

PETE AND ALICE DYE

Paul ("Pete") Dye's father designed and built a nine-hole golf course on his mother's farm in Urbana, Ohio, and Pete grew up playing and working on this course. Pete won the Ohio State High School Championship, was medalist in the Ohio State Amateur, won the 1958 Indiana State Amateur Championship, and played in the 1957 United States Open where he finished ahead of both Arnold Palmer and Jack Nicklaus.

Alice Dye won fifty amateur championships, including nine state championships in Indiana, three state championships in Florida, the Women's North and South, and the Eastern. She was a member of the 1970 Curtis Cup Team. She was the first female president of the American Society of Golf Course Architects.

As architects, Alice and Pete designed and constructed their first course, El Dorado, now called Royal Oak Country Club, in Indianapolis. They also co-designed such famous Dye courses as PGA West in La Quinta, California, and South Carolina tracks such as the Ocean Course at Kiawah Island Resort in Kiawah and Harbour Town Golf Links and Long Cove Club on Hilton Head Island. Pete and Alice also collaborated on Crooked Stick Golf Club in Carmel, Indiana; Teeth of the Dog in La Romana, Dominican Republic; and the Tournament Players Club at Sawgrass, the home of the PGA Tour, in Ponte Vedra Beach, Florida.

People often ask us how we got started.

Pete and I were members of the Country Club of Indianapolis and, as greens chairman, Pete finally killed most of the fairway grasses. He decided what he really wanted to do was build golf courses.

After unsuccessfully pursuing a job with Robert Trent Jones Sr., a local Indianapolis farmer-turned-developer gave us a job to build nine holes.

We tried to build a championship course with all the ideas we had from our national tournament experiences. Our carefully drawn routing crossed the creek thirteen times and included trees, bunkers, and small, severely con-toured greens. We were not hired to build the second nine.

The 17th hole at the TPC at Sawgrass, The Players Stadium Course, has one of the most famous greens in the world.

CHAPTER 33
AFTER THE BALL

JIM ENGH

Tullymore Golf Club, at the St. Ives Resort in Northern Michigan, has won national acclaim.

Jim Engh, principal of Engh Golf Design Group, based in Castle Rock, Colorado, spent several years learning the trade from established golf course architects such as Dick Nugent, Ken Dye, and Joe Finger. Engh eventually became the director of golf course design for IMG Developments at its European headquarters in London, England. Under Jim's direction, IMG Developments has worked with such golf legends as Bernhard Langer and Isao Aoki on a variety of projects in over a dozen countries worldwide. Engh designed the Club at Black Rock, in Couer D'Alene, Idhao; Tullymore Golf Club in Stanwood, Michigan; and, in Colorado, The Sanctuary in Sedalia, the Club at Pradera in Parker, and the Golf Club at Red Mesa in Grand Junction.

Tullymore's 535-yard, par-five 18th hole.

I singlehandedly lost the only golf ball in an entire country!

I was working for IMG and based in London in 1988, when a group of five of us traveled to Rega, Latvia, to discuss the possibility of building a hotel and golf resort. This was before the Berlin Wall had come down and travel was very interesting.

We were visiting the Latvian Golf Club, which consisted of a rebuilt house as the clubhouse, a wooden stand with a rubber mat, and a fifty-yard area that had been mown by a group of sheep and goats. Although there was no golf course, the scorecard for the club was a handmade leather notebook with blank pages.

The local members of the club knew little about golf but were very hospitable and eager to learn about the game. They insisted that one of us actually hit a ball from the wooden stand. I was elected. As it turned out, there was only one ball and a choice of hitting a three-iron or a five-iron. With a swamp to the right and tall grass all around, I tried to make an easy, safe pass at the ball. Of course, with a nice pass, I pured the ball into the long grass!

Two hours of searching was to no avail. Yep, I had lost the only golf ball in all of Latvia!

Before departing I took a bundle of stakes and located six holes for the boys to mow down and eventually play. Just like the old days!

Upon returning to London, I sent Latvia a dozen orange golf balls.

Yep, I had lost the only golf ball in all of Latvia!

CHAPTER 34
THE REWARDS OF COLD CALLING

KEN EZELL

Ken Ezell is a partner with the Florida-based Clifton, Ezell, Clifton Golf Design Group. He is the principal architect and master land use planner for The Villages. He's created Florida courses such as Forest Lake Golf Club of Ocoee, Remington Golf Club in Kissimmee, Grey Oaks Country Club's Pine Course in Naples, and Rock Springs Ridge Golf Club in Apopka. He also designed Highland Creek Golf Club and Linville Falls in North Carolina.

Back in 1989, a couple of years after George and Lloyd Clifton and I formed Clifton, Ezell, Clifton Golf Design Group, we were heading home from a project in Ocala, Florida. Along the way, I suggested to Lloyd that he should just stop in and say hello to a past golf consulting client of mine.

Those that know Lloyd know he is quite reserved and shy. George and I almost had to kick him out of the truck. About twenty minutes later, out popped Lloyd with a pronounced bounce in his step. He hopped into the truck.

"Boys, they were thinking about hiring us to do a new course but had not gotten around to calling us," said Lloyd. "We've got it."

The rest is history: Orange Blossom Gardens, as it was then named, evolved into what is now The Villages, the world's largest golf community!

The Villages will have twelve championship venues, ten of which are twenty-seven-hole configurations, plus thirty-five executive length nine-hole courses. These 621 holes of golf will host over 2.5 million rounds each year. The community also has over 30,000 individually personalized golf carts. And all this from a family ownership that doesn't even play golf.

I have been blessed to work on the front end of this project since 1989, master planning this dynamic community plus overseeing and orchestrating the construction, grow-in, and maintenance in addition to golf design services.

What a cold call!

CHAPTER 35
NO ONE LIKES TO BE TURNED DOWN
TOM FAZIO

The tumbling forests of Gaylord, Michigan, made Treetops Resort a great spot for the "Fazio Premier" course. This is the 472-yard, par-four 18th hole.

Tom Fazio was named the Top American Golf Architect by *Golf Digest* in 1991, and in 1995 received the Old Tom Morris Award given by the Golf Course Superintendents Association of America to individuals who have made outstanding contributions to the game. Fazio says he got an early start in the golf course design business from his uncle, George Fazio, and his contemporaries such as Byron Nelson, Jimmy Demaret, and Sam Snead. Tom Fazio has done restoration and redesign work on famed courses such as Augusta National and Pine Valley, but his original works are renowned destinations: the ocean courses at Pelican Hill; Corales at Punta Cana; Black Diamond Ranch; Old Overton; the National Golf Club of Canada; Emerald Dunes; Jupiter Hills Club; Lake Nona; PGA National Resort and Spa; World Woods; Butler National; Caves Valley; Dancing Rabbit; Edgewood Tahoe; Shadow Creek; Pinehurst #4, #6, and #8; Wade Hampton; and his home course, Champion Hills, in Hendersonville, North Carolina.

Q: Where and at what time of day do you find your inspiration? When are you most creative? How do you awaken your muse?

A: I can't even think of the answer. I wake up with high energy and I go to sleep with high energy. I don't believe in being tired. I don't believe in jetlag. No ups or downs. My personality is even-keeled. I've been doing this for so long that it's my job and I love it, but I don't think about it in other terms.

Q: Do you remember ever being nervous about a job? Do you still get nervous?

A: The only time I get nervous is when I have friends involved in a project. I was nervous when Peter Ueberroth forced me into the Pelican Hill Golf Club project in 1988. Ueberroth was the Major League Baseball commissioner and he was CEO of the Los Angeles Olympic Games. I really didn't want to design those Pelican Hill courses, but Ueberroth would not take no for an answer. My family was in North Carolina and I really didn't want to travel west to do it. I thought it was a difficult site. It was spectacular—both eighteen-hole courses at Pelican Hill would be on the edge of Pacific Ocean in Newport Beach, California's "high rent" district—so expectations were extremely high.

Q: At what stage in a project is the moment of satisfaction most palpable?

A: After people have played the golf course and my friends and critics start talking about it. After the fact, it's not about me, it's about the facts: do people like it? When it comes to design in the field, I can talk myself into anything and justify it. So can my clients. But the truth comes when the course is open and other people review it. The golfers know best—that's the real market. If the players don't like it, it isn't successful. Sure, most of the golfers don't know what resources I had available to me, or what my limitations were, but no one wants to hear that story. It's the final product that counts. The proof is in end results, regardless of what you started with.

Q: At what moment does your work feel like a job, and at what moment is it most like a pleasurable passion?

A: I never remember a moment when it felt like a job. It's not. We refer to projects as "jobs," but we don't call what we do a "job." The fun factor is so high. The reaction we get to our involvement in every project is so satisfying. And they're all different.

We ran into a guy named Weldon Wyatt at Sage Valley in Graniteville, South Carolina. He had a literally endless amount of acres. He asked me how many acres we'd like to have for the golf course, and told me if we wanted more than he had, he'd get us more! It was like being a kid in a candy store!

Take Quail Hollow Club in Charlotte, North Carolina. They had a PGA Tour event, the Kemper Open, from 1969 through 1979. George Cobb did the original design in 1961, but the course wasn't very well liked by the players. So the question became, how do we renovate it? A great renovation is harder than creating a new course, but we did it. In the end, after we implemented renovations in 1997 and 2003, the PGA Tour returned and the Wachovia Championship is one of the best-attended events in golf. That is very fulfilling.

Q: At what point in your career did you realize that people in the golf world truly accepted and valued you?

A: Never. I've never thought about it that way. I grew up in golf, so my career has never had a beginning or end. My uncle was a tournament player and my father was a club professional. I knew great players like Ben Hogan, Jimmy Demaret, Sam Snead, and Gene Sarazen. I was young, and then I grew up watching players in the Jack Nicklaus era, and some of those players—Nicklaus, Arnold Palmer, Tom Weiskopf, and Gary Player to name a few—became my competitors in the golf architecture business. But most of my competitors are my friends. Pete Dye is a good friend. It's not really competition. They're doing their thing and so am I. It's life.

Q: Was working on the Augusta National Golf Club the most delicate and high-profile redesign and renovation you've done?

A: I've done work on Winged Foot since 1971 and Oak Hill since 1975. I've been a member at Pine Valley for thirty-five years and it has been a great honor to be involved in additions at historic clubs such as Pine Valley, Merion, Rivera, Bel-Air, and Cypress Point. My involvement with Augusta National gets a lot of attention because it is the most high-profile. Augusta National is, after all, the only course in the world that has held a major championship each year since 1934. The great thing about Augusta is they are dedicated, committed people. Look what they've done decade after decade. Even the press votes the Masters as their favorite tournament to cover.

Augusta National has set a standard, but working on every one of those courses was an honor.

When I was a kid, I never would have dreamed of being a part of those clubs. Now, if I never did anything else, working with those clubs would constitute a dream career.

Q: Were there any golf course projects you turned down or lost the bid for that you still pine over or regret?

A: During the golf boom—there were two booms in the 1980s and 1990s—there were a lot of opportunities to design golf courses around the world. I didn't do that because I had children and I didn't want to travel and be away from home that much. But I've never looked back. It was the right thing to do.

People made offers and my answer was often "no" before they could finish making their offer. It's self-centered and unkind to turn down someone's generous offer. No one likes to be turned down. I always let potential clients know my thoughts well in advance and didn't let things get to the stage that I would have to turn down an offer. I made certain they knew my intent so they understood that my decision making was totally based on timing and the location of their proposed golf course.

Q: From which client did you learn the most about business?

A: Raymond Finch, the client for whom I created Wild Dunes in South Carolina, had a lot of influence on me. In 1981, he was in Washington working on the Ronald Reagan presidential transition team. He'd come back from D.C. and want to talk golf when we were building Wild Dunes. I didn't want to talk golf. Oh, sure, it was a great site on the ocean, but I wanted to talk to him and find out about the White House and why interest rates were 21 percent. I'm a political guy. I love to be "on the inside." He had insights business-wise, and I loved to listen to that.

Steve Wynn, the famed Las Vegas casino developer, wanted to build great golf settings on land he had in the desert. I told him we didn't have the suitable environment to do so. Wynn simply answered, "Well, let's build the suitable environment!" He's obviously a "can-do" guy who thinks outside the box.

William McKee was twenty-eight years old when he decided to found Wade Hampton Golf Club in North Carolina. He didn't have resources to do it, but he took a financial risk. He borrowed against his whole future! And he succeeded. To be a part of that is fabulous.

To see the energy these people had was fabulous. There have been so many of them in my career.

Things are always written about entrepreneurialism and the "American dream." Many of these developers were undercapitalized but they took risks, took chances, and remained dedicated, committed, and a little lucky. The common denominator these people had was that they were positive-minded and looking toward the future.

The future will be different for me. Our resources are better. Our knowledge is better. We build golf courses so much better than we used to. The expectation level is higher than ever.

Having my son Logan involved in our Jupiter, Florida office is great. He's pushing me to do things I resist doing because he wants to do them. Golf is a game of tradition, but in America, it's all about "what's next."

Q: What drives your designs?

A: My goal is to give golfers a feeling, a picture of the setting, so they say, "This is the greatest thing I've ever seen or experienced." I want them to say it again on the next hole, and next hole after that. By the time they get to the fourth hole of one of my courses I'd like them to think it may be the best place they've ever been to or seen. And then it just gets better. By the time they reach the ninth hole, I want them to say, "Obviously, this is the best nine holes I've ever played in my life." Then, by end of the eighteenth hole, I want them to think it was the best course they've ever played and ask when they can play it again.

Q: What contribution has America given to golf course design?

A: We've become a green society. Unfortunately, that is being pushed: green. When you think about green, it is a color and a texture that requires moisture and in some cases fertilizers. We get green programmed in our minds. If we could accept golf in the color brown and program in our minds that brown is good, we could do things differently. We could put less fertilizer on and do things differently in terms of design and maintenance. But unfortunately Americans go to play golf in Scotland, Ireland, Australia, and some of the old, arid environments and they see rough-hewn courses on windswept land, brown and sparse, and they talk about how great it is. Then they go back to their home courses in America and if they see some brown spots, they think the greens superintendent is not doing his job. It's incredible how our minds are like that.

CHAPTER 36
HUNGARIAN GOOSE CHASE

STEVE FORREST

Steve Forrest became an associate with Arthur Hills/Steve Forrest and Associates after earning his bachelor of landscape architecture degree from Virginia Tech in 1979. He became a principal in the firm in October 1999. He is immediate past president of the American Society of Golf Course Architects, and created the concept for this book. In recent years, Steve has been active with the expansion of the Arthur Hills portfolio in Europe. He has completed four new courses in Sweden and is currently working on projects in Norway, Russia, and Poland. Projects in North America take him from Maine to Southern California with an occasional side trip to the Caribbean. Some of Forrest's more notable courses are the Links at Lighthouse Sound in Ocean City, Maryland; Journey at Pechanga in Temecula, California; Sand Golf Club, in Jonkoping, Sweden; Forest Hills Resort and Golf Club outside Moscow, Russia; and White Clay Creek Country Club in Wilmington, Delaware.

The day was June 5th, 2006—a Monday. I was on a business development trip through Europe and had just spent a seemingly successful weekend trying to close our first project in Germany. One potential client had gotten us stuck in the mud near Munich on Friday, but the lunch that followed in the clothing-optional section of a thermal spa quickly took my mind off the earlier mishap.

Topping out at 122 miles per hour on the Autobahn and a tour of Heidelberg with another prospect on Saturday night had been memorable, too. Our timing was perfect—we caught the light show and fireworks that are displayed only four times a year at the famous castle there.

My next solid appointment was on Tuesday in Bratislava, Slovakia. I was to present a plan for a world-class resort course on a small island called Salt Cay in the Turks and Caicos Islands in the Caribbean. It was the best golf course site that our company had in the twenty-eight years that I'd been with Arthur Hills—superb ocean views from the entire course and ten holes directly on the water. We didn't officially have the project under contract yet, so it was very important that the presentation to the potential client go well.

Since that important appointment wasn't until Tuesday, I figured I would try to make Monday somewhat productive by agreeing to check out a potential project site about forty-five minutes north of Budapest in Hungary. This was one of those speculative projects where I didn't know much about the client, his site, or his country. I just took a chance that it might eventually turn into something.

After spending Sunday night at the Steigenberger Hotel at the airport in Frankfort, I caught a Lufthansa flight that landed in Budapest before noon. The good news was that while I was waiting to get off the plane, I received a call from Gyorgi, the man who was to meet me at the airport.

"I will be on the left after you clear customs," Gyorgi told me.

The international arrivals doors opened automatically and I begin surveying the faces of the people standing to the left. No sign of Gyorgi. Maybe he meant outside at the curb? Not there, either. Maybe he meant *his* left? So I went back inside the terminal and looked to the other left. No Gyorgi. I went back outside and tried to call Gyorgi on my cell phone. No answer. I left a message and began looking at faces in the cars stopped along the curb. No Gyorgi. My phone rang, and I answered it to learn that Gyorgi had been waiting on the left all right—sitting in a café, having a cup of coffee!

"Hi, Gyorgi. Steve Forrest. I'm pleased to meet you," I said, extending my hand and sitting at his table.

The 352-yard, par-four 5th hole at The Journey at Pechanga, Temecula, California.

"We will go look at the site and then I will bring you back to the airport," Gyorgi explained, finishing his coffee.

"I would like to travel on to Bratislava by train this afternoon, Gyorgi."

"No problem," he said. "There is a four o'clock p.m. departure which runs along the Danube to Bratislava."

He drove me first to the train station to buy the ticket. The train fare was 7,825 Hungarian Forint. Before I left America, I had printed out a currency exchange chart for the various countries that I knew I'd be visiting, but I hadn't committed it to memory and didn't bother to pull it out before purchasing the ticket. I thought perhaps Gyorgi might offer to help with the cost of my ticket since I had come this far with absolutely no expense to him other than the gas to drive us around, but he remained silent. After a proper intentional delay, I could no longer stand the awkward silence. I gave the ticket agent my credit card and hoped the fare wasn't outrageously high.

We then drove on out into the country on a slippery, winding, two-lane road up a mountain. Gyorgi began to look for the farm road that would lead down to the site. He slowed down at one turnoff, but then kept going. At the next road on the left, he turned in despite the fact there was a pile of dirt that had been placed in the center of the two-track road to discourage people from driving down it. Our compact car had just enough momentum to carry us over the hump, but at the bottom was a mud hole formed by recent rain. It all happened so fast, but I knew we were hopelessly stuck because he had absolutely no momentum or traction with which to reverse back over the hump, and if we went any further forward, the mud hole would've swallowed us up.

"This is the wrong road!" Gyorgi said.

He began to try to reach someone on his cell phone to come pull us out of the mud. I got out and begin to assess the damage and look for anything with which to create some traction. I realized it was hopeless, and then heard Gyorgi shout to me that he'd had no luck telephoning anyone.

Several punk-looking teenagers came walking up the country lane, but walked right past us without even an exchange of looks or bit of conversation. I thought it was eerie that Gyorgi didn't even try to solicit their help to push us out.

"I reached someone," said Gyorgi, fumbling with his phone. "The correct site entrance road is just down the hill. While we are waiting for someone to pull our car out, you should go ahead and see the site. I will walk down the hill with you and then come back to meet the person who is going to tow us out."

I had been traveling for several days in Europe at this point and had a large suitcase, a carry-on case, my briefcase, and a drawing tube containing a plan I was to present in Bratislava the next morning, all of which was locked out of sight in the car. I took my BlackBerry and my camera with me on the walk down the hill with Gyorgi.

About halfway down the hill, five minutes into the walk, Gyorgi spoke.

"I don't feel comfortable leaving the car unattended," he said. "I will go back and stay with the car."

I continued down to the site and took some pictures of a broad valley with a beautiful stream flowing through it—a nice site. After fifteen minutes, I finished taking pictures and headed back up the hill. Somewhere along the walk, my mobile phone rang. As soon as I heard Gyorgi's voice, I knew what he was going to say.

"Oh, Mr. Forrest, I have some terrible news! Someone smashed the window on the car and took everything."

I already had the vision of the open hatchback in my head before I actually reached the car and saw it. It was not a pretty sight. My briefcase was missing. It contained my laptop computer, travel documents, passport, plane tickets, and the train ticket I'd purchased earlier in the day. Also gone were my domestic cell phone, chargers, glasses, calculator, and various files and papers for my trip. The thieves also nabbed my big suitcase with all my clothes. The only things they missed were my street shoes and the tube containing the project drawing.

Gyorgi called the police, and when they arrived, it took ninety minutes to sort everything out. Afterwards, though, I was unable to go on to Bratislava because I had no passport. My deal with the great site in the Caribbean was in jeopardy because I would not make the meeting the next day. Two days later, I was supposed be back in the states to pick up my son from Ohio State University, but I figured I might not even have a new passport by then.

"Mr. Forrest, today is my sixtieth birthday and I have an appointment in one hour. Your golf course design fee is much too expensive for us. But I will take you to any hotel you wish on the way to my appointment," said Gyorgi. "The Kempinski downtown is very nice."

The mishap-filled visit had been for naught, but at the rate it was going, I could not afford Gyorgi much longer anyway.

I already had the vision of the open hatchback in my head before I actually reached the car and saw it. It was not a pretty sight.

"That's fine," I agreed.

Almost on cue, a very attractive woman in a low-cut blouse pulled up in a fancy car and gave ol' Gyorgi boy a passionate kiss. She drove us to the Kempinski in her sexy car.

Gyorgi walked me to the check-in desk and confirmed they had a room for me.

At that instant, my BlackBerry rang.

"Steve, it's Pam."

Pam is the manager from my office in Toledo.

"A police officer just called and said that they found your passport and suitcase, Steve. Quick, write down this phone number."

I gave the phone number to the front desk attendant, who called it and got directions. The hotel provided a driver who took me back out into the country. Forty-five minutes later, we pulled up to a farmhouse with a gate and a concrete walk on the side that led up to a small, covered shelter with a picnic table under it. There, stacked on the picnic table, were my large suitcase and carry-on case. In broken English, with some translation help from the driver, I learned they'd found everything up the road in a ditch. My passport, plane ticket, train ticket, and all my frequent flyer cards were still in the travel document case in the carry-on bag. Amazing! I thanked the finders profusely with a bunch of head nodding and we proceeded back to central Budapest.

On the ride back, I took inventory, and though my briefcase was not recovered, the thieves had dumped most its contents into the carry-on. The important thing missing was my laptop, which was three years old and at 95 percent capacity on the hard drive anyway. Good luck with that English version of Windows!

I called Pam back at the office and she restored all of my airline reservations for Wednesday, so I left an e-mail for the Bratislava clients to tell them our important meeting was back on for 9 a.m. Tuesday.

Once back at the hotel, the desk clerk checked train schedules for me, and there was a 7:45 p.m. departure to Bratislava, but from a different station than my original ticket. There was a 165 Forint surcharge for changing stations. I warily gave the train station attendant my credit card, and she explained that, in U.S. dollars, the original ticket was only $38.20 and the surcharge was $0.81! What a relief!

I got the job from the client in Bratislava the next day, and it was the best site we've ever worked with. Being on that small island in the Caribbean felt as if it was a million miles from Gyorgi and Budapest!

CHAPTER 37
BACK TO THE FUTURE
KEITH FOSTER

Keith Foster started his career as a golf course superintendent at a fifty-four-hole facility in Florida. From 1981 to 1986, he worked with Wadsworth Golf Construction as a construction project manager, and then joined the design firm of Arthur Hills, where he played a major role in the design and completion of sixteen acclaimed courses. In 1991, Keith established his own Paris, Kentucky–based design firm. He completed an extensive renovation of historic Colonial Country Club in Fort Worth, Texas, and the complete restoration of Southern Hills Country Club in Tulsa, Oklahoma, the site of the 2001 U.S. Open. Foster also designed The Quarry in San Antonio; The Tradition Course in Houston; Sunridge Canyon in Scottsdale; The Harvester in Ames, Iowa; and the River Marsh Course at Chesapeake Bay, Maryland.

I'm confident that all practicing golf course architects are rooted in their love of the game—often at an early age. I certainly am thankful for its imprint on my life.

I built a concept I call the Morris Course on my Kentucky farm. Within our farm rests a treeless, thirty-acre parcel with some stone accents and nice terrain.

The Morris Course is a nine-hole layout with seven greens, two of which are double greens with two pin positions. Most of the holes have two tees to create an alternate course with varied yardages and angles. Sixteen bunkers and interesting forms are dotted within the course.

The Morris Course is played with five clubs: a play club, three smooth-faced irons, and a putter, using an old gutty ball. The intent is to play an old-school course with pre-1900 clubs and ball, so the Morris Course is built to the scale of an 1885 golf course.

Golf is a great game, but it's also about relationships. Early in everyone's career, each one of us was given an opportunity and someone put their trust in us.

I worked with Wadsworth Golf Construction. The owner, Brent Wadsworth, saw something in me and had a profound impact on my career.

A few years later, I was working for Wadsworth Golf on a Georgia golf course project for Art Hills. Brent and Art spoke privately about me, and shortly after, Art met and hired me to be part of his wonderful firm.

I had worked with Brent Wadsworth for five years and then with Art Hills for another five years, but their early influence and confidence provided me with a great foundation. Now, twenty years later, I remain ever thankful to each of them.

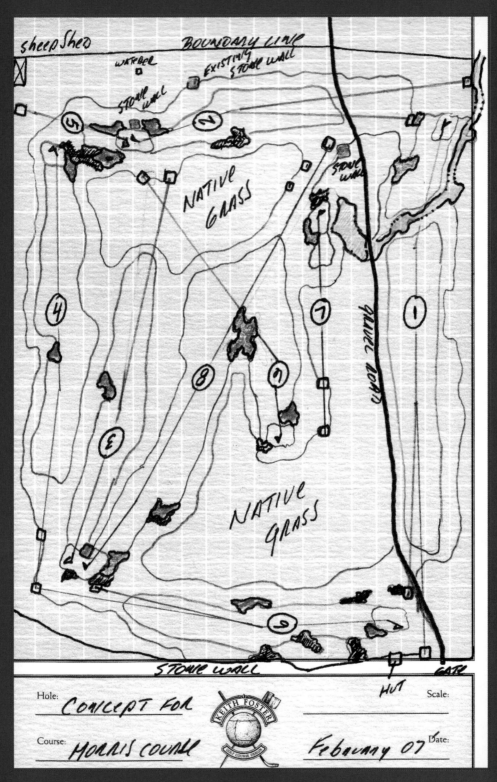

Concept drawing for Morris Course.

CHAPTER 38
ADMONISHED BY ONE OF
GOLF'S GREATEST

TIM FREELAND

Freeland Golf Group's president, Tim Freeland, has gained much of his experience working as a lead designer in the offices of Gary Player Design. Freeland has worked closely with hall-of-famer and golf legend Gary Player for over ten years and, until 2000, was the project architect on more than twenty Gary Player Signature courses and was also involved in collaborations with famed golf course architect Joe Lee. Freeland has helped create the Tournament Players Club at Jasna Polana, in Princeton, New Jersey; Raspberry Falls Golf and Hunt Club in Leesburg, Virginia; Cougar Point in Kiawah Island, South Carolina; Pinewild Country Club in Pinehurst, North Carolina; and the Laurel Oak east course in Sarasota, Florida.

It was my first golf course grand opening, and I could not have been more excited. I was working for Gary Player Design, and, after months of planning and work, finally the ribbon would be cut and golfers would be able to try out our new course.

After all of the speeches, media interviews, hand shaking, golf, dinner, and toasts to the new course, I drove Mr. Player back to his hotel. But he seemed oddly quiet during the short drive.

When we arrived at the hotel, Mr. Player opened his door and got out of the car, but then stopped. He turned, leaned back into the car, and looked me straight in the eye.

"Tim," he said in his South African accent, "if that course is the best you can do, you need to move on with your life's work."

Silence filled the air as I could only look back into Mr. Player's deep, sincere eyes.

I felt sorry for myself and was mad for a while until I realized that Gary Player does not accept a mediocre performance from himself, so why should he accept one from me? I decided that I would not move on, but rather, I would get better.

I went back to the course and spent days looking at it as a critic rather than as a proud father. I was embarrassed by the lack of aesthetic appeal and the flat look of the fairways.

To this day, when I find myself looking at an average hole under construction, just before I'm about to approve it for irrigation, I'll hear Mr. Player's words in my head and his hawklike eyes appear in my memory. Each time, I try to figure out why the hole is just average and then make the necessary changes to make it better.

CHAPTER 39
CONTINENTAL COMPLICATIONS

LES FURBER

GDS Golf Design Services Ltd. is located in Canmore, Alberta, Canada, and was established in 1980 by Les Furber and Jim Eremko. Their design philosophy was influenced in part by their long association with Robert Trent Jones Sr. GDS sports a unique international portfolio, including, in 1991, the first modern-day course in the Czech Republic and the first eighteen-hole course in Cuba, as well as courses in the United States, Switzerland, and Germany. GDS and Les Furber Design have undertaken a twenty-seven-hole project in Lithuania and, in Canada, created Glasgow Hills Golf Resort on Prince Edward Island, SilverTip Golf Resort in their hometown of Canmore, and The Links at Gleneagles in Cochrane, Alberta.

We designed the first modern, eighteen-hole course as part of the present twenty-seven-hole Karlstejn Golf Resort near Prague after the end of the communist rule in the Czech Republic.

During construction, the golf construction contractor refused to attempt to move dirt based on a cubic meter measurement because under the communist system, all the earthwork had been completed on a price per square meter depending on the depth of material to be excavated.

When it became obvious we were at an impasse, and they could not understand earthwork excavation by the cubic meter, it was agreed to complete all earthwork with equipment charging local hourly rates.

I made a site visit to a golf course in Portugal designed by my mentor, Robert Trent Jones Sr., in 1973.

I was staying at the Intercontinental Hotel in Lisbon when I received a phone call from our contractor advising me that the city of Lisbon was under siege and surrounded by the military. The television, radio, and all communications were taken over by the troops and all bank assets were frozen, as well as all border crossings and air travel cancelled.

The coup lasted three days and there was no bloodshed in the streets. As I was a tourist who had a return airfare out of Portugal, I was allowed to leave to go to our office in Spain on the fourth day. The golf course project was finally finished several years later by Cabell Robinson and Robert Trent Jones Sr.

CHAPTER 40
MY FATHER IS NOT JACK NICKLAUS

GARRETT GILL

River Falls, Wisconsin–based Garrett Gill grew up following in the business established by his late father, David Gill of St. Charles, Illinois. Garrett and David worked together for many years and completed numerous golf facilities, including Meadowbrook Links in Rapid City, South Dakota, and Hulman Links in Terre Haute, Indiana. Garrett, with partner George Williams, also designed, in California, Micke Grove Golf Links in Stockton and David L. Baker Memorial Golf Links in Orange County. His Minnesota courses include Inner Wood Golf Course in Inner Grove Heights; Majestic Oaks South in Ham Lake; Willingers Golf Club in Northfield; The Legends Golf Club and the Meadows at Mystic Lake Club, both in Prior Lake; Cedar Creek Golf Club in Albertville; Eagle Ridge Golf Course in Coleraine; and the new Wedgewood Cove Golf Club in Albert Lea.

I returned from Texas A&M in 1977 to work with my father, a prominent Chicago area–based golf course architect. He was given the commission to redesign portions of the St. Charles Country Club in our hometown. The acclaimed golf architect Tom Bendelow designed the original eighteen-hole course in 1924. The now-famed Arthur Anderson management company bought the clubhouse and portions of the front and back nines along the east banks of the Fox River south of town to build a training site. The club then purchased additional land up on the bluffs to replace the lost holes and to build a new clubhouse, which it desperately needed.

My father sited the clubhouse and parking lots and designed great new holes to complete the eighteen-hole layout. The golf course contractor selected to construct the project was the Wadsworth Company, based in Plainfield, Illinois. Wadsworth is a very reputable and highly sought-after firm with whom my father had worked many times. The Wadsworth foreman for the project was Bob Steele.

Naturally, on many occasions, Steele and my father walked the course during construction. On one eventful day, I was participating in one of these walkthroughs. My father was pointing out several items he wanted Steele to correct or modify. Several times, as my Dad would point out issues out, Steele, having just come off a Jack Nicklaus design job before coming to St. Charles, said, "Well, Mr. Nicklaus does it this way." Another time he said, "When I was working on the Nicklaus course, we did it this way."

My dad stopped dead in his tracks, turned and faced Steele square-on, and used a voice I had heard a few times before during my childhood. It was the voice that he'd used when we misbehaved.

"Goddamn it," he bellowed, "I am not Jack Nicklaus!"

Steele didn't bring up the Golden Bear's name again.

CHAPTER 41
NEARLY FATAL EXPERIENCES

LESTER GEORGE

Lester George, based in Richmond, Virginia, designed Kinloch Golf Club in Manakin Sabot, Virginia, and other home state courses such as the Colonial Golf Course in Williamsburg and Captain's Cove Golf Club in Greenbackville. George also created Newport Bay at Ocean City Golf and Yacht Club in Berlin, Maryland. He completely renovated the Old White Course at The Greenbrier in White Sulphur Springs, West Virginia; the DuPont Country Club's DuPont Course in Wilmington, Delaware; and the Country Club of Florida in Village of Golf, Florida. He's successfully transformed two brownfields into golf courses, converting overgrown, hazardous areas into plush, green, recreational turf. Among several other First Tee courses, Lester designed the First Tee Chesterfield, the premiere eighteen-hole First Tee course in the United States, and the First Tee Richmond (a brownfield site).

I was thirty-five years old and had previously owned a timber company, so I was familiar with all aspects of felling trees. I was out with two others in the process of clearing on a new golf course site. I was removing the stump from a large tree that had already been felled, and suddenly I heard a loud "crack!" The tree swung around and struck my leg. My leg was very nearly completely severed by the tree trunk, which had hit right above the boot line. Both lower leg bones were sticking out of my leg. I was losing a lot of blood, and knew I was in dire straits!

The two men with me quickly left to get help, so I was out there by myself, waiting. Lots of thoughts and emotions went through my mind. How could this happen now? Sitting on the golf course alone, I suddenly realized that I was mortal, and that I might lose my leg, maybe even my life.

Because of the extreme conditions of the site, it took almost two hours for the ambulance to get to me. Over the course of that time, I had splinted my own leg, and was in so much pain I could barely remain conscious. Once in the ambulance, the paramedics knew I'd be going right into surgery, so I couldn't be given anything to kill the pain because it would thin my blood. The ambulance even got stuck in the mud on the site at one stage, spinning its wheels until the other fellows pushed it out with a bulldozer. Every little bump in that ambulance caused unimaginable pain, but I was doing what I could to help direct them to get the ambulance unstuck. Time was of the essence in my situation!

When we arrived at the hospital, the pain was absolutely excruciating. The doctor told me my leg was shattered, and that he would try to save it by installing a series of plates and screws. He also had to continuously flush the wound because gangrene had started to set in. Because of the loss of blood, gangrene, and the severity of the fracture, he said the possibility existed that he may have to remove my leg altogether.

I was in such serious shock that I threatened the doctor.

"If I wake up without a leg, we are going to have a serious problem," I warned him. "You wake me up before you make a decision like that."

I will never forget the feeling when I woke up from surgery and saw that the doctor had indeed been able to save my leg. I cried tears of joy.

I was in the hospital for five days, and it took me an entire year to walk without the use of crutches or a cane. It had been such a gruesome experience. After that happened, it made me realize how short and precious life is, and that we must make the most of every day we are given.

You never quite know what other surprises await you on a course site until you actually get there and start working.

My company had just started shaping a golf course at Langley Air Force Base near Hampton, Virginia. Langley Air Force Base was the first military base built in the United States specifically for air power, having been acquired by the fledgling Aviation Section of the U.S. Army Signal Corps in December 1916. It is home to the First Fighter Wing and the Air Combat Command. However, when we started to work on the golf course there, we had no idea just how much history we were going to encounter.

A shaper was starting to install bunkers on one of the fairways when we discovered our first piece of history—a very large piece of history: a seventy-five-pound bomb that was left over from as early as World War I! The bomb, we later learned, still had a fuse on it and could possibly detonate.

We found several more large bombs at the site, and every time we did, we had to stop work to call in the appropriate authorities to remove them. Finally, our crew had had enough. We couldn't work in those conditions, nor did the Air Force want us to. Ultimately, the Air Force employed a highly sophisticated ultrasound sensor to x-ray the site to look for other "anomalies." They hoped the results would help to identify the locations of any more bombs. They could then dispose of them so we could get this course built.

The results showed 16,250 anomalies, including two five-hundred-pound bombs from the Vietnam War era! These bombs had a significant damage radius and would have destroyed everything within a few hundred yards if they'd been accidentally detonated!

It took two years and almost $3 million, but they finally safely cleared all of the bombs from the land and the course is now open.

> **After that happened, it made me realize how short and precious life is, and that we must make the most of every day we are given.**

CHAPTER 42
YOU CANNOT FAIL TO BE A SUCCESS
MICHAEL GLEASON

Pinehurst, North Carolina resident Michael Gleason began his career working with Ellis and Dan Maples, and during those sixteen years he worked on more than forty golf courses on the East Coast and abroad. In 1999, Gleason started his own firm, focusing on creating holes at such North Carolina courses as Olde Liberty in Youngsville and Linkhaw Farms in Lumberton, which provide a variety of alternate lines of play to the flagstick. Risk versus reward is a tenet of Gleason's design strategy. A great deal of his recent work has concentrated on remodeling the works of Ellis Maples and the Golden Age architect Donald Ross. He has worked on projects in Spain, Germany, and Japan, and has experience in preliminary master planning for large-scale developments, permitting, and environmental issues.

Through my many years as a golf course architect, I have seen my share of highs and lows. Every new project brings a new terrain, a new challenge, and a new group of people. I have been very lucky: the people that I have worked with have been very talented. But within every group of people there can be widely varying opinions about what is "good golf." It is my job to sift though these ideas and put together a design that is sensitive to the client, the environment, and the golfer.

When making their way around a golf course, most players have an opinion about how a golf hole should have been designed, but not many know of the sometimes impossible circumstances that affect the outcome of a golf hole. So many different things can happen during the design and construction of a modern golf course that it's a wonder that they can get built with any semblance of continuity at all. These problems can make my life miserable.

During my moments of self-doubt, I will usually retreat to my drafting table. On the wall in front of my desk I have a letter written by Donald Ross to Ellis Maples. It is dated May 27, 1927, and reads, in part:

Dear Ellis,

Mrs. Ross and I thank you for inviting us to your graduation exercises and we regret that we cannot be present. You are doing finely, Ellis, and I know you are going to make a fine man. My experience is that if a man follows the golden rule, gives consideration to others, and does some good (however small) every day of his life, and acts as a gentleman under all circumstances, he cannot fail to make a success of his life. However humble our occupation may be, we all have our little niche in this world's work.

I wish you every success,

Very sincerely yours,
Donald J. Ross

Mr. Ross's philosophy is a true inspiration to me and I try to follow that philosophy every day of my life. And when I take a moment to look at the overall picture, I come to the realization that I would not want to change my occupation for any other job in the world. What other endeavor would allow you to work in harmony with nature to expose its extraordinary beauty while at the same time providing an avenue of relaxation and sport for so many people, from every walk of life?

CHAPTER 43
ETERNAL OPTIMISM—MOVING HEAVEN AND EARTH

DENIS GRIFFITHS

Denis Griffiths has created golf courses all over the world, including, in Georgia, various courses at Chateau Elan Golf Club and Resort near Atlanta, Hard Labor Creek State Park in Rutledge, Brasstown Valley in Young Harris, and the Georgia Club in Statham. He also created St. Andrews Bay in Scotland and President's Reserve at the Hermitage in Nashville. Griffiths is holds a B.S. in landscape architecture from Iowa State University and is a past president of the American Society of Golf Course Architects.

I was working with Ron Kirby and Rodney Wright when we received a phone call from our project manager in Southeast Asia. He had been finishing up a new course on a small island republic there.

"You guys have to get out here immediately," he said. "I've got word that the wife of President Ferdinand Marcos, Imelda Marcos, wants to build a new golf course for her husband's sixtieth birthday. Since we're already working here, she's inquired about us."

Kirby, Griffiths, and "Huey."

Within the week we were in Asia and were flown to the site with the first lady in her private King Air aircraft. As we toured the site and discussed the project, the first lady made it very clear she would only commission the project if it could be finished and playable in time for the president's birthday in early September ... in three months. Three months! It was an impossible, unprecedented request.

It was at that moment reality set in, but we were eternal optimists and had never disappointed a client, so we told the first lady it was possible and agreed to the deadline. But, we told her, there would be certain things we would need: good base information, aerial photography, and topographical maps.

In about thirty minutes a black Ford with flashing red lights rolled up, and a general from the island's Air Force met us to discuss our needs.

We talked about flying over the property to obtain an aerial photograph, which the general indicated would be no problem. He meant it, because in a few more minutes a Huey helicopter landed and was made available to take us over the site.

The pilots took us wherever we wanted, but it was hard to keep focused as the military pilots skimmed along the ground or went vertical in the doorless beast. When we were done with the helicopter and returned to the hut for lunch, we spotted a C-47 flying back and forth at 2,000 feet, gridding the property!

The next morning we were awakened at 6:30 a.m. by two Air Force sergeants. They delivered a box of nearly fifty-meter-square aerial photos of the site

#18
Fox Lake
7/23/07

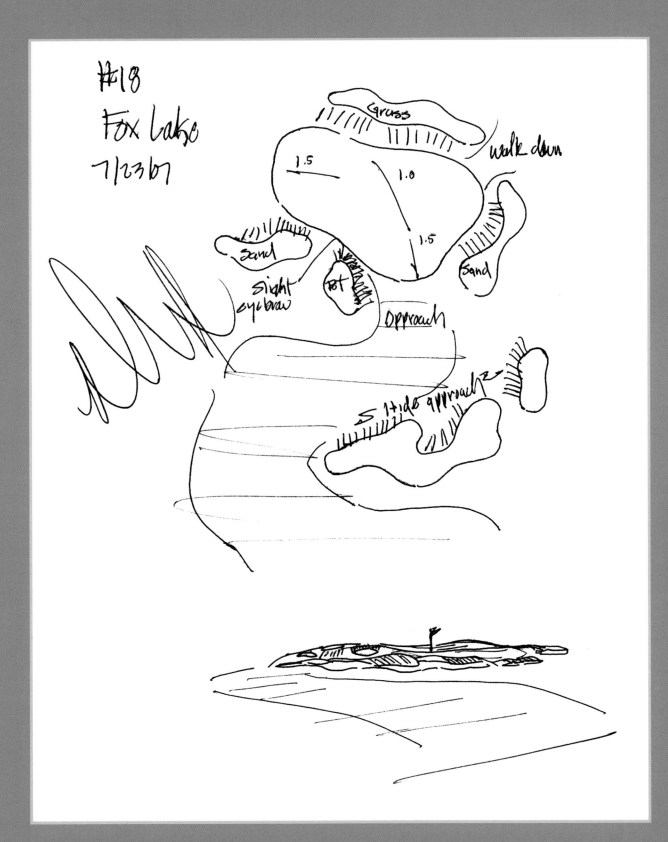

from the C-47 flight the day before. The photos were still wet, with unbelievable clarity! We took them to the hotel swimming pool deck and spread them in the sun to dry.

Over the next seventy-five days, we worked from a makeshift office in a hotel in the capital city, flying almost daily to the site on whatever military aircraft was available. We were headquartered in the capital city to maintain close communications with the president. Each afternoon, a call would come and a limousine would pick us up at a designated time to take us to the palace. The meeting with the president would usually take place on a royal three-hole golf course with a bandstand as the centerpiece, or on the sports courts, though sometimes the president would meet with us on his yacht!

This was the drill for some two and a half months while the government equipment toiled on the site to complete the president's birthday present.

We did get nine green, somewhat playable holes ready in time for his birthday party, through the miracles of rye grass in the tropics. Over the next nine months we completed the loose ends on the front nine while building the back nine. Mission completed!

"You guys have to get out here immediately," he said. "I've got word that the wife of President Ferdinand Marcos, Imelda Marcos, wants to build a new golf course for her husband's sixtieth birthday."

CHAPTER 44
THE CLIENT KNOWS BEST
... OR DOES HE?

JOHN F. HARBOTTLE III

John Harbottle, the son of Pacific Northwest Hall of Fame golfers, began his career in 1984 working on construction and design with the legendary golf architect Pete Dye, where he toiled in the office and on construction sites. He was influenced by trips to the British Isles and architecture books by classic designers George Thomas, Alister MacKenzie, Tom Simpson, Donald Ross, and Charles B. Macdonald. His Tacoma, Washington–based John Harbottle Design created courses such as the Olympic Course at Gold Mountain, Cinnabar Hills Golf Club in San Jose, Challenge Course at Arrow Creek in Reno, the Tony Lema Course at Monarch Bay, and the Resort Course at Genoa Lakes. Some of his remodeled or redesigned courses are Napa Valley Country Club, Saticoy Country Club, Hillcrest Country Club, Los Angeles Country Club's north course, and Park Meadows Country Club.

I don't mean to say that developers are difficult, but some clients are much more hands-on than others and they can definitely affect the design process, both positively and negatively.

One of my clients had lost a fortune making a movie. It seems they started filming before the script was finished. In my design process, I start with a rough concept for a design and then let it evolve in the field during construction. But this particularly hands-on owner asked me what I was planning to do with a certain hole, and when I told him I wasn't quite sure yet, he said, "You shouldn't start filming a movie if you haven't finished the script!"

I always loved that saying. He meant to impart to me that, because of his experience, I should not start building anything until I was sure of what I wanted to do.

The bottom line is, you need to appreciate that it's the client's money—and they can be a little nervous when someone else is waving their arms around a bunch of expensive machinery and spending it.

Another client once told me there would be no par-fours under four hundred yards long on his golf course.

"I want a man's course," he told me. "There will be no short holes."

This was the first course I designed after striking out on my own following six years working under Pete Dye, so I wanted my debut solo effort to be a great design. It took me months to convince the client how important variety was to the design and that a small group of interesting drive and pitch holes were going to make a big difference for the golf course. I used short holes like the tenth at Riviera Country Club to illustrate my point. It's one of the best holes on the course and is about three hundred yards long.

The final design took shape little by little, and as he saw the holes unfold, he began to understand what I had expressed to him.

By opening day, he was giving prospective members tours during which he boasted about the fact that they had par-fours that played from 310 to 480 yards.

CHAPTER 45
WORKING TOGETHER TO OVERCOME—
AND INCORPORATE—CHALLENGES

A. JOHN HARVEY

A John Harvey spent eight years with Robert Trent Jones Sr. as a junior design associate, and, in 1995, Harvey joined the Roger Rulewich Group as a design associate. In 2002, he joined forces with Morristown, New Jersey–based RBA Group, where he currently heads the golf course design division. Harvey has also served as a guest lecturer at Rutgers University for turfgrass courses. Some of his work includes Anglebrook Golf Club in Somers, New York; Ballyowen in Hardyston, New Jersey; Grande Dunes Golf and Beach Club in Myrtle Beach, South Carolina; and the Robert Trent Jones Trail's Silver Lakes course in Anniston, Alabama.

The consulting team of the RBA Group and the Roger Rulewich Group, with me as lead golf course architect, was awarded the contract to design a championship caliber, eighteen-hole golf course to be the most recent addition to the stable of courses owned and operated by the Morris County Park Commission.

The site selected for the course was an abandoned sand and gravel pit in the northwest portion of the county. The property was fallow for twelve years prior to the start of course construction in 2000.

During active mining, siltation ponds were created by wet excavation and dragline mining. They had been used to capture soil and sediment to prevent it from leaving the site and entering the adjoining pristine Rockaway River. Over time, these excavations became colonized by opportunistic wetland and transitional vegetation. We prepared a comprehensive development package from site feasibility to construction inspection for this eighteen-hole championship golf and practice facility on four hundred acres of challenging, yet dramatic property in northern New Jersey.

We evaluated all of the environmental constraints including wetlands, buffers, floodplains, soils, vegetation, endangered species, water quality, groundwater, zoning, and utilities. Based on these constraints, we obtained the seven required permits and came up with several layouts.

Final design plans and construction documents were then prepared for the eighteen-hole continuous layout, to include a clubhouse, maintenance facility, halfway house, pump house, and rain shelter.

The site constraints of this former sand and gravel operation necessitated the design of a 2,000-foot entrance roadway with a 10-foot concrete-block retaining wall. In addition, we had to import 230,000 cubic yards of recycled fill material to supplement earthwork and shaping needs.

We incorporated one of the more unique historic landmarks in the area, the stone ruins of a building that once housed the Ringling Brothers first traveling circus elephants in America, into the par-three, twelfth hole to serve as part of the wall containing the tee complex. The hole plays over the Rockaway River and related wetlands corridor to a green complex bordering the river and a waterfall created as part of iron mining operations in the late 1800s.

The challenge of this project was to balance the opportunities and constraints of this property and weave a golf course layout around the site to take advantage of the spectacular scenery without compromising the ecosystem that encompasses the development, while at the same time creating a strategic sequencing of holes that are both enjoyable and memorable.

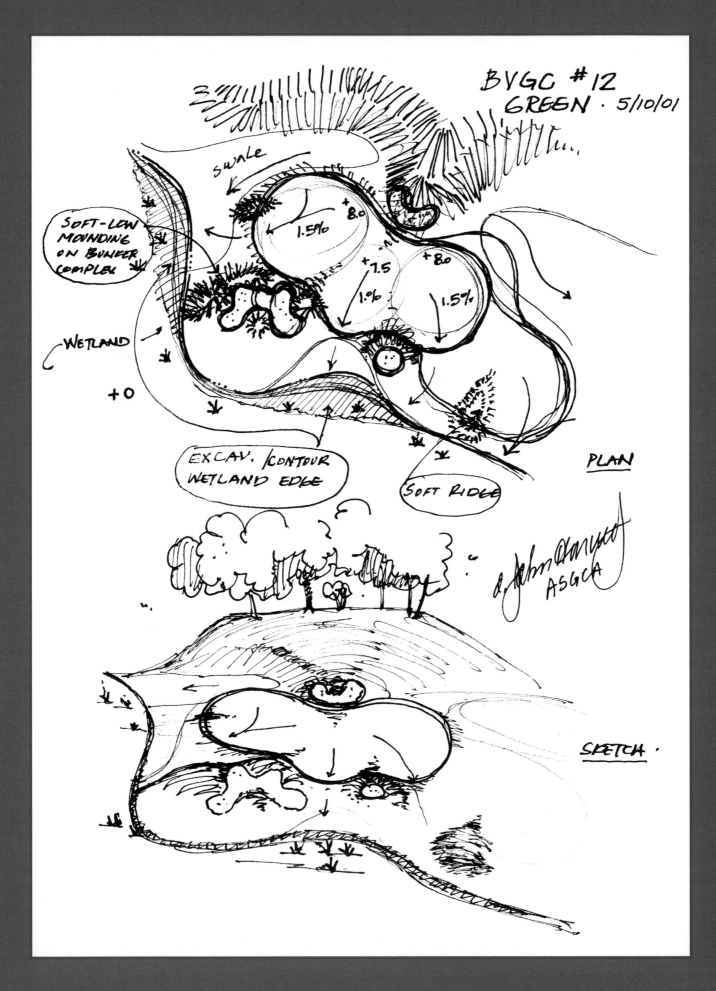

CHAPTER 46
FAR OUT FAR EAST

NEIL HAWORTH

Canadian Neil Haworth has overall responsibility for the operations of Nelson & Haworth worldwide, excepting the United States. He relocated from Singapore to Shanghai, China, and has designed, in China, Jade Dragon Snow Mountain Golf Club (the longest course in the world), Shenzhen Golf Club, and Sheshan International Golf Club (host of the European tour HSBC Champions); and in Malaysia, Shan Shui Golf and Country Club and Tiara Melaka Golf and Country Club. In Thailand, he created Royal Hills Golf Club.

On my first trip into China, in 1992, I took the train from Hong Kong to Guangzhou, where someone, amongst the millions of people loitering around the old train station, met me with a sign.

I was being driven, along with my Australian design partner, to the site, when we had to stop at a railway crossing because of a train. As soon as the train passed, cars on both sides of the road crammed in to try to get across first. Needless to say, nobody could pass through and it took an additional two hours just to make our way through the traffic jam.

Once we reached the site—a beautiful piece of land with rolling hills and mandarin orange and lychee trees dotting the landscape—we were to review the centerline staking and field the design. The Chinese surveyor followed our staking plan, which showed one-meter-high white stakes at thirty-meter spacing along the centerline of each hole.

One of the par-threes played over an existing, eight-meter-deep reservoir. The surveyor, following our instructions to the letter, had actually planted the stakes in the bottom of the lake! Sticking out of the water, exactly one meter high, were white stakes every thirty meters!

The next day the earthworks contractor was to mobilize. We thought we would meet with him, ask him about the machinery he had, and find out what schedule he was working on. It turned out the earthworks contractor was the head of a local village and the rice season had finished the day before, so more than 2,000 farmers showed up with their families ready to work on the golf course.

Each farmer could move three cubic meters a day, so each day the contractor moved 6,000 cubic meters—or 180,000 per month! That fit the construction schedule and gave me a new perspective on field changes: asking them to shift a mound ten meters involved a crew of several hundred people and lasted a week or so!

To get back to Hong Kong we had to board a train, which stopped at the local village. The driver dropped us off at the train station, but once we got inside, we noticed the train ticket was printed in Chinese. We knew what time the train was supposed to come, but could not read the signs to determine whether it was on time or which direction it would be going. Trains were stopping every ten minutes! As we studied the Chinese map, the sun position, and the stars trying to navigate our way out of there, a Chinese man came up and, in a perfect Australian accent, asked my Australian partner which part of Australia he was from. The fellow had returned home to his Chinese village for the first time in over twenty years and happened to be listening to our dilemma. I'm not sure what would have happened to us if he had not shown up.

About ten years ago we were asked by a famous Australian architect to visit a site in Myanmar on the Bay of Bengal. It was probably the best trip I have taken during my fifteen years living in Asia.

We left Yangon about 5 p.m. and drove for about three hours before stopping. There were no bridges at the time, and we had missed the last ferry across the river, so we had to stay overnight at a local government hotel.

Our Singaporean client had arranged for us to meet the local general, who showed up the next morning in his 4x4 accompanied by three flatbed trucks loaded with armed soldiers. We met with him briefly, and then set off to take the ferry.

After crossing the river we had to drive for about three hours. Since the main road had been washed out during the rainy season, we had to take a winding road over the mountains and down to a local fishing village. From there we took a local fishing boat with a military escort—because there were lots of pirates in the waters—about an hour down the coast. We viewed some of the most beautiful, unspoiled coastline anywhere in the world before we arrived at another local village. From there, accompanied by locals carrying our bags on their heads, we walked through rice paddies, and passed through villages full of people who I am sure had never seen white people before.

The monastery and the village chief were the only ones with electricity, but the power was only turned on between 7 and 9 p.m. We were treated to a home-cooked meal of fresh fish and vegetables before "lights-out."

The next morning we woke up and walked the site again.

I gave some of my opinions to the architect.

"We've come all this way, and the site is back in the hills with no views of the Bay of Bengal," I said. "It would be nice at least to have a few holes with sea views."

We agreed to have another look at the master when we got back.

On the way back, the client wanted to show the architect a potential source of stone for some of the buildings. While they did that, I walked to a high point that overlooked a beautiful piece of land, like Pebble Beach, Cypress, and Pacific Dunes all combined! When the client and architect got back I asked them a question.

"Could we put the golf course on this waterfront piece of land?"

"Sure," the client said. "We've got four thousand acres to work with."

It was getting a little late now and we had to make the same journey back: hiking through the rice fields, a boat ride, and then three hours in the car in order to catch the last ferry. If we missed the ferry, the closest hotel was in the local village where the dock was. After the hike and the boat ride, we were driving down the hills and had hit a perfectly straight and flat stretch of road for about forty-five minutes before getting to the river.

We were late, it was dark, and for forty-five minutes nobody said a word, but the screaming in the car was undeniably loud when we all suddenly saw the reflection of our headlights in the river! The car went airborne off the end of the road over the riverbank, with locals scattering out of the way. We landed in wheel-deep water.

Everyone was okay, and after laughing about it, we realized that we had missed the boat, which was docked on the other side of the river. The driver flashed his lights to get the attention of the ferry captain, and after a minute or so the captain flashed his lights in return, and then came back to get us. Apparently the general we had had breakfast with the day before had instructed the boat captain to look out for us in case we were late.

Unfortunately, after all that, what would have been an amazingly scenic course never got built.

The local Burmese people there in Myanmar, in my opinion, are the kindest and gentlest in all of Asia. The dictatorship there is obviously a tragic situation. One of my favorite spots is the Yangon Yacht Club on the lake, where all the generals live and where Aung San Suu Kyi (a pro-democracy leader and advocate of non-violent resistance) is kept under house arrest. The lake, therefore, has never been commercially developed. Since I can sit at a picnic table there and drink Labatt Blue and eat pizza, it reminds me of my home in Canada.

A day before the British handover of Hong Kong to Chinese rule, I was asked by Sun Hung Kai group to come and do a quick feasibility study for a forty-five-hole golf course they would build in conjunction with the Disney project, which, at that time, was in the planning stages.

They had already found a hotel room for me, and first class seats on Singapore Airlines, so I was on my way. I visited the site and did a quick study revealing they would have to cut thirty million cubic meters of rock and remove it from the site if they wanted to build the golf course. That news put them off of building the course!

CHAPTER 47
VIVE LA DIFFÉRENCE!
RAY HEARN

The 584-yard, par-five opening hole at Yarrow concludes with a well-guarded green.

Ray Hearn was an Evans Scholar at Michigan State University, where he earned dual degrees in landscape architecture and turfgrass science. His Holland, Michigan–based Raymond Hearn Golf Course Designs is working on Domaine de Lavagnac in Southern France, a development in Moscow, and Porto Marina, near El Alameen, Egypt. His other creations include home state courses Island Hills Golf Club in Centreville, Quail Ridge Golf Club in Ada, Moose Ridge Golf Club in Oakland County, The Grande Golf Club in Jackson, Royal Scot Golf Course in Lansing, Strategic Fox and Fox Hills in Plymouth, Ballantrae Country Club in Zeeland, Hemlock Golf Club in Ludington, The Golf Club at Yarrow in Augusta, and Macatawa Legends Golf and Country Club. Hearn also designed Sea Oaks Country Club in Little Egg Harbor Township, New Jersey; the Mistwood Golf Club in Chicago, Illinois; and the Traditions Golf Club in Edmond, Oklahoma.

Hearn's complicated 5th green at Yarrow Golf
and Conference Center in Augusta, Michigan.

My company has been fortunate to receive some great golf course architectural contracts around the world on some very special sites. Close personal friends have often lightheartedly commented that golf course design is easy, since most golf course sites are similar.

I tell them this couldn't be further from the truth.

Domaine de Lavagnac Golf Resort, in Languedoc, France, will use a historic, 1400 AD château as the resort's hotel and spa. The location has to be worked into the master land use plan. We have to avoid, but highlight, the Ancient Roman roads, which date back to 5 BC, that wind through the site. Maintaining and minimizing the impact to an active wine vineyard throughout the site, without compromising the golf layout, is another of our challenges at this site. All the while, we're expected to take advantage of views that extend thirty miles off the site in all directions.

At Hemlock Golf Club in Ludington, Michigan, we incorporated windswept, inland Lake Michigan dunes into the design and kept the amount of earth moved under 50,000 cubic yards by utilizing a "lay of the land" approach, while grassing the majority of the course into a pure sand subsoil. The client desired an award-winning golf course for a cost under $2 million. In doing this, we had to avoid oak, maple, and hemlock trees over a hundred years old. We are proud to report that the completed project won Best New Opening from *Golf Digest*.

In an ongoing redesign at Flossmoor Country Club in Chicago, I must be careful to respect the history and tradition of a classic, pre-1900 design with a star-studded past, including a PGA Championship,

U.S. Amateur Championship, and a Western Open. My challenge is to recapture lost shot value and play angles by selective tree removal, fairway expansions, and hazard placement, which will recapture the lost, classical playability and appearance of features from the early 1900s. Basically, we are remodeling, renovating, and restoring areas of the entire course.

Based on the above, I think we would all agree that a golf course architect's canvas is anything but typical or predictable, but most of us would also agree that we all love these challenges and enjoy what we do.

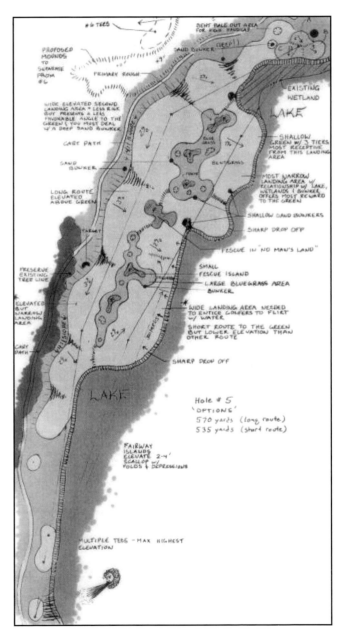

CHAPTER 48
MORNING IN INDIA

DAVE HEATWOLE

Since graduating from Penn State with a degree in landscape architecture, Dave Heatwole has been actively involved in golf course design. For nearly two decades, Dave Heatwole worked with Jack Nicklaus and served as senior designer for a number of award-winning courses, as well as courses that have hosted professional golf tournaments. Dave still serves as an independent design consultant for Nicklaus on select courses, but his company, Heatwole Golf Design, focuses on new course design as well as renovation, restoration, and master planning for existing courses. His collaborations and works include Great Bear Golf and Country Club in Marshals Creek, Pennsylvania; Pinehills Golf Club in Plymouth, Massachusetts; Twin Eagles in Naples, Florida; The Cliffs at Walnut Cove in Asheville, North Carolina; and Bay Creek Resort and Club in Cape Charles, Virginia.

While working for Jack Nicklaus, I had the opportunity to travel to some very exotic locations to build golf courses. I went everywhere from Europe to the South Pacific.

On one such adventure, in the early 1990s, I went to Delhi, India, to work on a brand new course: the Classic Golf Resort. I traveled to India in May—the time of year when India traditionally experiences monsoons. Perfect timing, right?

When I arrived in the evening, I was told that we would be inspecting the course the next morning at 4:30 a.m. This news was discouraging, considering it meant I would be getting only about five hours of sleep. However, it was necessary, given that by 10 a.m. the hot winds and sandstorms would be so bad we wouldn't be able to see a foot in front us.

India just amazed me. There were cows walking in the middle of the roads and people sleeping in the street. All of the sights and sounds were truly fascinating to me; it was all just so exotic and unlike anything I had ever before seen.

Bright and early, just at sunrise, I found myself walking around the job site. A few kids from the nearby village began to follow our party. After an hour or two the crowd grew to about fifteen kids following us around and giggling. Finally, I could no longer stand not knowing what the joke was.

"Why are these kids following us around?" I asked our guide.

"You are probably the first Caucasians they've ever seen," the guide answered. Then he pointed out a thin electric wire. "That that one wire provides the energy to an entire nearby village."

On that morning, when I was in awe of the splendor of exotic India, to those children, I was the most exotic thing they might ever see in their lifetimes. You would never have thought it, but we were the most foreign objects in that place.

CHAPTER 49
LOOK AT CHALLENGES FROM A NEW ANGLE: PLAY GOLF BACKWARDS

ARTHUR HILLS

The Ritz-Carlton at Half Moon Bay Ocean
Course, Half Moon Bay, California.

Arthur Hills, a past president of the American Society of Golf Course Architects, has over forty years of experience in designing and restoring golf courses for real estate development communities, private clubs, resorts, and upscale public golf facilities. His Toledo, Ohio–based firm has designed more than 180 new courses in the United States, Europe, and Asia, including Half Moon Bay, Bay Harbor, Quinta da Marinha Oitavos Golfe, Big Horn Golf Club, the Arthur Hills Course at Palmetto Hall, Shepherd's Hollow, The Club at Iron Bridge, Bonita Bay, LPGA International, The Golf Club of Georgia, Egypt Valley, Longaberger Golf Club, Hyatt Regency Hill Country, and TPC at Eagle Trace. They have also renovated more than 120 courses, including renowned clubs like Oakmont, Crystal Downs, Congressional Country Club, Oakmont, Inverness, and Oakland Hills.

A breathtaking view of the 14th hole at Ironbridge in Colorado.

As a kid, my father took me to the Toledo Open and I got to see the great Walter Hagen up close and shake his hand. He was impressive!

I went home and created a three-hole course around our farmhouse, mowing down "fairways" and "greens" with a push lawnmower, over and over, until I got the ground flat enough so my friends and I could putt on it. I guess that was technically my first course.

But after college, by 1966, I was a successful landscape architect with five children. One day I placed an ad in the yellow pages proclaiming myself a golf course architect. That is how I joined the ranks.

There were very few golf architects at the time, so, believe it or not, my phone rang and I got a job building a simple nine-hole course on a farm on the outskirts of Toledo.

One of my most high-profile and most challenging design jobs was the Legends Course at LPGA International near Daytona Beach, Florida, not far from the famous speedway, at the world headquarters of the LPGA. The land had teeming wetlands and dramatic stands of pine trees, and most of the site was covered with dense palmetto, so thick that when we went out to walk the site, we couldn't see through the stuff. It forced us to hack centerlines with machetes—three-foot wide slots down the center of each "hole." Drew Rogers and Mike Dasher from our staff had one heck of a time trying to mark the clearing limits (the limits that define the far right and far left edges of the holes for the construction teams to clear to). Since they could not get a measuring tape through the vegetation, they would pace their way outward from the centerlines through the thick growth, never knowing when they would step in a hole or on a snake, until they counted off enough steps.

When they each reached their respective edge, they couldn't see each other, so they had to throw marking tape up in the air to find each other and line up properly.

They faced mosquitoes, bugs, armadillos, water moccasins, rattlesnakes, and wild boar in developing the course with LPGA players Meg Mallon and Beth Daniel. The ladies had interesting viewpoints on the holes, and I taught them one of my secrets of golf

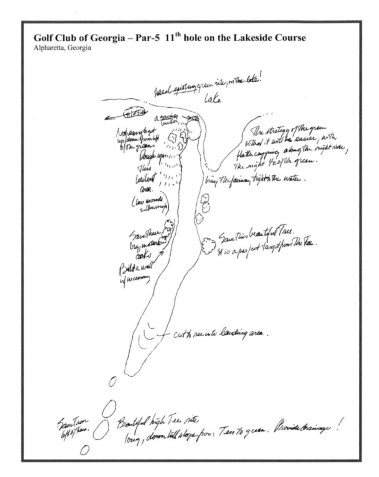

Golf Club of Georgia – Par-5 11th hole on the Lakeside Course
Alpharetta, Georgia

course architecture: design golf holes backwards—from the green to the tee; not the tee to the green. Turn around sometime when you're playing a hole and look back from the green. You'll spy a brand new view of how to create a golf hole.

Max Szturm, the deceased superintendent at Wildwood Country Club in Middletown, Ohio, and I, for years, played golf together for modest stakes at superintendents' meetings in southwest Ohio. One time we came to the ninth hole, a par-three, at Piqua Country Club. Max was a very good player. I teed up, hit my tee shot twelve feet from the hole and said to Max, "Beat that if you can." Max then took my breath away—and the wind out of my sails—when he hit his shot into the hole!

Bay Harbor's Links 9, at BOYNE Resorts in Petoskey, Michigan, overlooks Little Traverse Bay and Lake Michigan.

Bay Harbor's Quarry 9 was once the site of an unsightly cement factory.

CHAPTER 50
WHAT A TRIP!

BRIAN HUNTLEY

Brian Huntley is president of Uniontown, Ohio-based Brian Huntley Golf Sense, Inc. He earned his BSLA from The Ohio State University and began his design career with Arthur Hills and Associates before forming his own firm. Huntley has created Ohio courses such as Deer Creek in Bellville, Kennsington Golf Club in Canfield, Eagle Creek Golf Club in Norwalk and the Quarry Golf Club in East Canton.

Several years ago, while working for Arthur Hills and Associates, I had the opportunity to work on Bighorn Country Club for Westinghouse, a project that required numerous site visits to California. It was not unusual to get a phone call on a Monday requiring a site visit the next day. Typically, I would clear these emergency site visits with Art to get his approval. However, after one urgent phone call, I felt it was critical that a member of our firm be there. I was unable to contact Art in time to discuss the issues, so I made a judgment call and moved forward with the travel arrangements to Palm Springs.

The next afternoon, I was in Palm Springs working with their engineers to solve some lot and golf corridor issues. We worked well into the night, resolving most of the owners' concerns.

The next day, I had to inform the owners about some of the necessary changes to the course. Mainly, the fifth and sixth holes needed to get pushed up into some significantly steep, but interesting, terrain. The best way to quickly convey these changes was to go to the physical site itself, so the owners and I crawled by hand and foot to the new tee and green sites.

It was quite a feat to get up to the site, let alone tell the owners that it would cost them $200,000 to $300,000 more to implement these changes and continue to build the course. To ease this blow, I quickly explained how the new holes would work with the lots and how, in fact, several more million-dollar lots, with spec-

tacular views, were created. Needless to say, upon hearing this angle, the clients were relieved and, in fact, quite pleased!

I quickly said my goodbyes and hurried down the mountain toward my rental car. I was doing pretty well, dodging rocks and negotiating around swales, but my momentum was picking up! About halfway down, I tripped on a loose rock and went down hard. I tumbled down the rest of the mountain, and it seemed to take forever before I landed in a heap at the bottom.

I did a quick check and it seemed nothing was broken. So I returned to my quest to catch my flight. No one could have been more surprised than me that I actually made the flight! The plane doors were closed behind me and as I made my way to my seat, I noticed other passengers staring at me. It wasn't until I went to the bathroom and looked in the mirror that I knew why. I was cut up, bruised, and dirty, and had a ripped shirt. I looked as if I had been on the losing end of a fight. I cleaned up, settled back in my seat and reflected on how stressful but rewarding my visit had been.

A couple of years later the Skins game was played at Bighorn. I watched it on TV. The announcers were discussing the spectacular view from the tee of hole six, a par-four, 505-yard hole with a hundred-foot drop from tee to landing area. They even had a "hang time" stopwatch on the tee shots! I just watched and laughed to myself, remembering my first "trip" to that tee site.

CHAPTER 51
GOLF COURSE C RATIONS CREATED
A GOURMET FRIENDSHIP

DR. MICHAEL HURDZAN

An internationally recognized authority on golf course environmental issues, Dr. Michael Hurdzan, an American Society of Golf Course Architects past president, studied turf management at Ohio State University and earned a master's degree and a Ph.D. in environmental plant physiology at the University of Vermont. His course portfolio includes Devil's Pulpit Golf Course and Devil's Paintbrush Golf Course in Caledon, Ontario, Canada; Willowbend Country Club in Cape Cod, Massachusetts; River Course at Keystone in Keystone, Colorado; Bully Pulpit in Medora, North Dakota; Erin Hills in Hartford, Wisconsin; and Desert Willow in Palm Desert, California.

I've been involved with golf architecture for over forty years, and one of my fondest memories is sitting on a golf course construction site in the early 1970s, eating lunch with my mentor and partner, Jack Kidwell.

In those days, Jack and I would lay out centerlines of golf holes and we would grade-stake every single tee, green, bunker, pond, waterway, and the entire irrigation and drainage system. I don't know any golf course architect who still does that, as it takes a lot of time and can be very hard work in tough terrain, but it did keep us in shape.

At that time I was a young captain in the United States Army Special Forces Reserve. I was always nosing around for Army surplus, and I found someone selling cases of C rations. Combat rations, or "C rats," as GIs fondly called them, were introduced prior to World War II and persisted through the Vietnam War era. They came in a small brown box that contained a complete meal with a nutritional value of about 1,200 calories. C rations included a canned

entrée the GIs usually called "mystery meat," a can of crackers, cheese or peanut butter, dessert, and a syrupy fruit such as peaches or fruit cocktail. Everything a hungry soldier, or golf course architect, could hope for.

Jack and I would each take a C rat and a canteen of water when we went to work on a golf course site. I remember sitting back on a grassy knoll, big rock, or log, eating our lunch and talking. It was a bonding experience like none other, and perhaps the main reason why we enjoyed such a close relationship for nearly fifty years. I was the son he never had.

By the late 1980s, Parkinson's disease and cancer began to rob Jack of his mobility, but not of his mind, and his memory was sharp up until he died in 2001. During his last years he was confined to a wheelchair. Inevitably when we would sit and talk, Jack would bring up the subject of how much he enjoyed and missed our C ration lunches together, and it seemed to make his day a little brighter.

CHAPTER 52
SONGS AND STORIES
RICK JACOBSON

The second hole at Strawberry Creek GC, in Kenosha, Wisconsin, features a traditional heathland look.

In November of 1991, after a career that included work as a design associate with Jack Nicklaus Golf Services, Rick formed Jacobson Golf Course Design, Inc., in Libertyville, Illinois, which has created Virginia courses Augustine Golf Club in Stafford and Bull Run Country Club in Haymarket. Rick's portfolio of work includes Bear Trap Dunes in Ocean View, Delaware; The Club at Strawberry Creek in Kenosha, Wisconsin; Makefield Highlands in Lower Wakefield Township, Pennsylvania; Patriot Hills Golf Club in Stony Point, New York; Bear Lakes-Links Course in West Palm Beach, Florida; The Club at Nevillewood in Nevillewood, Pennsylvania; and Wynstone Golf Club, in North Barrington, Illinois. In Japan, he created Ishioka Golf Club in Ibaraki Prefecture, World Country Club in Osaka, Hananomori Golf Club in Miyagi Prefecture, and Komono Club in Mie Prefecture. Jacobson also provided the renovation of Des Moines Golf and Country Club for the 1999 U.S. Senior Open.

It was a simple example of how small this world truly is and that people can and do compassionately coexist on this planet.

My first American Society of Golf Course Architects meeting in Scotland was very memorable. The golf experience at the home of golf, the Old Course at St. Andrews, was also memorable for others ... at my expense!

We were exposed to the beauty of St. Andrews at the first tee because the Swedish women's golf team was teeing off in front of our group of golf course architects! We struggled to maintain our composure.

Eventually I met my classic Scottish caddy at this time. Before we started the round, I notified him of my somewhat erratic golf game—I had shot 76 and 103 in the same season—and my previous night's indulgence in pints of Guinness.

My round evolved in typical form, with a colorful blend of pars, bogies and "others"—until the eighteenth hole. On my tee shot I didn't quite get through the ball and pushed it slightly to the right ... right on top of our hotel! Being the swing doctor that I think I am, I made a minor adjustment, reloaded, and double-cross snap-hooked my next tee shot toward the beach on the far side of the first hole! (For those not familiar with St. Andrews, hole one and eighteen are parallel to each other and basically share a fairway that may be the widest on the planet!)

By this time Jeff Brauer was crying with laughter and my caddy offered words of encouragement. "Aye, Laddie, I've never seen that done before!"

During another ASGCA Annual meeting hosted in Northern Ireland, we had the opportunity to play one of the world's greatest golf courses: Royal County Down. The club was also hosting an international amateur tournament representing nearly twenty countries during our visit.

A large group of architects decided to visit a local pub that evening, and it happened to be karaoke night. This was the evening Brian and the Bullet Heads (Brian Curley and several other, as he would say, "follically challenged" ASGCA members) emerged as a self-proclaimed, leading golf industry entertainment group.

As an unbelievably entertaining evening was coming to a close, an elderly Irish gentleman rose and requested that an old Irish fisherman's ballad be played and displayed on the monitors in typical karaoke fashion to close the evening. The entire pub, with people from around the globe, engaged, arm-in-arm, and sang the ballad in unison. Now, this is not a life or death subject matter that the media covers, but it was a simple example of how small this world truly is and that people can and do compassionately coexist on this planet.

The Swedish women's golf team was teeing off in front of our group of golf course architects! We struggled to maintain our composure.

CHAPTER 53
BUGGED BY BUGS

CLYDE JOHNSTON

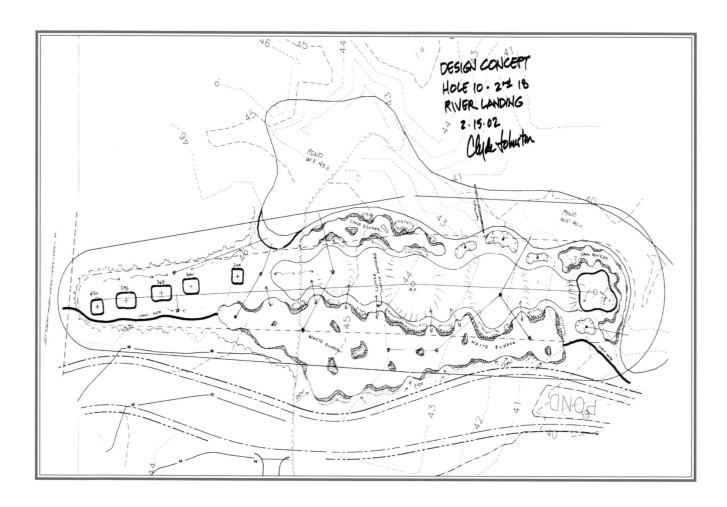

Clyde Johnston is a past president of the American Society of Golf Course Architects. He worked at Willard Byrd and Associates for fifteen years before founding Hilton Head Island–based Clyde Johnston Designs, Inc. in 1987. Johnston has designed such award-winning courses as Jacksonville Country Club, Cherry Blossom Golf Club, Ocean Harbour Golf Links, Heather Glen Golf Links, Old South Golf Links on Hilton Head, and Covered Bridge Golf Club, owned and co-designed by Masters and U.S. Open winner Fuzzy Zoeller. He also renovated Forest Oaks Country Club, home of the PGA Tour's Greater Greensboro Chrysler Classic. His Myrtle Beach courses include Glen Dornoch Golf Club and Wachesaw East Golf Club.

It was the middle of August and three of us were flagging the clearing for a new golf course near the coast of North Carolina. The temperature and humidity were extremely high and there was no breeze as we trudged through the trees and underbrush. The progress was slow since we had to watch every step for venomous snakes. But the worst part was the insects. The ticks and chiggers were bad enough, but it was like the mosquitoes were hosting their own blood drive.

My co-workers were Steve Manley and N. C. "Lee" Chang. Lee is originally from Taiwan and served in the Chinese Army before moving to the United States to study land planning at Georgia Tech.

It was the first time flagging the clearing for both Steve and Lee, so I walked the centerlines, keeping track of our position and shouting out instructions for which trees to flag.

By midafternoon, the heat, humidity, and mosquitoes were taking their toll on all of us. Lee was very unaccustomed to this environment and was particularly frustrated. I heard him yell a string of foul-sounding Chinese words, followed by the word "mosquitoes."

From the other side of the fairway, Steve responded:

"Lee, lighten up! It's not often they get to eat Chinese!"

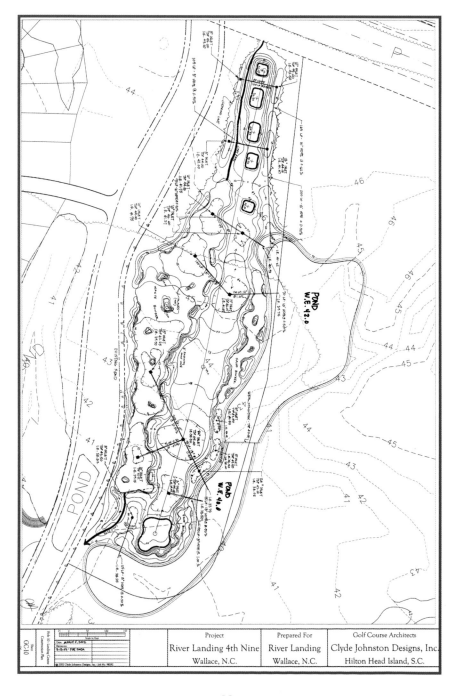

	Project	Prepared For	Golf Course Architects
	River Landing 4th Nine	River Landing	Clyde Johnston Designs, Inc.
	Wallace, N.C.	Wallace, N.C.	Hilton Head Island, S.C.

CHAPTER 54
WHO DO YOU THINK YOU ARE?

REES JONES

Ralston Creek Course's 424-yard, par-four 14th hole.

After college at Yale and graduate studies at Harvard, Rees, a former ASGCA president, went to work in 1964 as a principal in his father's firm, Robert Trent Jones, Inc. Ten years later he founded his own design firm, Rees Jones, Inc., headquartered in his hometown of Montclair, New Jersey. In the last thirty years, Jones has designed more than a hundred courses, including Nantucket Golf Club in Siasconset, Maryland; Ocean Forest Golf Club in Sea Island, Georgia; Black Lake Golf Club in Onaway, Michigan; Casata Golf Club in Boulder City, Nevada; and Atlantic Golf Club and Golf at the Bridge in Bridgehampton, New York. Jones's redesign of courses in preparation for major championships has earned him the nickname The Open Doctor. His remodeling skills have been applied to seven U.S. Open venues, five PGA courses, three Ryder Cup sites, and one Walker Cup redo, plus an original design for the 2001 Walker Cup. His redesign at East Lake has become the permanent site of the PGA Tour's Tour Championship.

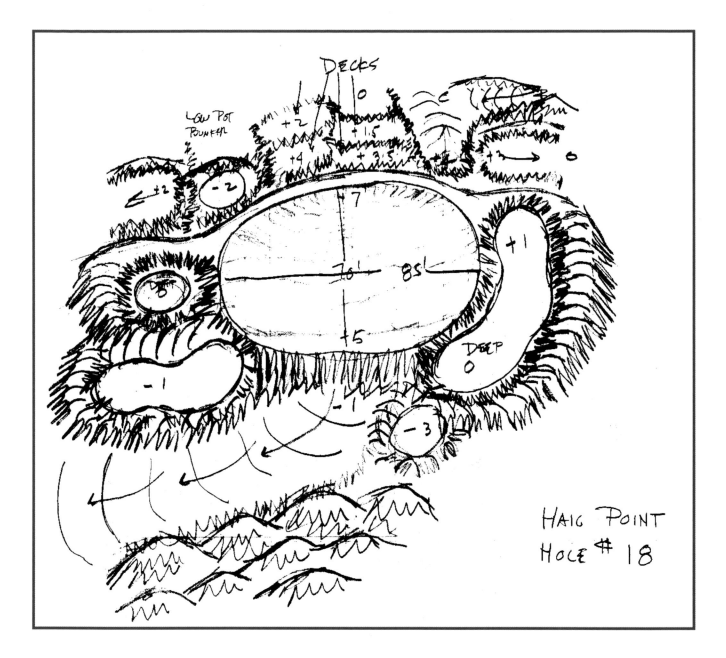

In the 1980s, I was vacationing on Nantucket with my family. I decided to go over to Sankaty Head Golf Club, an exclusive golf course I had heard much about but never seen. I wanted to do so without making a big fuss or telling them who I was. I just wanted to play this venerable old course

I entered the pro shop and asked the golf professional if I could play the course.

"Absolutely not," he told me. "This is a private club and you must play with a member."

"I have a few friends who are members," I told him. "May I see the club directory so that I can try to reach one of them?"

"Absolutely not," he repeated. "Our directory is solely for the use of our members."

At a loss as to what to do next, I explained that I was a golf course architect and that since Sankaty Head was a historic course, I was quite interested professionally in seeing it.

At that point the golf professional said, "Who do you think you are, Robert Trent Jones?"

"No," I answered. "But I am his son."

"Well, then, I'd be glad to play with you tomorrow morning."

At the finish of our round the next day, the entire green committee was waiting for me on the eighteenth green, anxious to ask me what I thought of their golf course.

235-yard 14th hole at Black Lake Golf Club in Onaway, Michigan.

GRASS

GRASS

GRASS

SAND

HAIG POINT
NUMBER 18
12/6/85

CHAPTER 55
FATHER'S DAY

ROBERT TRENT JONES JR.

The 6th hole on the aptly named Sunrise Course at Spanish Trail Golf & Country Club
in Las Vegas shows off the colorful "Rainbow Arch" of the Red Rock National Forest.

Yale graduate Robert Trent Jones Jr., a past president of the American Society of Golf Course
Architects, is the chairman of the board for Robert Trent Jones II LLC in Palo Alto, California.
He has designed more than 240 courses on six continents in forty-one countries, including
Chateau Whistler Golf Club in British Columbia; The Links at Spanish Bay in Pebble Beach, California;
Princeville Golf Resort courses on Kauai in Hawaii; Pine Lake and Golden Valley Golf Clubs in Japan;
Alcanada Golf in Mallorca, Spain; Turning Stone Oneida Nation's Kahluyat Course in New York;
Windsor Golf Club in Florida; and Chambers Bay near Tacoma, Washington, a future U.S. Open site.
He is the son of the late Robert Trent Jones Sr., a world-renowned golf course architect.

Some of my best memories have to do with my early days: apprenticing with my father at Mauna Kea in Hawaii and Spyglass Hill in California in the 1960s. Twenty-five years later, we went back to Spyglass Hill and recalled our many debates about the site where he, of course, made the final decisions.

One particular day we were visiting Spyglass to do some hole-by-hole videotaping and Dad, sitting in a golf cart, accidentally released the brake and somehow it got going down the hill at full speed. Fortunately, before accelerating into a steep ravine, it stopped abruptly by running into a Monterey Pine.

I was not in the cart at the time, since I had gotten out with the videographer. We raced down to Dad; he had a bloody forehead.

The first thing Dad said was, "Bobby, I told you we should have taken that tree out when we built the course!"

My dad had a great sense of humor and could turn anything into fun and glib comments. He loved the game of golf and he was not only my father but my mentor in golf course architecture. I now have wonderful professional memories of my times with him.

The sea-smashed 5th hole of the Beach Course at Waikoloa Beach Resort on Hawaii's Big Island.

CHAPTER 56
ONCE IN A LIFETIME JOB TURNED LABOR OF LOVE

STEPHEN KAY

Stephen Kay is principal of Stephen Kay/Doug Smith Golf Course Design of Egg Harbor, New Jersey. He has been an instructor in the Rutgers Turfgrass program since 1985, teaching golf construction, design, and surveying, and has done renovation work at over 250 golf courses. Stephen has done work in the Kingdom of Bhutan and has extensive experience restoring the classic old designs of such great architects as Donald Ross, A. W. Tillinghast, Devereux Emmet, and Charles Banks. His select course portfolio includes The Hamlet at Willow Creek, Long Island, New York; Manhattan Woods Golf Club (with Gary Player) in West Nyack, New York; Links of North Dakota in Williston, North Dakota; and, in New Jersey, Blue Heron Pines Golf Club in Galloway and Architects Golf Club in Phillipsburg.

When I was teaching at Rutgers University, one of my students approached me because they knew someone who was getting set to buy some land and build a golf resort.

"Would you be interested in designing a course in the Midwest?" the student asked me.

I considered it, but my wife had just had a baby, and we'd just left the Midwest to make our home

A golf course built on this site would have views of the water from everywhere.

in New York, so I wasn't keen on spending a lot of time traveling to North Dakota. But I knew a great shaper from Ohio, Marvin Schlauch. He was born in North Dakota and he didn't mind going there, so I

wouldn't have to travel so much. Plus, he knew the landscape, physically and politically.

There was no eighteen-hole course for hundreds of miles, which also intrigued me. The population of towns in North Dakota ranges from Bismark, population 70,000, to tiny hamlets with populations of four. Raw, unspoiled country.

So I phoned Marv, and it was on.

The developer was looking at three potential sites, so he took Marv on a Cessna to have a fly-over look at all of them and decide which site would be best for a golf course. Marv picked the one he liked best as the contractor, which was the one the developer liked least, because it was the farthest from town.

But what a site! When I finally traveled to North Dakota to see the site, I became much more enthused about the project.

It was 250 acres right on Lake Sakakawea, which was a huge, two-hundred-mile-long, seven-mile-wide body of water created when a section of the Missouri River was dammed. A golf course built on this site would have views of the water from everywhere. The topography was something you'd see in Ireland: sandy soil all over the site, several feet deep without a rock in it! The entire state of North Dakota is clay and horrible soil—except for this one little 250-acre hill with sandy loam soil. It was perfect for a golf course.

I rose from a crouched position and just stood quietly in the middle of the special site, with the wind blowing across a flat gray sky. I looked around and realized that the Good Lord was about to let me build my first Top 100 golf course.

Just standing there, I could envision green sites, fairways, and tees on the landscape.

The actual design and construction of the golf course required very little more than just standing there and imagining it. We could not improve upon Mother Nature. We simply marked the centerlines after surveying. We surveyed green sites and put down stakes for cut and fill.

We didn't even need to change the grade for six of the greens. We just sprayed the field grass with Roundup, and tilled it. The entire construction process, for eighteen holes, required us to move only 7,000 yards of dirt.

Even with the minimal construction costs, it was difficult for the developer to raise money. We tried to help raise $1.25 million to develop the site. We got $300,000. The developer was going to drop the project.

"You have got to see this through," I implored. "This will be a very special golf course. I could work until I'm ninety-two and never get a better site to work with."

The owner didn't believe me.

To put my money where my mouth was, and to get the project done, I left my fee on the table. So did the shaper. We used the $300,000 to pay for the laborers and to buy grass seed and fertilizer.

When the Links of North Dakota opened, with a small clubhouse, it was named second-best new golf course in America, and the best new affordable golf course in the country. And it cracked the Top 100 best modern golf courses list.

"I could work until I'm ninety-two and never get a better site to work with."

CHAPTER 57
TO DREAM THE IMPOSSIBLE DEADLINE

RON KIRBY

Ron Kirby, based in Palm Beach Gardens, designed the scenic Old Head Golf Links, in County Cork, Ireland—one of the most photographed golf courses in the world. He also created London Golf Club International Course in London, England; Dolphin Head Golf Course in Hilton Head, South Carolina; Sun City Golf Course in Bophuthatswana, South Africa; and La Moraleja Golf Club in Madrid, Spain.

I was in Wadesborough, North Carolina, in June, and Ron Kirby was giving the normal field instructions and input to the Wadsworth construction guys for the club's nine-hole addition. An assistant professional from the golf shop came out to find Ron.

"Mr. Kirby, there is an important phone call for you at the shop."

Ron went back with the assistant professional to take a call from Denis Griffiths, Kirby's associate, asking Kirby to wait right there for an overseas call. Within a few minutes, the overseas call came through. The discussion went like this:

Lady: Ron, my husband will be sixty years old this September.

Ron: Very nice.

Lady: To mark the occasion, we are renovating the church we were married in, and his old school, a park in the town center, and the jail he was held in for murder and successfully defended himself in.

Ron: Very nice.

Lady: As you know, my husband is a golf fanatic.

Ron: Yes, ma'am.

Lady: We want to give him a golf course for his birthday. Can you create it for us?

Ron: Well, yes, I would be very honored to have this assignment. But golf courses take a lot of time and effort to accomplish and it would not be possible to complete by September.

Lady: So an eighteen-hole course is not possible?

Ron: That's correct.

Lady: How about nine holes?

Ron: That's still not possible in the timeframe you have.

Lady: How about one hole?

Ron: Oh ... that would be no problem!

Lady: Well, perfect. We will have nine contractors build one hole each.

The lady on the phone was Imelda Marcos; and on a late afternoon in mid-September, President Ferdinand Marcos and his foursome played the first nine holes of the Lake Poway Golf Club in Ilocose North, Philippines.

CHAPTER 58
WE ARE NOT ALONE

DON KNOTT

Northern California native Don Knott is a past president of the American Society of Golf Course Architects and chairman of the ASGCA Foundation, as well as a tenured member of the environmental impact committee. He was, for more than twenty-five years, lead architect for the Robert Trent Jones II group, supervising the completion of more than sixty courses worldwide, including Princeville Resort's Prince Course in Hawaii, The Links at Spanish Bay in Pebble Beach, Long Island National Golf Club, and the National Golf Club of Australia. Knott has partnered with architect Gary Linn and PGA Tour player and 1996 PGA Champion Mark Brooks to form Knott Brooks Linn Golf Course Design.

In 1987, I made a site visit to the black free state of Transkei in South Africa. I was alone, walking the proposed site for the golf course, which was still in the planning stage, long before a single shovel of dirt was turned.

I was wrapped up in the scenery, the landscape features, and the solitude of it all when I got a peculiar feeling. I began to look a little closer at the details around me.

It turned out I was not alone on the site walk. The site was occupied by many, many natives living in grass huts. I began to notice bare-breasted women. And then I saw some not-so-friendly-looking men.

I was walking solo, and suddenly I felt as if I were intruding. The menacing looks I received were damned scary. My leisurely, peaceful stroll quickly became a hurried gait!

> **I was alone, walking the proposed site for the golf course, which was still in the planning stage, long before a single shovel of dirt was turned.**

CHAPTER 59
MY MAGNOLIA LANE MASTERS MEMORIES
JOHN LaFOY

John LaFoy, a past president of the American Society of Golf Course Architects, heads his own design firm based in Greenville, South Carolina. He began his design career with George W. Cobb. His opportunity to help Cobb with the remodeling of Augusta National Golf Club led to LaFoy remodeling many classic layouts, including those of architects A. W. Tillinghast, Alister MacKenzie, Seth Raynor, Charles Blair MacDonald, and numerous Donald Ross designs. John has also designed and renovated more than a hundred courses, including the Country Club of Charleston in Charleston, South Carolina; Country Club of Birmingham in Birmingham, Alabama; Linville Ridge Country Club and Neuse Golf Club in North Carolina; and Glenmore Country Club in Charlottesville, Virginia.

My first visit to the Augusta National Golf Club was in 1962 when I was a sophomore in high school. I knew a little about the golf course, since my best friend's dad, George Cobb, had designed the par-three course there, but like most teenagers, I never dreamed that I would one day be a golf course architect and actually work there.

Fast-forward about seven years—four years in college, three years in the Marines as a combat engineer officer—and I had a brand new job as an apprentice architect to George Cobb.

Mr. Cobb was a wonderfully talented architect who never really received the credit he is due. He also happened to be the consulting architect at the Augusta National. I was fortunate to have made all the trips to Augusta with him from 1973 through 1978, the year after Augusta National's legendary chairman Clifford Roberts died.

During our time there, it would have been nice to claim that we were the consulting architects for the Augusta National, but Mr. Cobb had a letter in his files from the green chairman saying that nothing from our office could promote or tout our work at the Augusta National Golf Club.

I'll never forget my first visit there to actually work. Mr. Cobb and I walked into a meeting a couple of minutes after it had commenced and Roberts was holding court. There were a number of Augusta

National members who were industry giants, including David Lilly, chairman of the Toro Company, in the room.

Roberts turned from them to face me and asked, "Are you George's bunker man?"

Before I could open my mouth, Mr. Cobb spoke up. "Mr. Roberts," he said, "I will be responsible for anything coming out of my office."

I soon understood that we were not there for casual conversation. I'm not sure that I opened my mouth the entire day, which I eventually figured out was probably smart!

After the brief, to-the-point meeting, we all piled into a van and started toward the first fairway. Mr. Roberts made a point to instruct that if any member of the group had anything to say, they should say it to the entire group. There would be no talking among ourselves.

About halfway up the first fairway, a couple of the high-ranking industry leaders started to chat.

"Stop the car!" Roberts commanded to the driver.

Then he turned around to the passengers and proceeded to scold them in a manner in which I wouldn't talk to a dog! They should have known better than to defy him, since they knew Clifford Roberts very well. As a Marine platoon commander whose primary job was to clear land mines and booby traps from the highway just south of Da Nang only a few years earlier, I was not intimidated by much. But I saw these grown men and captains of industry, with much more clout than me, wilt under a pretty good tongue lashing from Roberts.

I actually got along quite well with Mr. Roberts, and soon learned that he was one of those leaders who just wanted the truth. People got in trouble with him when they told him what they thought he wanted to hear instead of the truth. Roberts later referred to me as his "bunker man," and I was fortunate to have renovated many of the bunkers and many of the tees on the golf course, as well as several greens, including the famous thirteenth green.

I knew a little about the golf course, since my best friend's dad, George Cobb, had designed the par-three course there, but like most teenagers, I never dreamed that I would one day be a golf course architect and actually work there.

CHAPTER 60
ARNOLD PALMER'S DAM IDEA

ERIK LARSEN

Erik Larsen is executive vice president and Senior Golf Course Architect for Arnold Palmer Design Company. He serves on the executive board of the American Society of Golf Course Architects. He manages the company for Mr. Palmer and is completely involved with each project from contract negotiation to construction completion. Since joining the Orlando, Florida–based firm in 1983, Larson has been involved in the design of more than one hundred golf courses worldwide. His list of new layouts includes Deacon's Lodge in Brainard, Minnesota; Running Y Ranch in Klamath Falls, Oregon; Spencer T. Olin Community Golf Course in Alton, Illinois; and Links at Kuilima in Oahu, Hawaii.

Arnold Palmer stared at me, and his baleful glare seemed to drill holes right through me. What had I done to draw his ire?

I was a thirty-one-year-old golf course architect in 1985—my second year on staff at the Arnold Palmer Design Company. In those two years, I'd rarely been in the presence of "The King," so I was thrilled to be making my first site visit with Mr. Palmer. We traveled to Kingsmill, Virginia to walk a would-be golf course and review our plans. Mr. Palmer, Ed Seay (the co-founder of Palmer's company), and Harry Knight, the property owner, set out on foot, plans in hand.

Mr. Palmer was engaged in what we were doing and was considering my ideas. We were having a good time, getting along fine, and connecting. I was on top of the world: out in the fresh air playing in the dirt on a pretty site, creating a golf course with my hero, Arnold Palmer.

We reached what would be the ninth hole—a medium-length par-three hole played across a deep, dramatic ravine. Mr. Palmer took a long look at the ravine.

"I'd like to build a dam," he said, "and fill that ravine with water so the hole will play as a water hole."

I was tongue-tied. I wasn't crazy about the thought of converting this dramatic ravine into a pond. I stammered for a moment, and then blurted out my opposition to Mr. Palmer.

"Sir, I don't like your dam idea."

Everyone, including Mr. Palmer, stopped in their tracks. Knight hurriedly stepped back as Palmer turned and fixed his astonished gaze on me.

"What did you say to me?" Palmer said.

I realized he thought I'd said I didn't like his *damn* idea.

As Mr. Palmer stared daggers at me, he must have been wondering how a rookie on his first site visit could dare to speak to him in that manner!

Ed Seay, my direct boss, stepped in, as he always did, to smooth things out with Mr. Palmer.

"Arnold, what Erik's trying to say is that he likes the dramatic shot over the ravine rather than the water shot. Plus, this is an environmentally sensitive wetland area, and we will not be permitted to fill it in by building a dam," Seay said. "I'm afraid your dam idea, while inspired, won't be possible."

Mr. Palmer, who had never taken his eyes off me, said, "You'd better do something about this!"

Then he grinned.

I breathed a sigh of relief and didn't fully remove my foot from my mouth until later that evening when Mr. Palmer and I had a beer and laughed about the incident.

"You were tough," Mr. Palmer told me. "You were sticking up for your opinion. I like that."

Palmer must have meant what he said: twenty-two years later I am still in his employ and even running his company!

CHAPTER 61
JACK AND GARY

JEFF LAWRENCE

Jeff Lawrence's twenty years in the design business have given him the opportunity to work alongside some of the greatest golf course architects of our time: Gary Player, Jack Nicklaus, and Tom Fazio. Lawrence is currently working with Mr. Player on projects in Bulgaria; Abu Dhabi; Tenerife; Canada; and Costa Rica. Some of his other work includes Flint Hills National in Andover, Kansas; Stock Farm and Iron Horse in Montana; Members Club at Aldarra in Fall City, Washington; and Glenwild in Park City, Utah.

It's always a learning experience working with Gary Player, the most traveled man in the history of professional golf. Surprisingly, the most traveled man is a nervous flier!

Many times we'll take private jets and helicopters. Mr. Player talks to the pilots to make sure they have enough hours. He's always looking out the cockpit window and asking questions. We went through a thunderstorm in Florida once that had him very concerned.

I could not keep up with Mr. Player's work-out regimen, that's for sure … and he's over seventy years old!

Mr. Player's experience makes him the best when it comes to working with clients. He's got a passion for what he does and is charismatic. Some architects are standoffish, but, considering his accomplishments in his lifetime, he can still sit down with anyone, carry on a conversation, and really care.

There are times when Mr. Player's word goes a lot further than mine. When I get in a situation with the client, and the client needs some direction—particularly the ones in faraway lands who are new to golf—it's good to have that little extra push from Mr. Player. He has a way of wording things, and just because of who he is and the way he says it, he educates people about a certain design feature and why it is in their best interest, even if it means increasing the budget.

Mr. Player is open-minded. We talk through things. There are certain design philosophies he is adamant about, though. Playability for the average golfer is important to Mr. Player, and despite being recognized as the greatest bunker player who ever lived, he doesn't accept the long bunker shot as part of his design philosophy. Even though he is willing to debate most design strategies, he urges away from this design concept.

One of the most rewarding parts of my job is opening golf courses. Being able to play a game of golf on the course you personally designed gives you a feeling of pride unlike anything else. Opening a course also turns into a strategic report card: What do you like about the course? What could've been better? What changes should you make next time? You are able to critique your own performance.

Jack Nicklaus has very high standards for his work and is always trying to get things 100 percent correct. This is an excellent trait I learned from working for him.

When I was in college, I had the good fortune to caddy for Jack Nicklaus at the opening of the Desert Highlands course in Scottsdale, Arizona.

Early in the round, he asked for a yardage for his approach shot.

"What have we got here?" Nicklaus asked me.

"It looks like about one hundred forty-five or one hundred fifty yards," I answered.

Nicklaus turned and looked at me as if I were from Mars.

"Well, which is it?" he asked. "One forty-five or one fifty?"

I then understood the kind of precision he expected.

"One hundred forty-seven, to be exact," I said quickly!

CHAPTER 62
GOING GREEN IN GOLF:
THE LESSON OF LINKS

TIM LIDDY

Tim Liddy, is a Yorktown, Indiana–based course designer who has collaborated extensively with Pete Dye for two decades. Among his many solo projects are The Trophy Club in Lebanon, Indiana and a renovation of The Duke's in St. Andrews, Scotland.

Centuries-old links golf has much to teach us about the game. But I am afraid we are not listening or learning.

Although many of us—and by us I mean Americans—profess a huge love for links golf, the simple truth is that very few of us actually understand what it is or how to fully appreciate it.

This has become very clear to me in recent years while working in Scotland on a renovation. An increased exposure to the "real" game has enabled me to see the relevance of links golf to the game on a wider front.

For most Americans, links golf is a much-looked-forward-to trip to Scotland or Ireland that involves a manic chase around a few of the iconic coastal courses; a trip digitally recorded for posterity and for bragging rights back home. Inevitably, it will have been hugely enjoyable, but the truth is that at best it is largely a superficial experience. A few rounds on great links courses will set the golfing juices flowing, but they cannot begin to impart an understanding of what this form of golf is really all about.

There isn't enough time on a first visit truly to appreciate that links golf is one of nature's great gifts to us: seaside dunes tumbling down to the shoreline, the tawny coloring of fescue, the dark green gorse and purple heather against the rumpled green and brown fairways. It is one thing to feel the firm turf underfoot; quite another to experience a well-executed iron shot as the feeling travels up from the fingertips, through the hands and arms, and directly into the soul.

What I had not realized until I became immersed in the best of Scottish golf is just how vital the lessons of links golf and links golf course architecture are to the future of golf in America and elsewhere. Links golf courses, with their sandy soil, firm turf, and natural features, can teach us as much today as when they originated over five hundred years ago. Scottish golf writer Malcolm Campbell elegantly states in *The Scottish Golf Book*, "With few exceptions, golf in Scotland has remained true to the traditional principles of the game handed down over the generations. There are, thankfully, few examples of the tricked-up wares of self-styled architects—mostly, it has to be said, American—who arrogantly proclaim their creations as 'Scottish-style' championship links, when in fact they are as often as not nothing more than vaguely planned dumpings of dirt that turn honest countryside into fields of upturned egg-boxes to boost the sales of real estate."

On ecological grounds, links golf has much to teach us. In terms of sustainable maintenance practices at an affordable level that's playable for all levels of golfers, America, I am sorry to say, is lagging far behind.

We routinely irrigate over a million gallons of water a day on many of our golf courses. We judge the maintenance of our courses on something akin to a "scale of green"—usually against the most artificial golf course ever built, Augusta National. We have reached the point, in my view, where many searching questions now have to be asked. Among them:

- Is this high-maintenance, artificial form of the game sustainable?
- Is American golf now too expensive as a result?
- Are we making it harder for future generations to enjoy this great game?

Being green in golf is not the same as being green in other aspects of the environment. In America, dormant Bermuda grass is closer in playing condition to links turf than any other grass in the southern United States, and yet while we continually profess to want to emulate Scottish or Irish links golf, we consistently over-seed to achieve soft, green conditions for the winter golfer. It's an expensive and grotesquely wasteful use of resources.

Sustainability should be the new buzzword for golf in the United States, and for that, we need to look to the origins of the game. Links golf courses have been sustainable for centuries, requiring little or no water, low fertilization, and low maintenance costs. This explains why Scotland still enjoys inexpensive golf. Golf would not be the national pastime it is in Scotland if it were expensive.

Which begs another question: how much is a round of golf actually worth? $50? $100? $200? If we followed the example of links golf courses, our maintenance cost would be hugely reduced, our development of golf courses would cost less, and our green fees would go down—significantly! The benefits to the environment would be considerable.

The agronomics of links turf are pretty impressive: dry, lean, and firm. The ecology demonstrates proper maintenance practices developed over many centuries. There is no *Poa trivialis* on a links golf course (Poa being symptomatic of too much irrigation and fertilization). *Poa trivialis*, an annual bluegrass, is prominent in over-watered golf courses in America. It invades when superintendents, fearful for their jobs, over-water their golf courses in an attempt to keep their courses "Augusta" green and their members living an egotistical and unsustainable dream. Such a defensive maintenance regime allows Poa to overtake the drought-tolerant bents originally planted. Once the Poa is established, the superintendent is stuck with over-watering to keep alive what is essentially a weed.

With Poa endemic on your golf course, it is time seriously to look at maintenance practices. It will take time, maybe years, to be rid of it, but less water and fertilizer reduces disease growth, allows the bent grasses to return, and provides a firm turf, an ideal base for golf and essential for sustainable golf.

Links fairways in Scotland for the most part are not green in the summer but turn a golden tan color in dry conditions with only a hint of green here and there. And yet they not only remain alive and healthy, but provide a wonderful surface to play from. Minimal watering of putting surfaces, applied only in the driest conditions, ensures that greens remain firm and fast.

Playability for all levels of golfers is an important characteristic of a links course. Because of the way golf developed, particularly with the arrival of the Haskell rubber-core golf ball around 1902, golf on the ground was an integral part of the design strategy of the early links layouts. The ability to play golf more on the ground and less in the air adds

---

Golf, links-inspired golf, is the principal of working with nature, not against it.

---

greatly to the enjoyment of the game for the average player, while offering more options for the better player. It also encourages an improvement in skill levels.

Yardage means nothing, as the variable wind and firm conditions provide a test that differs every day. Five sets of tees are not needed because yardage differences are not as important without the forced carries and target golf so prevalent in the modern U.S.-led version of the game.

For example, the Old Course at St. Andrews, set up for the dry conditions of the 2000 Open, included fairways that in some cases rolled faster than the greens. These conditions defended the golf course against the power hitters. Tee shots traveled to the edges of the fairways where serious hazards awaited, and approach shots to firm greens had to be played from the right place. Course management was crucial.

Tiger Woods, the eventual winner, displayed wonderful strategic skills throughout the event with a classic example—his tee shot at the twelfth hole, named "Heathery." A moonscape of bunkers infests the fairway on this short par-four hole, where finding a safe placement for the drive is critical. Woods, with his tremendous power, opted to defend against the hazards not by laying up short, which would have left a difficult and unpredictable second to a severely contoured green. Instead, he elected to launch a driver over the green, and beyond all the fairway and approach hazards. This left him a relatively easy chip back into the green from beyond the golf hole, thereby taking out the fairway hazards and the pot bunker and severe tier at the front of the green.

It was the stroke of a master who had absorbed the essence of the game of golf as it is played under links conditions—the original and purest form of the game.

In his book, *The Spirit of St. Andrews*, Alister MacKenzie illustrated the playability of the Old Course with his diagram of the fourteenth hole, called "Long," showing four alternative routes to play the hole. The paths vary depending on a golfer's ability, the hole location on the green, and the prevailing breeze. Strategy is paramount and decisions that will have major impact on success or potentially embarrassing failure have to be made on this hole before any shot is played. Circumstances and decisions change quickly. The art of playing links golf is to appreciate the first and be able to respond with the second.

At its best, golf is a chess game—with different pieces and a different board every day. It requires as much, and perhaps more, skill and strategy than power. In America, by contrast, we play only one way. We fly the ball to the green, making golf a one-dimensional game.

Clearly it is not possible to have links golf courses everywhere. There has to be compromise and adaptation to natural ground conditions. But the guiding principals of the traditional form of the game in terms of sustainability and year-round playability are just as relevant today to every golf course.

A minimum of water and fertilization is paramount. Many inland golf courses on heavy soils would benefit from this sound agronomic principle. American golfers need to understand certain lessons carried over from links: the importance of top dressing heavy soils with sand; that Poa is the hallmark of too much water and fertilizer; and that green is not always the preferred color on a golf course.

Many golf courses throughout the world, including the heathland golf courses of England, such as Sunningdale and Swinley Forest, embody these virtues. That is why they are great golf courses and why they continue to stand the test of time.

To remain relevant, golf in America must take on its competition. Golf can offer solitude and natural elegance against the crass modern society, a private experience instead of mass media. But we need to stop building artificial golf courses, with cart paths, range finders, and yardage markers. If we drive our golf carts and play to yardages all day, why not just play to targets on a range? What's the difference?

To compete in today's society, golf needs to offer the antithesis of today's society, not a reflection of it. Links golf courses provide the natural, sustainable model for a healthy outdoor exercise that, in the words of David R. Forgan, son of the St. Andrews club maker, "affords the opportunity to play the man and act the gentlemen." Or as Malcolm Campbell states, "It opens up the joys of the great outdoors, the chance to pit one's skill against nature, an opponent and most importantly, one's self."

Golf, links-inspired golf, is the principal of working with nature, not against it. It's become increasingly vital to the future of golf in America that we understand the underlying message and act upon it before it is too late.

Because of its unique characteristics, the classic redan hole is one of my favorite designs. It combines a requirement for careful strategic thinking with precise shot making that sets it apart from the run-of-the-mill par-three. The angle and slant of the green away from the player present a choice of options, with the best alternatives usually being the right-to-left shot to run the ball into the green over the slope, or the high, soft cut aimed at checking the ball against the slope.

The redan hole at Charles Blair Macdonald's National Golf Links in Southampton, New York, was my inspiration for this important hole in our remodel of Princess Anne Country Club. The tee was raised to make the surface of the green visible and create a prominent view of Linkhorn Bay, an important feature of the golf course and surrounding area. The slight elevation restored an iconic view that the golf course had lost during previous remodels. This design is a refinement of the original redan hole at North Berwick, Scotland, which is semi-blind from the tee. I also added a foreshortening bunker on the right, which blinds the approach and deceives the eye, making the golf hole look closer to the golfer than its yardage.

CHAPTER 63
THE FIRST STEP'S A DOOZY!

JIM LIPE

Jim Lipe is a senior designer with Nicklaus Design. In that role, he was the lead design associate in the creation of Carlton Woods at The Woodlands in Woodlands, Texas; Spring Creek Ranch Country Club in Collierville, Tennessee; Mayacama Golf Club in Santa Rosa, California; Cordillera Ranch Golf Club in Boerne, Texas; Cabo Del Sol in Cabo San Lucas, Mexico; Sebonack Golf Club on Long Island, New York; and the May River Club at Palmetto Bluffs, Bluffton, South Carolina.

As a senior designer with Nicklaus Design for the past twenty-four years, I have been in numerous strange and hilarious situations. Not many people know this, but both Jack and Barbara are experts in pranks, gags, and playing tricks on unsuspecting friends. I have been the recipient of more than one "gotcha" through the years.

In some cases, I even inadvertently perpetrated a joke on myself, with less than flattering results.

In October 2006, we'd just finished an all-day site visit on a project in Cabo, Mexico. After driving all over the site for several hours in ATVs, our design team gathered back at the property owner's elegant home on the beach.

Earlier in the day, I was the last to arrive with one of my associates. Upon my entrance, Jack, who was already seated for lunch with about thirteen others, surprised me by leading the group in a verse of "Happy Birthday" to celebrate my sixtieth.

When it came time to leave, we were all migrating toward the front door, shaking hands with the client and contractor to thank them for their hospitality. In the excitement and commotion, after a long day, I turned from shaking hands and stepped right into a decorative reflection pool in the foyer! The pool, precariously near the front door, was four feet deep, so there I stood, in this elegant home, sunken in water up to my chest, holding both of my arms above my head to keep the blueprints from getting soaked.

Everyone got a tremendous laugh out of my clumsiness. Barbara Nicklaus came back in from the parking area when she heard the commotion, and immediately looked at Jack.

"Jim, you didn't?" she asked. Jack was laughing too hard to tell her he hadn't pushed me in, but I later learned that when he arrived at the home, he'd speculated that someone might fall in. Knowing me as well as he does, Jack wasn't surprised that I had accidentally taken the plunge, but he sure was amused by it!

The homeowner eased my ego a bit by explaining that I was the eighth person to fall in since he'd opened the home. My fall convinced him to cover the pool with a nice Plexiglas cover—good news for me, since we are now creating two new golf courses on his property!

Jack Nicklaus, through the years, has always tried to learn more and be a better designer. He has never been satisfied with designing a course just one way. In fact, he's always spoken with pride about the fact that players often don't know that he was the designer when they come off one of his courses the first time.

"That course was so much different than a previous Nicklaus course I've played," is a phrase that is music to Jack's ears.

Like our client in Cabo, Jack has had many developers hire him to do multiple courses on the same property, mainly because Jack has the ability and vision to approach each design in a different way. He provides different looks and varying playability.

Just as Jack wants his courses to evolve during construction, he also wants to evolve as a designer and never be satisfied. It is his famous drive, the same internal drive that made him the great golfer he became, that makes him continually improve as a designer.

Jack is also renowned for his attention to detail. His powers of recollection have astounded me and others through the years. He rarely forgets anything related to his designs throughout the entire design and construction process.

Jack is also very cognizant of and sympathetic to spending as little of a client's money as possible. Jack doesn't make demands on a client to move extraordinary amounts of earth or build expensive water features just because the client has the means. He works very hard to work with the land given to him and, whenever possible, disturbs as little as possible of that land to produce a memorable golf experience. Jack is as serious about that as he is about doing whatever it takes to design a first-class golf facility and to meet the client's objectives. It is this class associated with Nicklaus-designed projects that continues to make him one of the most sought-after designers of his time.

The thing that stands out most about the man, to me, is his generosity. He keeps most of his good works quiet, so even though I could list example after example, just know that he is a generous, loving family man who is also very generous to those that have been associated with him in the design business.

I am blessed and fortunate to have had the opportunity to work side by side with Jack Nicklaus for so many years, and I will cherish those times forever.

Jack Nicklaus, through the years, has always tried to learn more and be a better designer. He has never been satisfied with designing a course just one way.

CHAPTER 64
CLOUD NINE OR FIELD OF DREAMS?

BOB LOHMANN

Lohmann Golf Designs, Inc. was founded in suburban Chicago in 1984 by Robert Lohmann, who served as president of the American Society of Golf Course Architects from 1998 to 1999. His company's services include construction management services and agronomic and environmental consultation. Some of his courses include Mattaponi Springs Golf Course in Virginia, and in Wisconsin, Bishops Bay Country Club in Madison, Whispering Springs Golf Club in Fond du Lac, and Cedar Creek Country Club in Onalaska. In Illinois, Lohmann designed Boulder Ridge Country Club at Lake in the Hills, The Merit Club in Libertyville, and Canyata in Marshall.

Heaven forbid the phone should ever stop ringing but, like most golf course architects, I have experienced my share of new course projects that never happened. In fact, if I had a dollar for every new design job that seemed like a sure thing but, for any number of reasons, never got built, I'd be a pretty rich man.

The story of Jim Oliff, for instance, really hits home with me. Jim's a lawyer who approached us a while back about designing a golf course on 320 acres he owned in Ruther Glen, Virginia, just north of Richmond. He approached my firm, and several others, in fact. He actually drove from Virginia to our offices, outside Chicago, to interview us. He apparently drove all over the U.S. interviewing architects before choosing us.

He turned out to be the most hands-on client you could ever imagine. The first time I traveled to Virginia to see the property, Jim picked me up at the airport himself. All the way from Baltimore, and back again the next day, we talked design and construction, routing, and wetlands permitting. From the way he talked, it was clear Jim was determined to build the course himself, with local crews, using equipment he planned to purchase.

Upon arrival in Ruther Glen, we immediately began walking the 320-acre property; at lunch he sent someone for sandwiches, which we ate in an old barn on site. Three hundred twenty acres is a lot of land, enough for twenty-seven to thirty-six holes, or eighteen and enough housing to pay for the whole venture.

But Jim made it clear that he wanted eighteen holes of golf and no housing. That evening, we had dinner at truck stop on the way to his home, where he kindly put me up.

I have to admit at the time I couldn't help but wonder if Jim Oliff really was a hands-on guy throwing himself totally into the golf development process, or whether he was some fly-by-nighter on a shoestring who would drop me back in Baltimore and never contact us again. It turned out Jim Oliff had his own way of doing things, and he made it all work.

He ended up buying all of the construction equipment we used to clear, grade, and irrigate the golf course. Even professional course builders lease most of their equipment, but not Jim. When we were finished, he sold that equipment. In fact, my construction division bought one of the bulldozers.

We provided shapers to build the features in Ruther Glen, where we more or less taught his local help how to build the golf course. This complicated matters for us but we made most of our site visits, especially when the greens were built. We ended up working very closely on greens construction with a local 'dozer operator who had learned a great deal from one of the shapers we brought on site. He was a real quick study, and he now works for us.

In short, the entire construction process was completely unorthodox. Jim spent a lot of time out of the country attending to other business. When he was on site, things moved right along. One day, Jim called me to say they needed a tee leveler. The next thing I knew, one of Jim's employees showed up at our offices outside Chicago to pick it up! When Jim was gone, however, things tended to languish. Jim didn't seem to care, though. He was in no hurry to complete the project and we wondered if he ever would. The construction proceeded in this way, in fits and starts, for years.

Mattaponi Springs Golf Club did eventually get built. The grand opening took place in the fall of 2004, and it proved well worth the wait, earning all manner of national and regional "best new" awards; it ranks among the top three public courses in the state of Virginia, and folks are still lining up to play it. It's some of our very best design work.

The experience working with Jim, for me, reinforced some important things—delegating is important!—but it also reminded me, and continues to remind me, why I got into this business: No matter how many deals fall through or never pan out, that next project could well be someone's field of dreams. And who wouldn't want to be part of that?

No matter how many deals fall through or never pan out, that next project could well be someone's field of dreams.

CHAPTER 65
LETTING THE SITE CREATE
THE NATURE OF A COURSE

BILL LOVE

Bill Love, an ASGCA past president, has worked on more than a hundred projects throughout North America and abroad, and authored *An Environmental Approach to Golf Course Development* for the American Society of Golf Course Architects. His experience includes the development of all types of new golf facilities and extensive renovation work with existing courses. His College Park, Maryland–based firm specializes in land planning and design for golf communities, enhancement and master planning for older courses, and environmentally sensitive golf design for both new and existing facilities. Examples of Love's projects are Hunting Hawk Golf Club and Laurel Hill Golf Club in Virginia, Bellport Country Club in New York, the Olympic Club in California, and Guadalajara Country Club and Club Campestre de Monterrey in Mexico.

Ever since I was a little kid, my brothers and I were constantly outside playing sports or spending countless hours in a large tract of undeveloped parkland near the house exploring the terrain, streams, ands woods. When my dad introduced us to golf at a small, local nine-hole course one summer vacation, we didn't think it could get any better than playing a new sport outside all day. This confluence of interests produced a profound appreciation for the unique way golf utilizes the environment and provides an unending variety of strategies, challenges, and settings.

It is always great opportunity to work on a site with conducive terrain and a lot of natural features. When these qualities exist in a site, they can provide a new course with an inherent character indicative of the regional landscape. Sometimes those opportunities occur in areas of the country that haven't yet been pressured by development or in foreign countries where the landscape has changed little over the years. I am currently working on a project in northern Mexico where the golf course will be developed within the confines of a nature preserve. The site contains such beautiful trees and scenic waterways that it was just a matter of exploring and discovering the right holes for the course. It helps to have an enlightened, environmentally sensitive owner who has given us free rein to lay out the golf course in areas of the site that would fully incorporate the character of the preserve. The golf course provides a green space buffer for the environmentally sensitive areas on the site and creates wildlife corridors so existing inhabitants are not confined. A limited amount of residential area has also been planned to lie lightly on the land in the most unobtrusive areas of the site. The owner is adopting an environmental management program for the site to utilize best management practices for resource conservation and sustainability. The end result will be a very unique golf course that is a great experience by blending into the natural landscape and allowing players, residents, and wildlife to coexist.

CHAPTER 66
ADVENTURELAND

JEFFREY LUCOVSKY

Jeffrey Lucovsky, with Jacksonville, Florida–based Mark McCumber & Associates, has created Hidden Cypress Golf Club in Bluffton, South Carolina; The Brickyard at Riverside Golf Club in Macon, Georgia; Tunica National Golf and Tennis in Robinsonville, Mississippi. In Florida, he worked to create Hunters Run (south course) in Boynton Beach and the Golf Club of South Hampton, in St. Augustine.

Travel is one of the fun, exciting, dangerous, and unique parts of working as a golf course architect. After working domestically for most of my career, our firm has begun to aggressively branch out into the international marketplace. Other than a few close calls with amateur pilots on small planes, some bad weather during flights, and lots of travel delays, nothing has compared to my last couple of years of travel to Central America.

Even though I live in the country, my horseback experience was limited to a few rides over a span of twenty years. I have now logged over sixty hours riding in steep jungle terrain on horses that are smaller than their American counterparts, with an architect that is not much smaller than an average NFL linebacker.

An easier way to view a property was on a seven-passenger Eurocopter. Seeing the site from the air was an exciting way to see the difficult terrain. Of course you can't see the entire site by helicopter, so two weeks later, clad in work clothes and boots, we hiked the site. Any missteps might mean a fall of a couple of hundred feet. Grabbing onto a vine to climb up vertical embankments would be the only way to get back up the slopes.

The most unique site visit I ever took was via a zip-line, often known as a "canopy tour." We were suspended above a coffee plantation by wires, strung tree to tree about seventy-five feet off the ground, and zoomed through the jungle to look at the site. To be honest, I was more worried about getting from tree to tree than paying that much attention to what the ground looked like below in terms of a golf course.

The best part was rappelling down to the ground. The guide told me to guide my hands on the ropes, but not to hold the rope. He explained that a man at the bottom of the tree would catch me. I was the first to go. After jumping off the platform and freefalling below, I was sure that I was going the crush the man on the ground. They did some trick with the ropes and I stopped safely.

There can't be many jobs where every day is an adventure, and that is what I love about my job.

CHAPTER 67
DON'T BE AFRAID TO GET DIRTY
GREG MARTIN

Greg Martin founded Martin Design Partnership, Ltd., headquartered in Batavia, Illinois, in 1991. Martin's critically acclaimed projects are seen as environmentally beneficial, time and budget sensitive, site specific, economically successful, creative, and thorough. Some of his projects include The Links at Carillon in Illinois; Millwood Golf and Racquet Club in Missouri; and in Wisconsin, Wildridge at Mill Run, Glen Erin Golf Club, and The Oaks Golf Course.

We get dirty every time we begin a project.

There is a perception of glamour associated with our profession. There is a certain degree of truth to that perception, but the profession of golf course architecture is like no other. We are a small band of like-minded individuals who have very distinct ideas about our craft.

Everyone sees the grand opening. Everyone sees us playing golf, or the media shot: holding a set of plans pointing at a faraway feature. But very few see the challenges of our job. We walk the rocky slopes during the early days of construction and we walk through brush on a hot August day trying to locate center points. We give pressure-packed presentations of renovation plans to three hundred pessimistic club members. We elicit changes during construction while keeping contractors enthusiastic.

We wear many hats, and they all get dirty. Every job is messy, whether trying to iron out construction issues, stretch budgets, or walk muddy paths. We get muddy. We get sunburned. We get sweaty and covered with silt. We get tired and put in too many miles between job sites.

And yet I wouldn't trade it for anything.

I didn't choose it. Golf course architecture sits at the intersection of creativity, logic, a love of sport and the game of golf, an appreciation of the natural environment, and ego. That's where I reside.

A fitting tribute to getting dirty? Golf course design is a craft and I get my inspiration on the soles of my feet while walking the property. There is a boot of mine stuck in a muddy grave at Carillon Golf Club. I stepped into a soft spot and pulled so hard that my boot came off about one foot below grade. It was never recovered!

Carillon was a ninety-five-day miracle. As part of a new "active adult" community in Chicago—the first such development outside of the Sunbelt—I was commissioned to develop a twenty-seven-hole golf course. The permitting, approvals, and plan prepara-

---

Golf course architecture sits at the intersection of creativity, logic, a love of sport and the game of golf, an appreciation of the natural environment, and ego. That's where I reside.

---

tion for the community were fast-tracked, but only left time to develop the golf course in one growing season. By the time plans were prepared and bids accepted we had a total of only ninety-five days to construct the golf course.

This was a large project under any scenario, but given the tight timeframe, I was on site approximately three times per week with Superintendent Renny Jacobson. It was my first golf course and

Minimalism is very popular in golden age and modern architecture.

maybe my biggest challenge. I had to ignore the audacity of the deadline.

Obviously each client or owner differs in what they're willing to accept. Jerry Rich had a vision to develop the most exclusive and intriguing golf course possible. With a local contractor he had constructed three holes. Each of the holes could be played as a par-three, par-four, or a par-five by using multiple tees. He continued this project until nine holes were completed over multiple phases. At that point, though, the difficulty of routing, circulation, theme, character, and balance became a bit more daunting than Mr. Rich expected. I was hired to help complete his vision.

Over the next year or so, we conceived of a new nine holes that would be introduced to complement the existing nine. Mr. Rich was interested in a variety of concepts and aesthetics, with each hole possessing a different image and each with incredible challenges. We had a particularly difficult time with the new eighth hole. This hole was a long, 450-yard par-four. Playing the hole required driving the ball uphill and then hitting a second shot back downhill, over water, into a beautiful setting. We'd moved the green and repositioned it numerous times. After the third or fourth adjustment Mr. Rich settled on a size and shape for the green: very wide from left to right, and very narrow from front to back.

After studying the new green configuration and reviewing the requirements of the hole—the challenging uphill drive, the tough downhill shot over water to a narrow target—I finally said, "Jerry, the average golfer can't play this hole!"

Mr. Rich responded, with plenty of assurance, "Greg … I don't want average golfers playing this hole!"

Design decisions were much easier after that.

Here are a few of the guiding principles I've come to learn and embrace:

- Par is less important than shot values.
- Golf is a pedestrian event, even if you are in a cart.
- The site dictates the routing and feature placement (the site dictates everything!).
- Golf architecture is not static art, it is dynamic theater.
- Fun is more important than length.
- Creativity and shotmaking should be rewarded.
- Golf should be emotionally engaging and mentally stimulating.
- What the golfer feels is more important than what the golfer sees.
- Less is often better.

We are stewards of the environment and caretakers of the game. As golf course architects, we are privileged to offer services that will be recognized as classic tests of golf for generations to come.

CHAPTER 68
LISTENING CAN OVERCOME
BARRIERS AND EARN RESPECT

VICTORIA MARTZ

Victoria Martz is vice president and senior golf course architect for the Arnold Palmer Design Company and serves as director of environmental design, responsible for assisting in preparing environmental site assessments including wetland management, permitting, native grass, plant selection, and evaluation of wildlife habitat. Martz is also a member of the Urban Land Institute and serves on the American Society of Golf Course Architects Board of Governors. Her projects include the Victoria Clube de Golfe in Portugal, which hosted the World Cup in 2005, and the Classic Club in Palm Desert, host of the PGA Tour's annual Bob Hope Chrysler Invitational.

In the late 1990s I became the project architect for a Tournament Players Club course in Blaine, Minnesota, a suburb of the Twin Cities. At that point in my career I had been lead architect for about a half-dozen courses for the Palmer Design Company. I had worked for the company for about fifteen years and my bosses, Ed Seay and Arnold Palmer, had been my mentors and advocates in bringing me from the design boards into the field. Mr. Seay cautioned me, though.

"It might be difficult for you, as a woman, to give direction to construction crews," he warned. "Construction crews are tough and not necessarily 'gender blind.'"

The construction for the TPC course was very complicated due to the fact that the site sat on a deep layer of peat. This layer had to be removed and thus the grades had to be reviewed and approved two feet below final grade. Once approved, irrigation would go in and two feet of sand would plate the grade work. All of the crew understood the difficulty of this method and together we shared ideas for this complicated process.

I was reviewing the project with the construction superintendent, the shaper, and representatives from the PGA Tour. As we walked one of the more complicated holes, a grizzled, older bulldozer operator, who I was told was a Vietnam veteran, watched me from his bulldozer. He climbed down and approached me.

"I can't tell you how much it means to me to be a member of a team that cares about my opinions. Thank you very much for including me," he said.

This macho construction worker then presented me with a gift he'd selected for me: a beautiful golf pin. I knew then that it was okay to bring a "softer" side to this business and that being a woman in the midst of construction crews would not be a problem.

Everyone wants to be treated with respect and have his or her opinions count. That pin is one of my favorite possessions and is a great reminder that we can do anything if we remember to do it with consideration of others.

CHAPTER 69
ARTISTIC COMPOSITIONS PAINTED BY ARCHITECTS AND NATURE

TOM MARZOLF

Hendersonville, North Carolina–based Tom Marzolf is a past president of the American Society of Golf Course Architects who studied landscape architecture, art, and art history at Virginia Tech University. Marzolf is senior design associate with Fazio Golf Course Designers, Inc. Among the notable layouts Marzolf has designed with Fazio are the Ritz Carlton Members Course in Sarasota, Florida; the Greenbrier Sporting Club's Snead Course in White Sulphur Springs, Virginia; the Capital City Club's Crabapple Course in Atlanta, Georgia; the Green Monkey Course in Barbados; and Corales Golf Club in the Dominican Republic. Marzolf has also been a consulting architect for a number of golf tournaments, including the 2009 and 2010 U.S. Women's Open; the 2006 and 2007 U.S. Opens; the 2002 U.S. Senior Open; the 2003, 2004, and 2005 U.S. Amateurs; and the 1997 and 2003 PGA Championships.

The most important aspect of golf course design is strategy. Playing golf is "placing" your ball so that you are always in the best position to play your next shot. Good players review the shot options by first studying the green. They consider the angle of the green's position, its shape, the hole location, and best route of attack in order to plot their course backward from the green. They always aim for a spot that best allows for success on the next shot. In this regard, golf is very similar to a game of billiards, or a game of chess. Golf, at its best, is a thinking game. The smart player is rewarded for thinking, and the non-thinking player is penalized.

The golf architect creates the playing field for the sport. The best courses make players think and hold their interest longer. The element of strategy is designed into a good golf course by a skilled golf architect. Only the best strategic courses are among the top ten courses in the United States because strategy has lasting value. Without it, the game is reduced to a walk in the park. There is nothing wrong with a walk-in-the-park, average course with little strategic emphasis. A course like that may be fun and user-friendly. However, this type of course will never be considered great and could never serve as the course for a major championship. Life is short, and with my work, I have focused on trying to build courses of lasting value, which means that strategy must be included.

The second most important aspect is beauty.

The golf architect puts a golf hole together with the same elements of composition an artist uses to paint a picture. How the human brain breaks down a picture dictates the rules of composition. The design process includes the desire to create interest through beauty.

The average golfer may not understand strategy, but he will recognize beauty. A beautiful course will have value.

The best golf architects have a skill to combine beauty and strategy. This is a winning combination, and is the key to a successful career in golf course design. Without this skill, your work will be weak and soon forgotten. The average golfer demands beauty, and the game's best players strive to be tested. Strategy creates the lasting challenge, which few can master.

CHAPTER 70
HOG HEAVEN
JERRY MATTHEWS

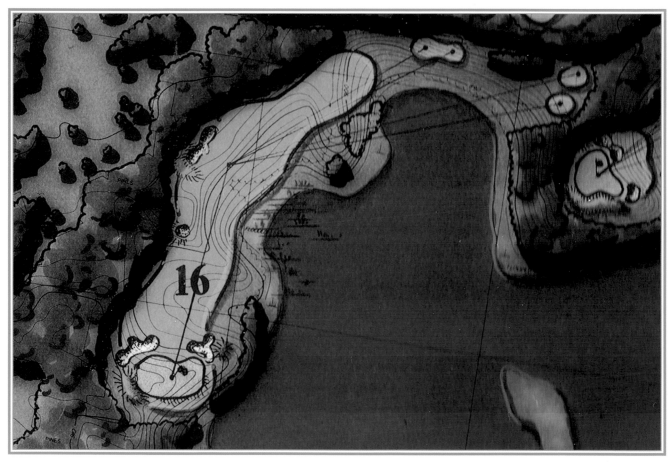

Risk and reward at Elk Ridge in Atlanta, Michigan.

Jerry Matthews, a past president of the American Society of Golf Course Architects, began his career when he was twelve years old by working for his father on the maintenance crew at Green Ridge Country Club. Upon completion of his education at Michigan State University in 1960, Matthews teamed with his father to form the golf course design firm of W. Bruce Matthews & Son. In 1979 he took over as president of Matthews & Associates, PC as Bruce settled into retirement at the family-owned Grand Haven Golf Club. Jerry designed Michigan courses The Lakes Course at Michaywé in Gaylord, Timber Ridge Golf Course in East Lansing, Elk Ridge Golf Course in Atlanta, St. Ives Golf Club in Stanwood, Timberstone Golf Course in Iron Mountain, Bucks Run Golf Club in Mt. Pleasant, and Sundance at A-Ga-Ming Golf Resort in Kewadin. Jerry also teaches golf course design and construction techniques for the Turfgrass program at Michigan State University.

I designed Elk Ridge Golf Course in Atlanta, Michigan, in 1990 for Lou and Mary Schmidt, owners of the Honey Baked Ham Company. This company invented and patented the first spiral-sliced, flavor-coated hams in the country. They have sales outlets across the United States.

The course has become known for what started out as a tongue-in-cheek attempt at humor and became a landmark—a pig-shaped bunker to be seen from an airplane!

The original idea was to design a water feature on the par-three fourth hole, which was also to serve as the irrigation supply reservoir. The shape of this water feature was to be that of a pig, as seen from above. The design and shape were included in all construction drawings and the irrigation plan. Since it was slightly tongue-in-cheek I wanted to have someone—the owner, contractor, supplier, or superintendent—make the discovery in the plans that the irrigation lake was going to resemble a pig. But I got no response from anyone. I decided to simply carry it out and figured some pilot someday would look down and finally recognize a small water pig.

I proceeded to stake it out on the ground as best I could to maintain the pig shape, and then the excavation began. Unfortunately, water sand was encountered below the four-foot level, which made just stabilizing the banks a problem, let alone trying to maintain the pig shape. Thwarted, but not defeated, I decided to design a sand bunker in the shape of a pig. Construction had progressed toward the end of the project, but as luck would have it, the tenth green was one of the last ones built, and it was located nearly one hundred vertical feet directly below the clubhouse site. This afforded a very good elevated view of the tenth hole, a par-three, which could be seen from the deck of the clubhouse. A perfect spot for the visual effect of a Honey Baked Ham symbol.

To carry out my desire that someone else discover the shape of an animal on a set of golf course plans, I sketched a pig-shaped bunker on the number ten green. The person who finally recognized the shape is unknown, but someone finally did, and that's when the supposed joke took a strange turn. The golf course superintendent, John Maddern, voiced his opposition.

"No way!" he said.

However, the owner, Lou Schmidt, said he liked it. So John carefully staked it out and constructed a very good-looking pig bunker, complete with curly tail. The shape is very carefully maintained to this day.

Thus an attempt at humor and trying something different ended up as a very unique, eye-catching golf feature, which not only is a delight for golfers and non-golfers to see from the deck of the clubhouse, but also adorns a full-sized billboard on Interstate 75, between Detroit and Atlanta, Michigan.

Cutters Ridge at Manistee National Golf & Resort in Michigan had ample forest for Matthews to carve through, as he did here for the 421-yard, par-four 7th hole.

CHAPTER 71
WHY AM I IN THIS BUSINESS?

W. BRUCE MATTHEWS III

Since 1991, Bruce Matthews, of Lansing, Michigan, has designed over forty-five new courses and renovated over sixty, and is known for his ability to design upscale courses at affordable prices. He was a superintendent at high-end private clubs and ran a public course. His father managed Grand Haven Golf Club for thirty years, where Bruce learned the golf business from the bottom up: cleaning clubs, picking the range, and filling pop machines before being promoted to the grounds crew. Bruce is a third-generation member of the American Society of Golf Course Architects. Matthews's grandfather designed and built golf courses and his uncle Jerry is also an accomplished architect. Some of Bruce's Michigan courses include Angels Crossing in Vicksburg, Hidden River Golf and Casting Club in Brutus, and Beeches Golf Club in South Haven. He also remodeled Grosse Ile Country Club and the Country Club of Lansing.

A golf course is an undefined field of play and is open to personal interpretation. Not all people have the same tastes. I am as passionate and serious as other golf course architects. I pull on my education, experiences, and skills to put my personal thumbprint on the earth's surface. To me, being a golf course architect is about making people happy.

Last year at a local golf show I was standing by a booth of a course I designed. A gentleman reading the materials said, "Hey—this course was designed by Bruce Matthews. I know all about his courses." Naturally, I asked him what he knew about the courses. "He designs long par-threes on each of his courses," he replied, and on he went. He was genuinely happy and excited about golf.

I really enjoy sitting on the porch or in the bar of a course that I have designed. In the crowded room I'm that quiet guy sitting at the table. I can hear a lot from the table. There are happy people, talking about how they mastered a golf hole. Others are explaining that the match will be different next time. The big guy is telling his foursome how the eighth hole could have been better with another bunker. His buddy says that the ninth hole is the best

par-four he has ever played. The instant feedback can be quite euphoric.

I spend countless hours compiling and recording base information and mapping the site's opportunities and constraints. I spend hours listening, questioning, and listening again, making sure the parameters of design are understood and incorporated. The strategic routing flows through the open areas and woodlots avoiding the wetlands. One owner's sacred, half-buried, rusty Ford Pinto still sits by the fence post in the trees behind the new eighteenth tee. The owner walks back behind the trees, looks, and comes back to the tee, smiling with another Ford Pinto story.

It's about the process, properly lining up all components of the design and interlocking where necessary. There is the constant push, pull compromise with government agencies, engineers, consultants, and contractors. Consider the case of the oak tree in the middle of the fairway. Everyone tells me the tree should not be there. They say the tree obscures the view of a very scenic golf hole. It knocks down the good tee shots that otherwise would be in the middle of the fairway. I have pled my case of where, why, and how it should happen. For the good of the game, it must go ... except I played the hole recently and worked my tee shot around the oak tree into the fairway beyond. As I picked up my tee I looked up and the owner and grinned. "See, I guess it's not that hard."

Much of what I do is convey the technical elements of golf course architecture into layman's language. It never ceases to amaze me that as we walk through the site during construction the client says, "How did you find that hill for that green site?" or "I never knew I owned that property."

To me, being a golf course architect is about making people happy.

CHAPTER 72
A FAMILY LABOR OF LOVE

MARK McCUMBER

Mark McCumber, professional golfer and golf course architect, joined the PGA Tour in 1978. Among his ten PGA Tour victories were two wins at Doral, two Western Opens, the Tour Championship, and the 1988 Players Championship, in his hometown of Jacksonville, Florida. He was also a member of the United State Ryder Cup team. He now heads up Mark McCumber and Associates, the design arm of McCumber Golf, which he operates with his oldest brother, Jim. McCumber has designed such Florida courses as the Tournament Players Club at Heron Bay in Coral Springs, Ravines Golf and Country Club in Middleburg, The Golf Club of Amelia Island, and South Hampton Golf Club in St. Augustine. He's also designed Hidden Cypress Golf Club in Bluffton, South Carolina, GreyStone Golf Club in Dickson, Tennessee, and, in Georgia, Osprey Cove in St. Mary's and The Brickyard at Riverside in Macon.

I have been very fortunate to work on many wonderful design projects for a lot of great owners throughout my career.

A project with great owners, a beautiful piece of land, and a healthy budget is truly the perfect combination, and we had that combination for our Macon, Georgia project.

A lifelong friend called me up to tell me about a project his employer was working on. His employer's father was a tremendous amateur golfer. Whenever he traveled to a tournament he would take the family along with him. The result was that they all grew to love and appreciate the game of golf as much he did.

A local hometown golf course was struggling under private membership, and the Sams family made a decision to buy it and renovate it into something special. This was their opportunity to honor their father's love of the game of golf, as well as to give something back to their hometown.

The day they closed on the property we began work. Their brick manufacturing business has been in the family for over a hundred years, and because they mined their own clay they owned lots of heavy machinery. They mined clay only six months out of the year, so we had equipment and operators at our disposal for the run of the golf course project.

Alfred Jr. and Kenneth Sams went above and beyond the call of duty in every way. We told them eight-inch drainage pipe would work. The next morning we had stacks of twenty-four-inch pipe at the ready. We wanted to know the depth of the rock on the driving range. Fifteen minutes later Kenneth was on the backhoe digging a test hole.

Working with this wonderful family was a joy for us from start to finish. The unbeatable combination of great owners, beautiful land, and a healthy budget came together in Macon, Georgia. The course was a dream project for us, and The Brickyard at Riverside, in its first year of eligibility, was ranked by *Golf Digest* as the twelfth best course in the state of Georgia.

CHAPTER 73
GROUNDBREAKING DESIGN
NEAL MEAGHER

BELMONT COUNTRY CLUB
Fresno, California
Proposed Improvement for Hole No. 7
July 2007

Neal Meagher worked for Robert Muir Graves and Damian Pascuzzo, two past presidents of the ASGCA, and during that time he had the privilege of guiding golf greats Johnny Miller and Sam Snead through designs. He founded Neal Meagher Golf in Pleasanton, California, in 2000. His California designs include Seven Oaks Country Club in Bakersfield, Woodcreek Golf Club in Roseville, Sterling Hills Golf Club in Camarillo, The Institute in Morgan Hill, and Maderas Golf Club in Poway.

A close-up of Ancient Oak Farms.

Growing up in southern Mississippi, I knew quite well the consequences of the odd hurricane blowing through now and then. But after moving to northern California I quickly learned about that other big disaster-in-waiting: the earthquake.

Less than one year after moving to the San Francisco Bay area, while diligently working late one afternoon in the office of my original mentor, Robert Muir Graves, the earth began to buck and fold in what turned out to be the 7.1 magnitude Loma Prieta earthquake. In the ensuing years, I learned to grow used to the swarms of small quakes that occurred with some regularity, but had always occurred while I was indoors.

Another sketch of Ancient Oak Farms.

USE SLOPE TO ACCESS

SHOULDER

YARDAGE DECEIVING BUNKER

HOLE 14 - APPROACH TO GREEN

I will never forget being on site at the Glendale Country Club, near Seattle, Washington, on the morning of February 28, 2001, when Mother Nature awakened again. As I was deep into a comprehensive bunker renovation project, spray paint gun in hand, I found myself walking along the top of a new bunker-to-be that featured a fairly steep face and supporting ridge behind. Being very sure of foot normally, I was surprised to find myself tippling about in that way that can ordinarily only be felt after a couple of martinis.

It took several seconds, but it finally dawned on me, as it did on the construction crew I was working with, that we were in the middle of an earthquake right there and then! Having only felt them indoors before, I was surprised at how it literally felt like I was standing on a pat of butter that was starting to melt. It turned out to be the 6.8 magnitude Nisqually Earthquake, which was strong enough to wreck the control tower at the Seattle airport.

After a very short period of time we all simply got back to what we were doing there on site, but it did occur to me how fortunate I was to be outside, albeit on a cold winter day, doing what I loved with no fear of a roof bearing down on me.

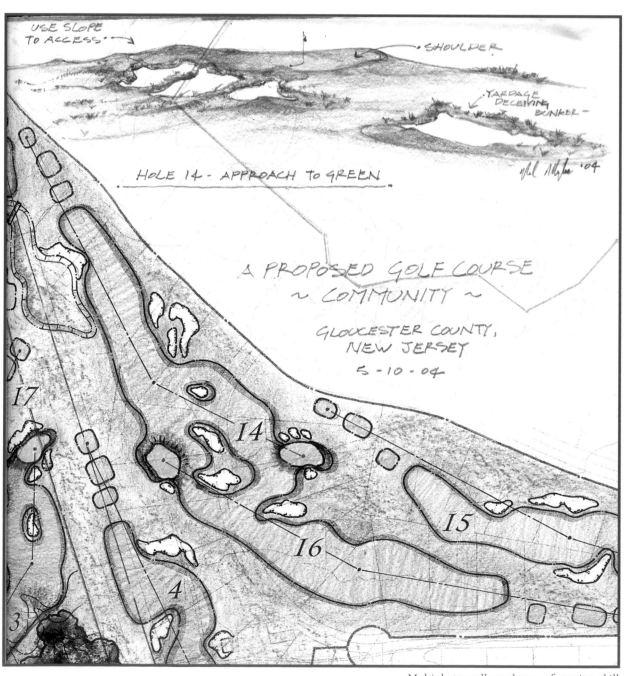

Multiple tees allow players of varying skill
levels to enjoy Ancient Oak Farms.

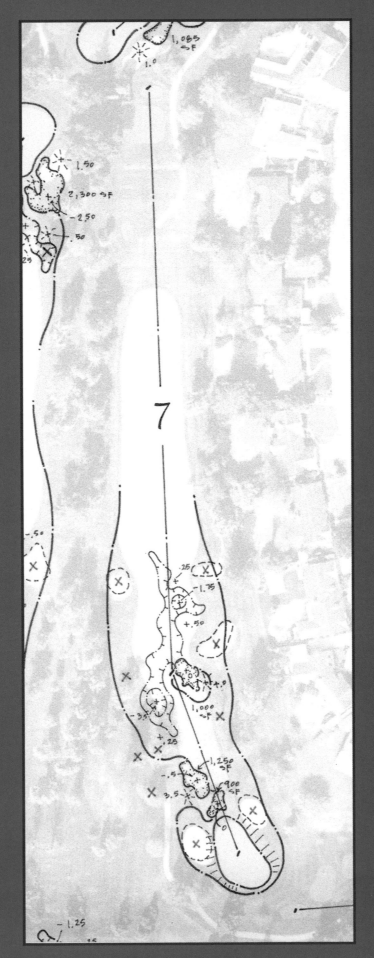

Redesign in progress—a
new look at an old hole.

CHAPTER 74
A BENEVOLENT KING
HARRISON MINCHEW

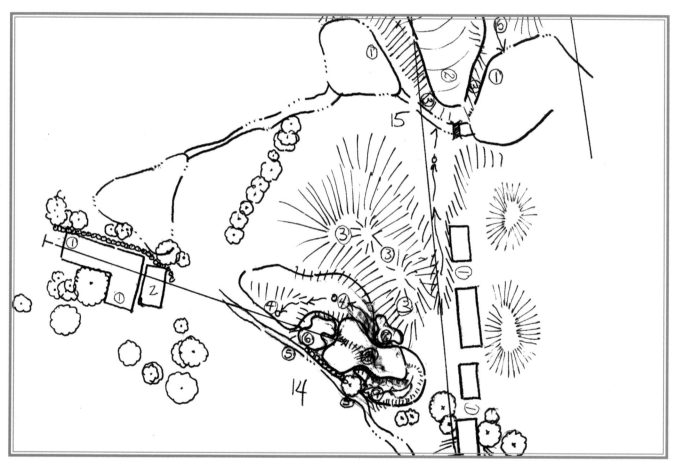

Follow Minchew's thought process as he designed Milverton in the following images.

Harrison Minchew joined Arnold Palmer Design Company in 1982, and as vice president, director of design services, and senior golf course architect, he was completely involved the design of over 140 golf courses worldwide. Today, as president of Signature Golf Design, Minchew's nearly three decades of personal interaction with the finest golfers on the globe and a huge cadre of celebrities has given him unique insight into the courses professionals prefer, as well as the process, management, and marketing involved in producing a successful outcome for all. He worked on Four Seasons Resort Aviara in Carlsbad, the Palmer Course at PGA West, and Tradition Golf Club in LaQuinta, California. Minchew's other credits include Seattle Golf Club and, in Florida, Adios Golf Club in Deerfield Beach, and the King and Bear at the World Golf Village in St. Augustine. He also, with Palmer, designed the Palmer and Smurfit Courses in County Straffan, Ireland, site of the 2006 Ryder Cup, and Tralee Golf Club in County Kerry. He worked closely Palmer's right-hand man, the late Ed Seay.

I grew up in Augusta, Georgia, and didn't really realize how big the Masters Tournament was when I was growing up. I went to the tournament as a child, and by the age of fifteen, I had a job carrying cameras for an Associated Press photographer who had been a war correspondent in Vietnam, so he wasn't the type to sit around. We were always on the move up and down the hills and through the trees at Augusta National.

After seeing him play in the Masters as a kid, I ended up working for Arnold Palmer for twenty-seven years before I started my own company. During the time I worked for Palmer, I was able to work on a lot of great teams, and with some pretty exceptional leaders. One of those leaders was Ed Seay.

Ed was a people person. He was the type of person who included everybody in the process—even the toothless bulldozer driver. Ed made sure everyone respected that bulldozer driver because he was part of the team—part of the team that was going to make everyone look good. We were just hired guns who drew lines on a paper. The construction people were the ones who made our vision happen. Ed really taught us how to treat people and get the most out of them. He was such an inspiration because I really wasn't much of a people person. Ed taught me a lot of life lessons in that way.

Arnold didn't let too many people get close to him, but he let Ed in. Ed knew how to handle Arnold.

There was one particular time, when we were working on Tralee in Ireland, that Ed wanted to include everybody in an outing. He was trying to organize everyone on the project, all the laborers, architects, and engineers, to go to local pub in Tralee. All the laborers were headed there anyway, but Ed convinced everyone else to come along as well so we could really bond as a team. Everyone—including Mr. Arnold Palmer.

That pub was completely packed, and Arnold stayed at the pub with everyone for about five hours, enjoying the music, conversation, and color. The team just loved being able to spend time with Arnold because usually they didn't have much access to him. Bringing in Arnold, who was a hero to all of us, was Ed's way of rewarding the team for a job well done.

Construct back tee at least 20 meters from edge of road. Grade of main tee slightly above existing grade at far right corner. A stacked rock retaining wall along left side may be necessary to construct tee 12-18 meters wide.

2. Forward tee .5-.75 below main tee.

3. Construct a huge hillock left side of approach and green. Hillock to have two or three broad tops. approximately 2-4 meters above approach and green.

4) Construct a broad swale that extends from left bunker across to stream

5 Relocate stream along right front of green and down centerline so it is clearly visible from tees. Expose existing wall along green or construct a ½:1 grass slope down to stream, Wall at tree will need to remain.

6. front bunker to be 1.5-2 meters below de of front portion of green

7. Angle green along 1 meter deep bunker so that back left pin placement will need to carry corner of bunker

8. enter portion of hour glass green is no more than 8 meters wide

9. Cut a distinct .75 meter deep swale along right side of grn

#15 Continued

9. Fairway area beyond center bunker begin a two broad swale that join into a broad valley that extends beyond right side green.

10 & 11. Broad valley in fairway is flanked by very broad ridge on either side of fairway. Broad ridge #10 extends down left approach to green. A broad deep swale is between ridge and entry road

12. Construct a very large bunker with a large island. Left side of bunker has a distinct sharp shoulder.

13. Construct a subtle, broad bowl between shoulder of bunker, front left of green and ridge along left side of approach. Bottom of bowl approximately .75 meter below green.

14. Front right of green is a distinct lowest portion of green. Front bunker is .75 meters below front right of green. Rear bunker is to be 1.75–2 meters below back elevation of green.

#15   425 METERS

1. Locate back tee to + save trees on either side of center line. Adjust elevation of tees so beginning of fairway & at least a portion of lakes on either side of center line are visible

2. Slightly crown fairway from beginning to angle turn stake

3. Construct a distinct 5-8:1 upslope to give crowned fairway a plateau appearance.

4. Construct large mounds to block view of cars from tees.

5. Fairway bunkers on either side of landing area are at the top of a broad swale. Far bunkers are 1 meter above front bunker

6. Cut a distinct slot in right side of landing area 20 meters short right of angle turn stake. Slot extends down to a lower fairway between center bunker ⑦ and right side bunker ⑤

7. Large center bunker is constructed against a small hillock. Hillock will partially block view of large bunker at green from portions of upper crowned fairway.

8. Construct large hillocks. Far left portion of fairway slopes up face of first hillock.

CHAPTER 75
SIZE MATTERS

JAY MORRISH

Jay Morrish has been active since the 1960s, when he served an internship with Robert Trent Jones and worked with George Fazio. Throughout the 1970s, he worked with Jack Nicklaus. In the 1980s, Morrish partnered with Tom Weiskopf to create more than twenty courses, including Troon Golf and Country Club, Tournament Players Club of Scottsdale, Forrest Highlands, and Shadow Glen. Morrish now works with his son Carter in Texas. He was president of the American Society of Golf Course Architects in 2002.

Many years ago, while working for Jack Nicklaus, I received a telephone call from a supposed developer with a property in Fort Lauderdale. It was the kind of call a golf architect dreams of receiving.

"I want to build a world class golf course capable of hosting PGA tournaments," he said. "Money is not a problem."

I was elated!

"How many acres do you have?" I asked.

"Twenty-seven," he replied.

The conversation ended shortly after that.

CHAPTER 76
WILD RIDE

GREG MUIRHEAD

Greg Muirhead is a senior designer at Rees Jones, Inc. and a past president of the American Society of Golf Course Architects. Muirhead joined Rees Jones, Inc. in 1984 upon graduating from Ball State University. Among his notable projects are Ocean Forest Golf Club in Sea Island, Georgia; Nantucket Golf Club in Nantucket, Massachusetts; Sandpines Golf Club in Florence, Oregon; and 3 Creek Ranch Golf Club in Jackson Hole, Wyoming.

I was fortunate to know I wanted to be a golf architect very early in my life. My friends recall me doodling golf holes during seventh-grade social studies class.

Unfortunately, my professional career was almost derailed before it ever got started. While completing my landscape architecture degree in 1982, I consulted with Pete Dye at Crooked Stick Golf Club, which was then my home course, about how to break into the golf course design business. Pete was kind enough to offer me a summer internship position participating in the construction of his new Austin Country Club project in Austin, Texas.

Having completed all necessary arrangements and having received all appropriate approvals from my school administrators, I secured housing in Austin and arrived on site after a two-day drive from Indianapolis, ready to learn.

I quickly located Pete's on-site project architect, Rod Whitman, and introduced myself. The long silence and look on Rod's face made it clear he had no idea who I was, or why I was there! It seems Pete had neglected to let Rod know that help was on the way.

Rod made it clear he didn't need any interns, but eventually agreed to give me a week to "see what happens." I worked very hard that week, and I was very relieved when Rod agreed to let me stay for the summer, as well as to return the following summer to participate in the course completion and grow-in.

After graduation, I worked for Rod on another of Pete's courses in Denver, Colorado, before Alice Dye, Pete's wife, helped me secure my current position.

One of my first big projects was the design of the Charleston National Golf Club in Mt. Pleasant, South Carolina. The sandy site, featuring a blend of towering pines and century-old live oaks, was bordered by a tidal marsh and panoramic water views of the Isle of Palms. At the time, it was one of the most naturally diverse and scenic parcels of property I'd ever seen. The club itself was conceived as a very high-end and exclusive facility, with a course intended to both challenge and impress its national membership. After the considerable efforts and expense of many, the course was completed and set to open in absolutely pristine condition.

Two days prior to opening, Hurricane Hugo and its accompanying fifteen-foot-high storm surge swept across the site. As a kid in Indiana, I'd seen tornado damage; however, the overwhelming devastation I witnessed when touring the course a few days after the storm was beyond my comprehension and very disheartening.

While conducting a site evaluation trip in St. Lucia, my potential client suggested we tour the site via helicopter. I agreed and he proceeded to make the appropriate arrangements. After I took my seat in front, the pilot began to remove the door on my side.

"An unobstructed view will provide you with the best feel for the property," he said.

After some inner reflection, I went along with him. As I began adjusting my headset, I noticed the pilot encapsulating the latch of my seatbelt buckle in duct tape. This state of the art safety precaution was intended to keep me from inadvertently bumping the latch and falling out of the plane. Before I could protest, we were airborne and I was enjoying one of the most exhilarating site tours of my life.

One of the most rewarding projects I've been associated with was the restoration of the East Lake Golf Club. In this case, golf functioned as something significantly more than just a game.

Local philanthropist and developer Tom Cousins purchased the club, in the early 1990s. Mr. Cousins had the vision to use the game of golf as a vehicle to attract and combine both public and private resources in a landmark effort to revitalize an entire community and change lives. Today, the East Lake community is a proven success, featuring new, mixed-income housing, a neighborhood charter school, a YMCA, the Charlie Yates public golf course, and various outlets. Hopefully, this model will be replicated in communities throughout the country.

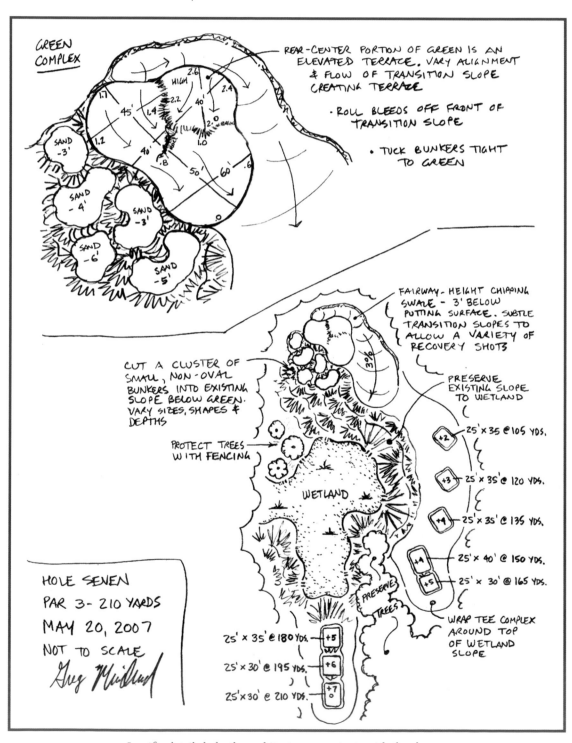

Specific details help the architect communicate with the shaper.

CHAPTER 77
HIDDEN VIEWS AND NATURAL FEATURES

MARK MUNGEAM

Mark Mungeam is a principal with Mungeam Cornish Golf Design in Uxbridge, Massachusetts, a firm he joined in 1987. His notable course designs include Shaker Hills and Cyprian Keyes in Massachusetts, The Links at Hiawatha Landing in New York, and the Golf Club at Oxford Greens in Connecticut. In 1999 Mungeam oversaw the renovation of Olympia Fields Country Club in Chicago in preparation for the 2003 U.S. Open.

I have to admit that I like quirky design features that make use of natural features the best. Whether it's a tree, an outcropping of rock, or grasses, if it can be incorporated into the design I think that's great.

My favorite design feature is to obscure visibility of the putting surface from a portion of the fairway. I don't mean the steeply uphill approach where you can't see the surface of the green; what I'm talking about is a hole where if you hit it to one side of the fairway you can't see the green, but hit to the other side and the green is clearly visible. Using this feature, you can reward a player for hitting to a certain area, much as you would with a bunker.

This is a subtle variation of design that is often missing from today's eye candy designs.

Stampeding cows were a natural feature I hadn't counted on, though.

Several years ago we were hired to design a course in rural Kentucky. The site was a farm with rolling fields and groves of trees. It was very pretty land, but there was still a herd of cows in one field. We weren't paying them much mind. It was a quiet morning and the cows were all munching on the dew-soaked grass.

I had heard about stampedes but had never experienced one. All of sudden these cows started running after the four of us on the site walk. We had to scatter and run for the fences, each of us diving over or under the rails and barbed wire.

I've been pretty excited on site walks at seeing potentially great new holes, but my heart never beat as fast as it did in that field in Kentucky!

My favorite design feature is to obscure visibility of the putting surface from a portion of the fairway.

Hole: 4

Course: Oxford Greens Golf Club

Hole # 4

Michael -
Thank you for helping the ASGCA with the "A Day in the Life" book. Best wishes.
Mark A. Mungeam

Notes:

GREEN:

- SIZE +/- 6,265 SF
- FILL 5.0' AT CENTER OF GREEN TO SUBGRADE
- Green slopes primarily right to left with sand and grass bunker left, fairway "kick" slope to right.
- Shift green forward +/- 35' to save large maple tree behind green

FAIRWAY

- Fill, create mounds, left side of approach about 200' in front of green
- Lower grade along existing wall to right of landing area, but don't cut too high up slope
- Fill 2-5' along left edge of proposed fairway
- Add fairway bunker left at ridge at 235 yards from back tee
- Add bunker series on right, 125 - 175 yards, stepping up slope
- Lower grade 5-8' along centerline and to right from old roadway to beyond bunker group to create visibility of landing area from tees.

TEES:

1176 SF	• E	• 28' x 42'	FILL +/- 1.0' AT CENTER
1350 SF	• D	• 27' x 50'	FILL +/- 1.0' AT CENTER
2400 SF	• C	• 40' x 60'	FILL +/- 0.5' AT CENTER
1500 SF	• B	• 30' x 50'	FILL +/- 1.5' AT CENTER
1125 SF	• A	• 25' x 45'	FILL +/- 5' AT CENTER

(shift "A" tee back +/- 30')

TOTAL TEE SURFACE AREA - 7551 SF

Scale: 1"=100' Date: 10.31.03
REVISED: 3-8-04
Cornish, Silva & Mungeam, Inc.

CHAPTER 78
STORMY WEATHER

JEFFREY MYERS

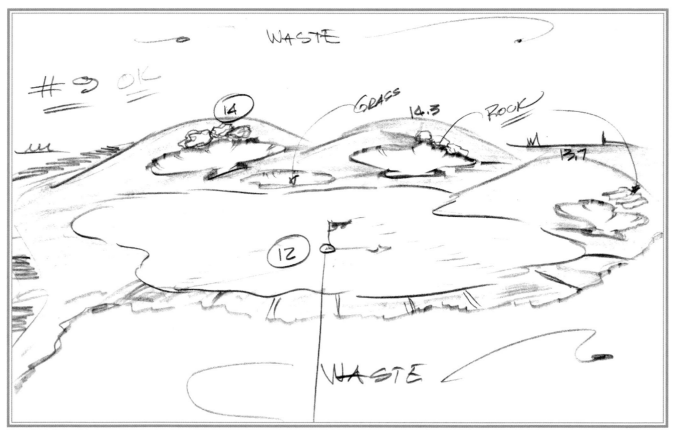

Construction begins after an approved plan.

Jeffrey Myers designed Laurel Oak Country Club in Sarasota and Baytree National in Melbourne, Florida. He also created Summit Golf Club in Panama City, Panama; The Links at Shirley in Shirley, New York; and Hilton Head National in Bluffton, South Carolina. Myers served as vice president of design with Gary Player Design Company and earned a bachelors degree in agronomy from The Ohio State University. He currently heads his own golf course architecture firm, JCM Group.

I was working on Hilton Head National Golf Course in Bluffton, South Carolina, on a beautiful, warm, sunny day.

A few members of my team and I were driving to the site on this clear, gorgeous day when we noticed a thick, black cloud hanging directly over our golf course.

Suddenly, on the radio, we heard the weather report: "It's a beautiful day out, wonderful weather, except for an area over in Bluffton. There seems to be an isolated storm system starting up. Stay tuned for further updates."

We hurried to the site, nervous about the strange storm that loomed ahead of us.

It turned out the laborers at our course had to dispose of the trees that had been cut down to clear the area and had made a large bonfire with all the timber. It was a still day, so there was no wind to push the smoke away. The result was a large black cloud hanging over the open fire.

We had a good laugh about altering the weather report!

CHAPTER 79
HOW A BAD AIRPLANE SEAT TAUGHT ME COURAGE

DOUG MYSLINSKI

After earning a landscape degree at West Virginia University, Doug Myslinski entered the golf course industry though the construction discipline with the highly respected Wadsworth Golf Construction Company. He built his first course, Diamond Run Golf Course in Pennsylvania, with Gary Player. He became senior designer for Jacobson Golf Course Design and created Thornberry Creek Country Club, Hunters Glen, the Club at Strawberry Creek, The Broadlands, and Morningstar Golf Club in Wisconsin, and Vista Links in Virginia.

One of the most important things I've learned in business is a moral lesson: one truly should never judge a person by a first impression.

I was in the Kansas City Airport with Rick Jacobson after an all-day site visit, awaiting a flight back to Chicago. Before we went to the gate, Rick and I, exhausted, sat down for a quick bite to eat in the airport bar, an outdated sports memorabilia shrine and eatery.

We overheard a couple sitting next to us. They sounded similar to the old television series couple Edith and Archie Bunker, except this Archie didn't say much. The woman must have asked her husband twenty questions, answered them, elaborated on them, and then rephrased them in a twenty-second span. The husband said not one word, nor did he need to.

I don't remember too much about the one-sided tongue lashing, but I do recall her asking if he took his ten medications (many of which, I speculated, had to be taken as a direct consequence of her). She was afraid maybe his food was too spicy or maybe he wouldn't digest it well or maybe the bread was too starchy and stale. I'm sure she truly loved this man, but the only thing Rick and I thought was that he must be a glutton for punishment.

We finally boarded our plane. Rick and I wearily slithered into our assigned seats, which were rows apart. I closed my eyes for about ten seconds, when I opened them to see a sight which couldn't have been worse had Albert Pujols been hitting me in the forehead with a baseball bat full of five-inch nails. It was the wife! And guess what seat she had?

Within the first ten seconds she'd given me—her new seatmate—countless questions, comments, suggestions, and orders.

I am normally the lucky one that gets the open seat next to me. Not this time! I had no choice but to engage in a conversation, as every trick in the book seemed to bounce off this woman like a rubber ball on concrete. I even tried the old "turn my back to look out the window and act like I'm looking at something interesting on the tarmac" trick, but this lady was determined!

She told me she was of Jewish faith and heritage. Her youth had been spent in a small village with her brother and parents, but her dad was a soldier in World War II—he fought all over Europe.

"We did not hear from my father for several years during the war," she said. "When we finally received news, it was word that my father had been killed in battle."

She was a young, Jewish teenager when, during the war, German troops attacked her village and captured her, her mom, and her brother.

"I was aware of my fate when they took me. The soldiers separated my brother and me from our mother. It was the last time we ever saw my mother."

The woman went on to tell me that she and her brother were locked in a room with many other Jews for several weeks, where she waited for what she feared would be their death. They were given very little food and almost no water, and there was just enough room to sit down in the extremely crowded space.

"My brother and I survived only on fear and our hope to, somehow, escape," she told me. "My brother finally reached a breaking point and decided he had to do something. He kissed me goodbye and slipped by the German guard as he opened the door. I heard commotion and chaos, and could only pray."

So many bad things happened to this young girl during the war that she could not have possibly anticipated what happened next. "I knew a bit of German. Each day I would say a word or two to the guard. One day I asked the guard to set me free. To my surprise, he slid the door open a bit and turned his back," she told me. "I don't know if he was tired of hearing me cry, or he felt sorry for me, or maybe he respected the fact I spoke German, but I went through the door and didn't look back."

The problem was that her home and city were destroyed, her mother and father were dead, and she did not know if her brother had survived his escape attempt. She had escaped to the shocking sadness of no one and nowhere.

The army helped her find a foster home where she grew up and awaited the end of the war. She did not mention much about it, so I could only imagine it did not bring her any joy to discuss it. She did say that she received some type of education, got a job, and managed to meet her husband. As soon as they could, they moved to the United States in hopes of living a better life—and they found it.

"Two years ago," she continued, "I received a letter from my brother! Can you believe he'd survived and somehow managed to find me in America?"

She was trying to get him documentation so he could move to the U.S. I sure wish I could have been there for that reunion.

So my story is really not about the game of golf, but had I not been with Rick in Kansas City making a construction visit, my life would not have been changed by someone I originally thought was going to make that airplane trip the worst ever. Instead, she made it the best!

> **One of the most important things I've learned in business is a moral lesson: one truly should never judge a person by a first impression.**

CHAPTER 80
URBAN LEGEND IN THE FAR EAST

ERIC NELSON

Eric Nelson studied parks and recreation at Michigan State University and landscape architecture at Texas A&M before embarking on a golf architecture career that yielded the likes of Avocet Golf Club in Conway, South Carolina; Centennial Golf Club in Acworth, Georgia; Woodland Hills Golf Club in Eagle, Nebraska; and, in Texas, Brookhaven Golf Club in Dallas and Great Southwest Golf Club in Grand Prairie. Nelson is Senior Project Architect with GolfScapes, based in Arlington, Texas.

We were completing a job in Singapore when I began investigating a job lead in Jakarta. Two men met me at the airport with a sign that had my name on it—my first clue that they did not speak English.

After a long, silent car ride, we reached the outskirts of the property and then proceeded to drive another few miles along a narrow, twisting road deep into a secluded forest. When we arrived at the site, we had no base maps, property corners, or bearing points of any kind. To top it off, there wasn't another human being within thirty miles. These guys started to look awfully shifty to me. We have all heard these urban legends about thugs who knock people off and steal their organs to sell on the black market. I was in a perfect situation for that to occur, and the thought had weighed heavily on my mind since we'd turned down the winding road.

Over the next few hours we toured the site, got a feel for the property, and then made the long, silent journey back to the airport. I was never so glad to get to an airport in all my life.

When we arrived at the site, we had no base maps, property corners, or bearing points of any kind. To top it off, there wasn't another human being within thirty miles.

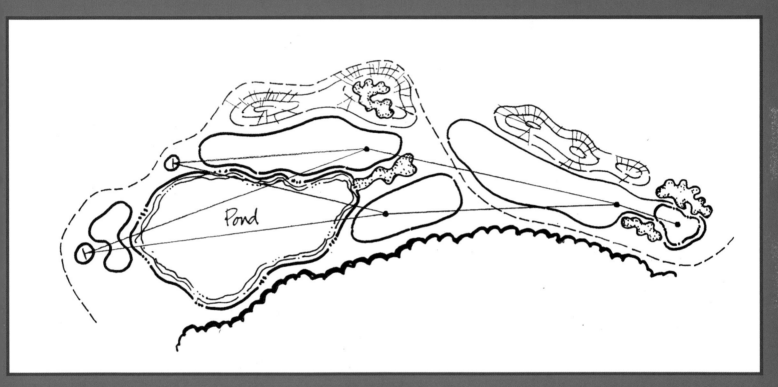

Pond

An early sketch of the 18th hole at Tangle Ridge Golf Course.

CHAPTER 81
TYPHOON TROUBLE
ROBIN NELSON

Mangilao Golf Course's famous 188-yard, par-three 12th hole, the most striking in Guam.

Mill Valley, California's Robin Nelson, of Nelson & Haworth, Golf Course Architects, designed Mauna Lani Golf Courses on the Kohala Coast in Hawaii; Bali Golf and Country Club in Nusa Dua, Bali; Ravenwood Golf Club in Victor, New York; The Dragon at Gold Mountain in Portola, California; and Shenzhen Golf Club, in Shenzhen, China. A graduate of the University of California, Berkeley, Nelson earned his AB in landscape architecture.

The original, nearly impassible site for the 12th hole.

We were asked to design a new eighteen-hole golf course, Mangilao Golf Course, on the island of Guam in early 1990. Guam's location in the middle of the Pacific Ocean exposes it to some of the most extreme weather on our planet, including super typhoons, with winds over two hundred miles per hour, along with numerous category three and four hurricanes.

Guam is also home to one of the greatest ocean par-threes in the world: the twelfth at Mangilao, which measures 188 yards from the tips and 99 yards from the forward tees. Its beauty is surpassed only by its story.

The peninsula upon which the twelfth green rests was very difficult to discover, even with the best topographic maps. The terrain was so rough that even crawling though the vegetation was impossible. It was only after helicopter reconnaissance that we found it, but once the hole was identified, the rest of the course was designed around it.

Getting permits from the Environmental Protection Agency in Washington, DC proved to be quite difficult, as the regulatory body needed to inspect the green area because it was within the shoreline setback zone. That meant we had to place a ribbon around its entirety, which, in turn, meant I had to swim over to the rock and do my best climb its twenty-five-foot-high sheer face.

We then had an approximate six- to nine-month period for the permit to take effect. Super Typhoon Russ was on our side in this instance though. Two weeks after placing the ribbon, the storm showed its fury and removed all the vegetation for us! Presto—no vegetation: no permit needed!

So we were on our way.

The green was built and grassed. However, during grow-in later that year, Typhoon Yuri hit and wiped out everything, including cart paths, irrigation lines, trees, and concrete thrust blocks. This storm was well forecast and everyone decided to

Mangilao's reinforced 12, now more impervious to extreme Pacific weather.

witness it this time. One of the shapers was caught on the green when a hundred-foot wave hit and almost washed him out to sea. Luckily he wasn't killed.

The decision was made to rebuild the green, knowing that these storms could hit every ten years or so. The green's infrastructure was rebuilt in reinforced concrete, and a par-three, nineteenth hole was built out of harm's way so that its sod could easily be used to rebuild the twelfth green quickly.

Less than one year after that, Typhoon Omar hit and totally destroyed the green, but because of the planning, the concrete infrastructure, and the nineteenth hole, we were able to get the green back into place and playable in three weeks.

Typhoon Paka unofficially recorded sustained winds of over 225 miles per hour, which are still being debated to this day as possibly the strongest winds ever recorded on the planet. But due to creative structural solutions and lifestyle of the maintenance staff and superintendent Ken Gokey, who take these massive storms as facts of life, the twelfth hole at Mangilao will live on, and continues to be one of the most beautiful par-three holes in the world.

CHAPTER 82
A GOLDEN AGE FOR THE GOLDEN BEAR
JACK NICKLAUS

The Cordillera Summit Course's 412-yard, par-four 14th hole, near Vail, Colorado.

Jack Nicklaus is one of only five men to have won all four Grand Slam championships in his career. The native of Columbus, Ohio, now living in North Palm Beach, Florida, won a record eighteen professional major championship titles: six Masters, five PGA Championships, four U.S. Opens, and three British Opens. He also won two U.S. Amateur titles. After playing numerous tournaments and exhibitions throughout the early 1960s on courses designed by the greens chairman or superintendent at those clubs, Jack developed an eye and an interest in what was good in golf course design. Then, in the mid 1960s, Jack was invited by Pete Dye to the Golf Club in Jack's hometown of Columbus, Ohio. Dye was designing the course, and asked Jack to look at what he was doing and offer suggestions. A hobby and budding passion was born.

A few years later, Jack and Dye teamed to design Harbour Town Golf Links in Hilton Head Island, South Carolina. Harbour Town quickly earned its place among the Top 100 courses in the country, followed closely by Jack's design at Muirfield Village Golf Club in Dublin, Ohio. Considered a breakthrough design in the 1970s, Muirfield Village has been a fixture among the Top 50 courses in the world. Nicklaus Design, as a company, has more than 330 courses open for play in thirty-two countries, including Sebonack Golf Club in Southampton, New York; Shoal Creek in Birmingham, Alabama; Castle Pines Golf Club in Castle Rock, Colorado; and Desert Highlands in Scottsdale, Arizona.

The question comes often these days: Now that you are a few years removed from your tournament career, what motivates you? What makes you tick?

In a word, it's the ability to create. To take a piece of raw land and challenge myself and my own limits to create a beautiful golf course for generations to enjoy. To create opportunities in new countries and emerging markets to introduce and grow the game. To create ways to give back to the game that has given me and my family so much. To create a vehicle to quench my love of competition.

We all get just one life, one shot at it, and you need to make the most of it. You not only want to be satisfied with yourself and your accomplishments, but you hope that along the way, you have made a difference in a life or two.

I am fortunate to be able to say that I not only lived out a blessed career through playing the game of golf, but I have enjoyed—and still enjoy tremendously—a second career through the business of golf.

Perhaps it is difficult to believe, but I am having

Golf course design is about realizing a vision, and I truly believe that teamwork makes the dream work.

as much fun in this second life of mine as I did in the first, traveling the world, designing golf courses in every corner of the globe. In many ways, I am finding even more personal satisfaction in this second career, because I am able to give back to the game that has been so good to me; I am able to impact the growth of the game worldwide, and, as we would all like to do, touch lives along the way.

It has been said that too often in business or life we overexaggerate yesterday, we overestimate tomorrow, and we underestimate today. In other words, we dwell too much on the good or bad that happened yesterday, and bank too much on what might happen tomorrow. Today matters. And I like to think that throughout my career and life I have tried to make the most of today.

It's just like when I played golf. I always wanted to make the most out of each round. I tried to focus on the shot at hand—forgetting about the last shot and not worrying about the next. It's the same approach in business or life, when you make today and every day count.

Golf was always my vehicle to competition. Now golf course design is that vehicle. It is a competition with myself, my creativity, and a piece of ground.

It is, for me, the challenge of going into new countries and markets and shaping the game of golf—and through golf, impacting tourism, economies, and lives around the globe. I will admit to being proud of the fact that our company, Nicklaus Design, has designed close to 330 courses around the world, and we have courses open for play in thirty-two countries and thirty-eight states. I am even more proud of the fact we have golf courses under development in forty-five different countries, and even more excited with the fact that thirty of those countries are ones in which we have never been involved before.

When you look at Eastern Europe, its countries combined account for only 2 percent of all courses on the continent. Yet we are now working in Croatia, Bulgaria, and the Czech Republic, to name a few. Until recently, Croatia had three golf courses to service 4.5 million people and one of Europe's fastest-growing tourism industries. I was fortunate a couple of years ago to meet with Croatia's prime minister, Ivo Sanader, and his cabinet to discuss golf's impact on tourism. Not long ago, I also sat down with Yury Luzhkov, the mayor of Moscow, Russia, about his hope to create with golf what Russia successfully did with tennis. I was approached probably twenty or so years ago to design a course in Russia, but at the time, I did not want to be involved with the current government and I declined the opportunity. Now that it is a new Russia, I embrace the opportunity to be a part of its future.

The same can be said with South Africa. I always loved the beauty of South Africa, and books authored by Wilbur Smith that used the country as the backdrop were among my favorites. So when apartheid was officially abolished in 1994, I wanted to become a part of the new South Africa. Since 1998, we have opened four golf courses, with at least another six under development. That is exciting to be a part of a country's future!

I would never have imagined a decade ago working in Panama, Cambodia, or Vietnam. Yet we are. We are hoping to shape the game and, in some ways, economies worldwide, from Central Asia and Kazakhstan to Central America and Nicaragua, where there is only one eighteen-hole golf course. A little more than a year ago, we opened our first golf course in the Dominican Republic at a place called Cap Cana, near Punta Cana on the eastern coastline. It is gratifying to hear that, thanks in part to golf, the developer at Cap Cana has set worldwide records in property sales, and in less than a year has secured a high-profile Champions Tour event. What's more exciting is to know that the project created more than 4,000 jobs, most of them for Dominicans from Punta Cana to Santo Domingo. And when the project is built out, they will employ more than 28,000 people, with housing, health care, and a school on site.

It is about making a difference. It is about making a difference for others. And what I am most proud of is being able to make a difference for others with others. It's true that you are only as good as the people you surround yourself with, and in my business and my life, I have been blessed to have wonderful people surround me.

Golf course design is about realizing a vision, and I truly believe that teamwork makes the dream work. I am proud that at least twenty-two of our past and present designers have earned memberships to the American Society of Golf Course Architects. I am honored that a third of the twenty design associates we use worldwide have been with us for at least eighteen years.

These talented individuals have become the backbone of the Nicklaus Design family. But there is no greater joy to a father than the ability to work side by side with his own family, his own children. I am proud to say that all five of my children have played a part in our business. In fact, my four sons and my son-in-law have combined to contribute to close to sixty courses our firm has designed worldwide, and my oldest, Jack II, is not only president of Nicklaus Design, he is a member of the ASGCA. We are truly a family business.

And when you talk about the business of family, that is truly where I am the luckiest. I have five wonderful children, twenty-one beautiful grandchildren, and a life partner who has been by my side for over forty-seven years. No one I know has made more of a difference in my life and in so many lives than my wife Barbara.

Barbara gets the credit for the many lives she touches through her support and involvement with

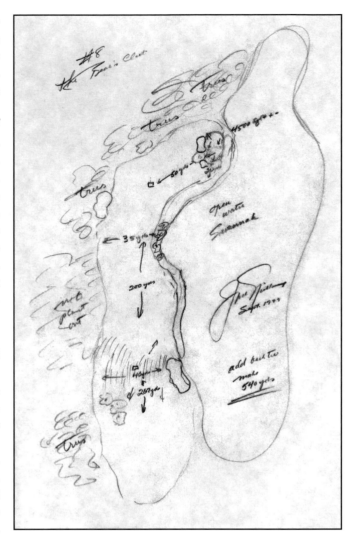

An early rendering of the 8th hole at The Bear's Club, one of the world-class courses designed by Nicklaus.

numerous charities, including the Nicklaus Children's Health Care Foundation, which supports pediatric health care in a five-county area of South Florida. Whether she's raising money to fight children's cancer or making cookies for a grandkid's school bake sale, both Barbara and I have enjoyed and been gratified by being involved in the community, and hopefully we have many more years to continue trying to make a positive impact. At the same time, we hope we have made an impression on the lives of our own children and instilled in them the values and the motivation to carry on what Barbara and I have tried to start.

I have always said that no matter what I did in my tournament career, golf course design will be my lasting legacy. But if I could rewrite that, I would say that if Barbara and I did our jobs right, the most important legacy we have created rests with our children and their children.

CHAPTER 83
BEAR TRACKS AND CLAW PRINTS IN THE MUD

JACK NICKLAUS II

Jack Nicklaus II, president of Nicklaus Design, is the oldest of Jack and Barbara Nicklaus's five children. He has established himself as a course designer, with thirty-one courses opened worldwide: sixteen solo designs and fifteen co-designs with his father, including Superstition Mountain-Lost Gold and the Golf Club at Estrella in Arizona; Cherry Creek Country Club in Denver, Colorado; and Pinehills Golf Club in Plymouth, Massachusetts. Not only have numerous Jack II designs or co-designs earned national and international accolades, but many have hosted tour or professional events. The Club at TwinEagles in Naples, Florida, was host to the Champions Tour's ACE Group Classic and served as the host venue for the 1999 Office Depot Father/Son Challenge, won by his father and brother Gary. Jack II's Heritage Course at Ibis Golf and Country Club in West Palm Beach was one of two Nicklaus Design courses used for the LPGA's 1999 season-opening event. Legacy Golf Links in Aberdeen, North Carolina, hosted the 2000 U.S. Women's Amateur Public Links. Internationally, Hanbury Manor has hosted the English Open.

My mother tells the story much better than I do, but when I was six or seven years old, somebody asked me, "Well, what does your dad do for work?" My response was, "My dad doesn't work, he just plays golf."

Four decades later, I long ago realized that my father not only played golf—and very well—for a living, he changed the face of the game. And he still does. Several years removed from the end of his record-setting career, my father continues to shape the game of golf and leave another legacy through his golf course design work worldwide. I have been asked countless times growing up what it was like being the son of the greatest golfer in history, and what it was and is like to follow in his footsteps. Jack Nicklaus is an amazing man. Most people see the public image of my dad making the birdie and eagle putts, raising trophies to the sky in celebration, or slipping on a size 44 green jacket. But to me and my four siblings, he's simply "Dad," and he's been

as great a family man and role model to us as he has been an icon for the rest of the world.

In terms of business, my dad has enjoyed a great deal of success, and at sixty-eight, he's in the prime of his second career as a designer.

I thoroughly enjoy being on a golf course site with him, watching him work his masterful creativity as a designer. His imagination is truly wonderful. You get a sense of that imagination each time you go out there, walk around in the mud with him, and watch him stare at a piece of property like a blank canvas, and then seconds later scribble his vision for golf on a piece of paper. I did that with him as a little kid in 1972, trudging around what is now Muirfield Village Golf Club, watching him create his course. I was not quite eleven years old at the time, and it is my first recollection of being on a golf course site with him.

Dad's got a great ability to see the total project as it should unfold. Where a lot of us get caught up in the forest, he's able to get up to about 40,000 feet

> **You get a sense of that imagination each time you go out there, walk around in the mud with him, and watch him stare at a piece of property like a blank canvas, and then seconds later scribble his vision for golf on a piece of paper.**

and decide what is best for the developer or owner, what's best for the overall project, and what's best for that piece of property. The developer might have a vision for the end result, but my father has the mind and the mind's eye to get the developer to the end.

These are just some of the characteristics I observed while following in my dad's footsteps. The bonus was my dad allowing me to work side by side with him, share some of my thoughts on the design process, and eventually do some designs on my own. It's been a wonderful trek, a great education for me, and I see those lessons paying off now in my own career.

As a son, you're never going to meet your father's highest standards. As a father myself, I know that you place higher thresholds on your own children than you do on others'. My dad has allowed me to do my own work as well as complete his directives on different courses in which he's heavily involved.

At Nicklaus Design, my father has assembled a tremendous group of design associates and support staff, who are the most highly skilled in the golf architecture industry. I am able to work closely with them, just as my dad has over the years. We've got a great team, and we take our cue from a tremendous leader. It is absolutely a collaborative process, and I think we make good decisions along the way for both the quality of the design and the betterment of the overall project.

Most of us are in this business because we love the game of golf, yet I find myself playing very little golf anymore. If you ask anyone on staff, you'd find that none of us get to play as much as we would like.

I had some minor successes in both amateur and professional golf, and while I don't play the game as much as I used to, I still love to compete. I guess you could liken me to Don Quixote—always chasing the impossible dream. I still have aspirations to one day compete again at the highest level, and with age fifty closing in, perhaps the Champions Tour awaits with a second chance at success like it has given so many careers. On the other hand, what makes me think I could beat those same guys at fifty that I could not beat when I was thirty? Still, as a golfer and competitor, I don't want to give up that last hope. So if you see me at the range, digging in the dirt to resurrect my golf game, just know that the work comes with a lot of fun.

After all, didn't someone once say that playing golf is not really work?

CHAPTER 84
CULTURAL CURIOSITIES AND DANGEROUS DECISIONS

TIM NUGENT

Tim Nugent designed the Phoenix Links Golf Course in Columbus, Ohio; White Deer Run Country Club in his hometown of Vernon Hills, Illinois; White Hawk Country Club in Crown Point, Indiana; Harborside International Golf Center in Chicago, Illinois, and Green Bay Country Club in Wisconsin. He earned his MBA in construction management from Arizona State University.

Coming back from Croatia the first time, our team had an overnight connection in Frankfort, Germany. Everybody's luggage had arrived, except for ours. After about a thirty-minute wait, our bags finally turned up, but it was obvious they'd had been thoroughly searched because everything was a complete mess. We wondered why our luggage had been singled out, until I finally realized that inside my checked luggage was a sand sample I had in an old coffee can. Evidently coffee cans were used to smuggle drugs from Turkey to Croatia and on to other parts of Europe!

A couple of years later I was flying from St. Petersburg, Russia to a site visit in Helsinki, Finland via a connecting flight in Copenhagen. I had a sand sample, and I knew my luggage would have to pass through several security and customs checkpoints. I didn't want to go through the same scrutiny and delay, so I took the sand sample with me in my carry-on bag. The security and customs officials I met along the way thought I was nuts for carrying sand with me, but this time stopped me to conduct thorough reviews of the sets of plans I was carrying! It turned out they were all on the lookout for artwork being smuggled out of Russia.

Most of my international intrigue was of that pesky variety, but not all of my experiences were so harmless.

In the early 1990s, we were part of a group attempting to develop a resort on the Adriatic Coast of what was then Yugoslavia. During the planning process, the country fractured and the site, located outside the city of Zadar, ended up being in Croatia once the borders were redrawn. Although there was an airport near Zadar, the facility was within range of Serbian artillery, so I had to fly to the city of Spilt, several hours to the south.

I thought the drive to the site, along a narrow coastal road with hairpin turns and a driver that thought he was a Grand Prix driver, would be the most dangerous part of the trip, but I was mistaken. While the rest of our group was in the capital at Zagreb, Jon Shapland, from Wadsworth Golf Construction, and I were to spend a couple of days exploring the site and sourcing materials. We stayed in a nice resort hotel that had very few happy resort guests. Most of the occupants were either European Union military observers or peasant refugees the government was housing.

The site was basically a huge mountain that rose from the coast. It was mostly rock, but supposedly there was farmland in the valley on the eastern side. Naturally, we wanted to get an idea of how much farmland was there and how deep it was, and we wanted to get some samples for analysis. Our translator was resistant to drive us around to the valley, but we couldn't spend the time or effort to hike up and down a three-hundred-foot tall mountain twice. Shapland and I tried to persuade the driver.

"Who will even know we're going there?" we asked her. "Why would anyone want to bother us? What would they do?"

She was adamant, though, refusing to drive us.

When the rest of our design party arrived, the newspapers reported that an American group was in town. Unfortunately, the Serbs read the newspapers and they decided to flex their muscle by lobbing several rounds of artillery into the city.

We were told that, for our safety, we would stay up the coast on the island of Pag.

We only experienced one more shelling (three rounds, though) while we there.

When we went back to Spilt to exit the country, Shapland went to a hotel bar where he ran into television reporters from CNN and the BBC. He said at first they thought he was just another reporter covering the siege of Sarajevo, but when he told them why he had really come to Croatia, they could not believe someone, in the middle of the military and political strife, would show up trying to build a golf course.

A shot of Willow Hill Golf Course in Northbrook, Illinois.

CHAPTER 85
QUESTIONS WITH THE KING
ARNOLD PALMER

Arnold Palmer furthered his legend by designing courses such as The Legend at Shanty Creek Resort in Bellaire, Michigan.

A rnold Palmer won ninety-two professional events, capturing the Masters Tournament title four times, twice winning the British Open, and fashioning a dramatic victory at the 1960 U.S. Open. "The King" played on seven Ryder Cup teams, and captained two. His charity work, business acumen, and aviation skills are legendary. Arnold Palmer Design Company was founded in 1971 when Palmer joined forces with longtime friend Ed Seay to create what was then known as Palmer Course Design Company. The company has designed over three hundred courses and clubs worldwide, including The Tradition Golf Club in California, Ireland's K Club—the 2006 Ryder Cup course—and Spring Island in Okatie, South Carolina, as well as design modifications to Bay Hill Club and Lodge, home of the Arnold Palmer Invitational, and Laurel Valley in Pennsylvania, which was ranked one of the fifty best golf courses in 2006.

Michael Patrick Shiels interviewed Arnold Palmer on the Hawaiian Island of Maui, on the practice range at the famed Kaanapali Golf Club, where The King was practicing between rounds of the 2008 Wendy's Champions Skins Game.

MPS: My eleven-year-old son Harrison went skiing recently, and before he left he told me he wanted a little money. When I asked him what he wanted the money for, he told me he wanted to get a hot dog and an "Arnold Palmer." Do you ever stop and realize you really are an icon? Your name has gone beyond "you." You're Mickey Mantle. You're Frank Sinatra. Do you ever feel that way?

AP: I don't. That's one thing about golf. When you play the game and play it as long as I have you have moments where you think you can do what you want to do … but then just wait awhile and it will all come back and you'll feel that you're just like everyone else. You have to work at it. You have to be humble. And you have to make sure you can do what you think you can do, and a lot of times that becomes very difficult.

MPS: You came to Michigan and built a course called The Legend at Shanty Creek Resort, and that spawned a whole new industry of big-name northern Michigan golf courses. That kind of impact is undeniable.

AP: I enjoyed building that course. The fact that a lot of people enjoy it makes me feel pretty good.

MPS: When it comes to golf architecture, when do you feel most like a golf architect? When do you say to yourself, "Yeah, I'm a member of the American Society of Golf Course Architects?"

AP: I don't think I ever forget that. When I am playing or when I am looking to build a golf course, it's the same thing all the time. There are times when I see one hundred or two hundred acres of land and I think, "My goodness, what a golf course that could be!" I almost see the holes, and then I get into the details of where I want to put sand traps and what kind of greens I'd like to build. There's a never-ending desire to create. You try to create something that is fun for people, environmentally correct, and aesthetically the kind of thing people will go out and enjoy.

MPS: When you built Shanty Creek there was a man involved, a man I worked for, named J. P. McCarthy,

a morning show host from a big radio station in Detroit. You used to be available for him any time. In fact, he called you the morning after you made consecutive aces on the same hole in two rounds of the Kemper Open. Are the demands of the media greater on you now than in those days?

AP: The media wants to know more than they used to. If they had a story they wanted to talk about it was pretty instant. You did it and got on with what you were doing. Now, they want more detail into what is going on. Without question, the media wants more information than we used to give.

MPS: You built the first modern golf course in China. That's another way you've crossed borders and had an impact on the game and the industry.

AP: Building the golf course in China was quite an experience for me. I've built golf courses since the early 1960s around the world, and having the experience of going to China and seeing what they have and how you to go to work to build a golf course. When I went there they were using wheelbarrows, shovels by hand, and no equipment of any kind. They had a dump truck, but the rest of it was manual labor. It was an exciting thing for me to do. One of the things that would happen was that the people had no idea. They were totally out of it when it came to what you had to do to build a golf course. I told the owner we needed some help to get the irrigation system in. They told me they could not get extra help and that we'd have to put the irrigation system in with the workers we had been given. When I went back to check on the project, I found they'd installed the irrigation system on top of the ground, not in the ground. Things like that happened. But the people I worked with were fantastic. They were hard workers. When we got the message to them, they did what we asked them to do.

MPS: We're coming up on St. Patrick's Day. I know you created Tralee Golf Club in County Kerry and the K Club near Dublin, which hosted the Ryder Cup matches. Ireland seems more like your kind of place than China.

AP: It was great doing the K Club and Tralee. In both instances it was a bit unusual. Michael Smurfit, the owner of the K Club, was a great guy and a good guy to work for. He knew what he wanted and he got that message across to us and we built that for him. I feel like we were fairly successful with what we did.

Palmer designed courses into the autumn of his life with his longtime, trusted right-hand man, Ed Seay.

CHAPTER 86
HOW TO SPOT GOOD GOLF COURSE DESIGN

GARY PANKS

Gary Panks captained the Michigan State University golf team and won eighteen amateur titles. By 1978 he began designing golf courses exclusively as Gary Panks Associates, including acclaimed Arizona courses Silver Creek Golf Club in White Mountain Lakes and Sedona Golf Resort. Panks and PGA Tour player David Graham combined to produce ten outstanding courses under the name Graham & Panks International, including Grayhawk in Scottsdale; The Raven at South Mountain in Phoenix; Turtle Point Golf Course at Laguna Quays Resort in Queensland, Australia; and Chaparral Pines, in the high country of Payson, Arizona.

There are a number of basic things that go into most of my routing plans. I strive to balance the number of doglegs so that the course does not favor a particular type of shotmaking. A typical routing plan includes four par-three holes, each playing in a different direction to make golfers encounter the elements differently on each of the holes. I try to include a sporty, short hole of 110 to 135 yards, one in the 150- to 165-yard range, another of 180 to 195 yards, and a long one of 220 to 250 yards, which would require a tee shot with a fairway metal. Of course I familiarize myself with the prevailing wind so these different distances are not negated.

Whenever possible I include one or two short par-four holes with lots of options for the golfer to consider. These can vary in length from 300 to 350 yards. Holes of this type are a particular favorite of mine and of other golfers, as well.

Par-five holes should also play to different points on the compass and vary in length. I like to make sure one of the par-fives is not reachable in two shots by anyone, and another that is reachable by most strong players. The other two par-fives are marginally reachable by the strongest of hitters.

In designing the remaining par-fours, a lengthy hole or two of 470 to 500 yards is good. Often I will not include any bunkers or water hazards on these holes due to the length. Most golfers will not hit the green in the regulation two strokes, so it gives

me a chance to design the green complex in a way that favors an imaginative short game.

You will seldom find a course of my design with more than three par-four holes in succession, since I believe more than that is boring to golfers.

After completing the routing plan, grading studies begin. As the cuts and fills are developed on paper, I pay particular attention to good shotmaking strategy and the desired appearance of the hole. Matching the course to its surroundings is always paramount in my thinking in order to provide a seamless transition. In the case of a great natural site, we use the lay of the land as-is, or grade in such a way that the finished product appears quite natural. Should changes in elevation be lacking on a site, cuts and fills will be made to achieve them. This is not too difficult a task, since a ten-foot cut near a ten-foot fill makes for a nice twenty-foot change in elevation. All grading plans are done by hand and then inputted to a CAD system for printing. Very little design is done on the computer.

Hazards such as bunkers and water provide options for golfers, and are important to help define fairway landing zones and guard greenside cupping locations. The style of the bunker design is often done in harmony with the course environment. Beside the ocean, we create bunkers resembling water swells or whitecaps. In the mountains we go for a more jagged effect. Bunkers in the hill country will have a

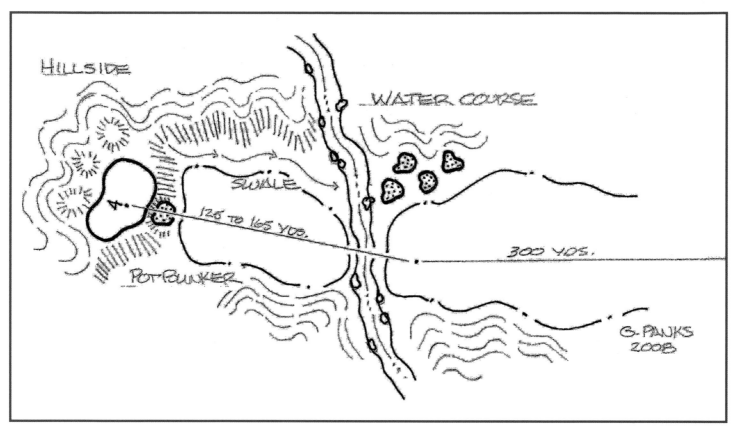

HILLSIDE

WATER COURSE

SWALE

125 TO 165 YDS.

300 YDS.

POT BUNKER

G. PANKS
2008

In defense of par: a well-guarded green.

more compatible rounded appearance. The depth of bunkers can vary, but we always make sure they are deep enough to compensate for the normal shallowing that occurs over time.

Green contours in my designs normally provide for changes in elevation without being too wild or difficult to maintain. Slopes between cupping areas are usually graded at 7 percent or less, with actual cupping areas from 1 to 3 percent.

Green shapes allow for easy access without forced carries to some cup locations, and include others that do require a forced carry over a hazard.

Finally, landscaping is an important consideration on any course, and as a registered landscape architect, I prepare these plans as well. Locations and varieties of trees, shrubs, and groundcover are critical to the playability of a course. Landscape materials should always be compatible with those encountered on the periphery of the golf course.

Matching the course to its surroundings is always paramount in my thinking in order to provide a seamless transition.

CHAPTER 87
THE GOOD, THE BAD, AND THE UGLY
DAMIAN PASCUZZO

A past president of the American Society of Golf Course Architects, Damian Pascuzzo partnered with the famed designer Robert Muir Graves in El Dorado Hills, California. In 2006, Pascuzzo formed Pascuzzo and Pate with PGA Tour veteran Steve Pate, who competed on the great courses of the world during a playing career that yielded six Tour wins and membership on two Ryder Cup teams. Some of his courses include The Ranch Golf Club and Indian Pond Country Club, both in Massachusetts; and in California, Maderas Country Club, Paradise Valley Golf Course, and Monarch Dunes Golf Course.

Like people in any industry or profession, golf course architects experience enriching moments ... and frustrating ones, but there seems to be a lesson in either case. Especially when it comes to leadership.

Early in my career I was a design associate working with Robert Muir Graves.

We'd been commissioned to design a new municipal golf course that was to be part of a large hotel and convention center project. As time went on and the project moved into its more critical stages, the city council insisted that they get an in-person report from the various designers on the project every two weeks. So every other Tuesday I had to pack up all the project files, leave the office after work, and drive ninety minutes to the city for a 7 p.m. council meeting.

Sometimes the council would move the consultant presentations up to the front of the night's agenda so that we'd be out of there by 8:30 or 9 p.m. and I could be home before 11 p.m., but on most nights, we were the last item on the agenda. There was nothing I could do but sit and wait for them to slog their way through the night's business, hoping that they would get to me before midnight—which rarely happened. By the time I got home I would have logged a seventeen- to eighteen-hour workday.

Once the council did get to the consultant reports, they were as tired and cranky as we were. Needless to say the dialogue would get a little strained between everyone at 2 a.m. The council

members thought it great sport to second-guess the consultants, although none of them had any experience as a designer.

The worst of all was when they would make me wait all night only to tell me, at the end, they had no questions for me. They had just made me sit there for six hours for absolutely nothing, other than to show me who was boss. This happened about twenty years ago, but in all the time since, I have never dealt with such a group of inconsiderate and unprofessional city leaders.

On the other hand, I was once hired by a private club in northern Japan, Otaru Country Club in Sapporo, to do an extensive remodeling of their course. I made many trips there over a number of years as we completed the master plan and then went into the reconstruction of the course. The club president was a much older gentleman and always insisted that we play golf together on at least one occasion during each visit. The games were fun but I never thought of them as more than "client golf."

After about four years, the project was completed and I was in Japan for a wrap-up visit. This was our first chance to play all of the newly renovated holes on the golf course. The club president and I made our usual 1,000-yen wager and teed it up. He was really playing well that day, and he insisted we play from the back tees.

Late in the round, I commented to the superintendent, who also acted as translator, that the president was playing very well.

"The president is in his late seventies, but he still plays golf almost every day at one of the several clubs where he holds memberships," the superintendent told me.

After we finished the round, I took advantage of the traditional Japanese bath available at the club before I went to a dinner hosted by the club president. The dinner was elaborate and wonderful. During our conversation, I learned the president came from an old-line, well-to-do industrial family in Tokyo. I began to wonder how they made it through the war when I realized the club president would have been a young man during the time of World War II ... just like my father! My dad had served in the Navy and was stationed in the South Pacific during the war.

It was amazing to think that as young men they would have been sworn enemies, but that here, now, some fifty-five years later, things were very different. Here I was halfway around the world enjoying this great experience, and getting paid nicely for it, all because I could help an old Japanese man fix his golf course.

Like people in any industry or profession, golf course architects experience enriching moments ... and frustrating ones, but there seems to be a lesson in either case.

CHAPTER 88
BEGIN IN DOUBT, END IN CERTAINTY

RICK PHELPS

Rick Phelps graduated with a degree in environmental design from the University of Colorado. His Evergreen, Colorado–based Phelps-Atkinson Golf Course Design has created the Devil's Thumb course in Delta, Colorado; the Panther Creek Country Club in Springfield, Illinois; Twelve Bridges Golf Club in Lincoln, California; and the Southern Woods Country Club in Homosassa Springs, Florida. He also remodeled and renovated the Pinnacle Peak Country Club in Scottsdale, Arizona; the Pinehurst Country Club in Denver; and the Eagle-Vail Golf Club in Avon, Colorado.

I am a second-generation golf course architect, but the route that I took to my profession is a bit unique.

By the time I was ten, I was working for my dad during the summer, spending a few weekends helping him with construction staking on two local projects in Colorado. My brother Scott and I took turns holding the survey rod and pounding grade stakes. I remember working on the Englewood golf course, which was one of the first golf courses in the United States to be built on an old landfill. We had to wade through all kinds of nasty things in order to set the stakes for the grading operation.

In my early teens, when my dad was really busy, I helped around the office by running prints, learning how to draft green details, and assembling bid documents for shipping.

As I entered my high school years, Dad started encouraging me to look in other directions in terms of a career path. In hindsight, I'm fairly certain he was trying to do two things: He wanted to make sure that golf course architecture was truly my passion and not just his; and he was probably trying to save me from diving into such a wildly inconsistent way of life.

As a result I spent two summers working with our next-door neighbor as a medical research assistant. I was doing some incredibly fascinating neurological research and learning a tremendous amount about neurosurgery, neurology and, occasionally, nurses! I was allowed to scrub in a few times to observe various surgeries—an experience I will never forget.

I entered college with the intent of getting a BS in engineering while taking my prerequisites for medical school. At the time I had thoughts of either practicing medicine or perhaps designing medical instruments. However, it didn't take long for me to realize that I needed a more creative outlet. I did not want my work to be limited by a mathematical formula or a textbook answer.

After transferring to the University of Colorado and entering the College of Environmental Design, I was fairly well convinced that I was destined to be a golf course architect. I did have one more interesting diversion, though. There was a job opening on campus for the sports director position at the campus radio station. I interviewed for the job and was hired! As a result, I spent two years as the play-by-play announcer for the Buffalos football broadcasts and also did some announcing for the basketball games. I was able to do an internship with the big sports station in Denver, 850 KOA, which allowed me to sit in the press box for a few Broncos games, help with player interviews (including John Elway), and even work as the field reporter for the state high school football championship. It was fun, but still not what I was most interested in as a career.

So, while it took me a long time to make up my mind, I came to realize that by far the most enjoyable job I had ever had was creating a golf course: a place where thousands of people could get outdoors and enjoy the wonderful game. Seeing a project evolve, from a few lines on a piece of paper through earthmoving and grass planting to a beautiful playground for the greatest game ever invented, has to be the most rewarding work anyone can ever undertake.

CHAPTER 89
DOING BUSINESS IN JAPAN

MARK RATHERT

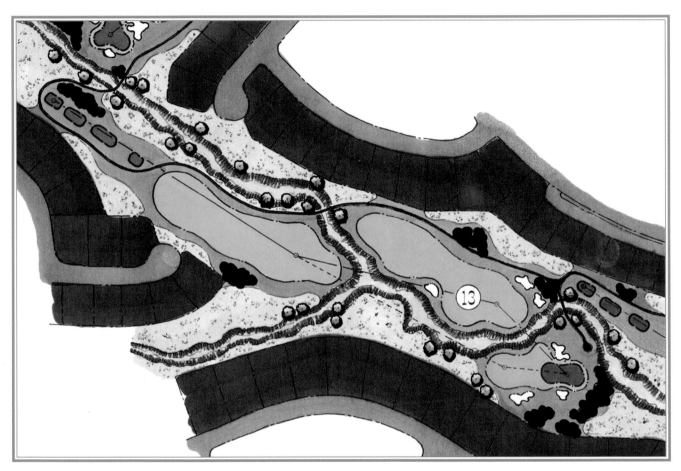

A forced carry with plenty of bail out left.

Mark Rathert, a Kansas State graduate, is based in Greenwood Village, Colorado, and designed courses worldwide and domestically in Boulder Creek Golf Club in Boulder City, Nevada; Kissing Camels Golf Club in Colorado Springs, Colorado; Prairie Falls Golf Club in Post Falls, Idaho; Gainey Ranch Golf Course in Scottsdale, Arizona; and Indian Creek Golf Course in Elkhorn, Nebraska. He has also remodeled and renovated courses including Sharon Heights Country Club in Menlo Park, California; Broadmoor Golf Resort in Colorado Springs, Colorado; and Hayden Lake Country Club in Hayden Lake, Idaho.

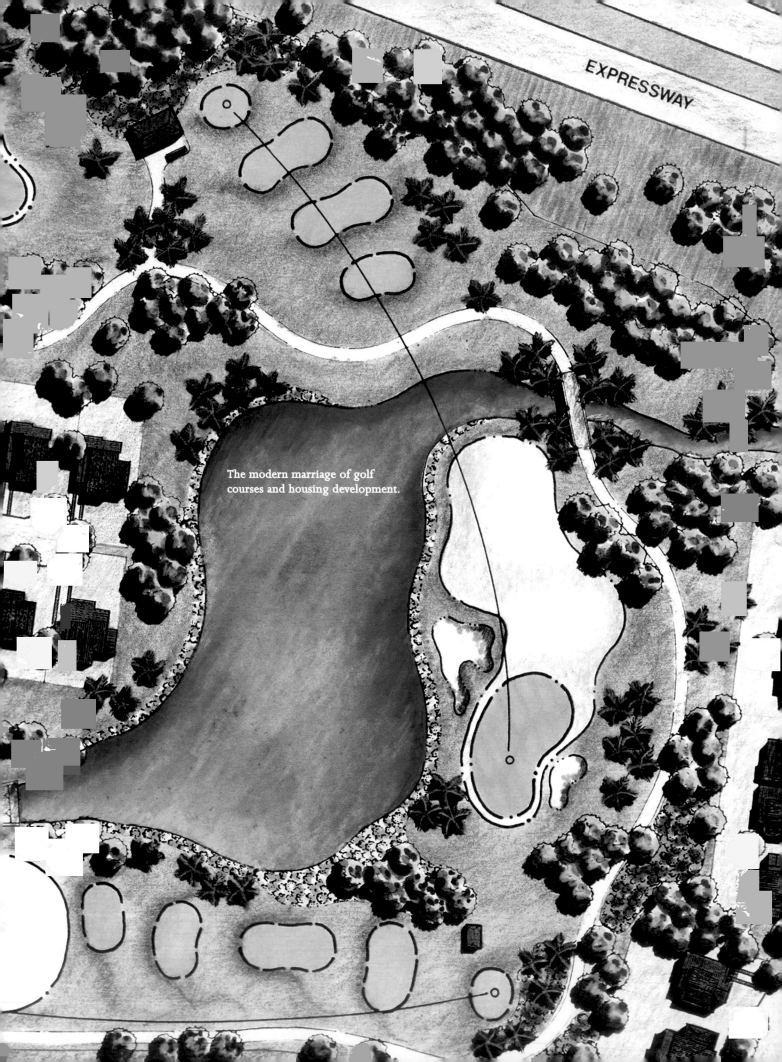

The modern marriage of golf
courses and housing development.

EXPRESSWAY

In the mid 1980s we were very busy doing projects in Japan. We discovered cultural differences as soon as the projects progressed.

Typically, most golf projects required that as many as three hundred property owners agree to sell their land in order for enough property to be obtained to construct a golf course. Approval processes, because they were complicated and time-consuming, would often take place prior to securing all of the land. But there were always some land-owners who held out for more money, so the golf course routing was constantly being changed to work around these pieces of property.

What further complicated this design work was that most of the sites were in mountainous areas of Japan. Farmland was rarely used for a golf course, so massive amounts of earth needed to be moved in order to flatten out areas for the golf holes. That, too, was not always easy due to approval restrictions. These restrictions dictated how much area on a site could be disturbed and required that storm water be retained before being released onto adjacent farmland.

Culturally speaking, doing business in Japan was quite different than working in the United States because each golf course developer hired large engineering firms to get the approvals. Consequently, the engineering firms developed golf course plans suitable to obtain the approval. After the preliminary approval for the project was given, the owners would hire a foreign golf course architect. I remember one project required the routing to be changed fifteen times before the owner finally secured all the property and final approvals to construct the course.

Getting the project engineers to then accept our design concept was another story. Typically they had some reason they wouldn't be able to do it our way. It was only after working on three or four Japanese projects that I realized their disagreements with our ideas were usually business-based on their part: the owner had negotiated a lump sum price with them to construct the course before hiring us. The owners often told us to make the course magnificent: that money was no object. But that wasn't really true. It took a tremendous amount of patience and persistence to get the course constructed our way.

Developing trust with both the client and the engineering firm was critical for success. Having the professional skill set to be able to sit in a hotel room or site office and design or revise a grading plan was critical. In order to keep the machines running, I often had to quickly redesign the plan and recalculate the earthwork quantities. This ability went a long way in perpetuating their trust and confidence in my abilities.

Getting the project engineers to then accept our design concept was another story. Typically they had some reason they wouldn't be able to do it our way.

CHAPTER 90
BEHIND THE IRON CURTAIN
FORREST RICHARDSON

Forrest Richardson studied golf architecture throughout the Fife region of Scotland. He learned under the direction of his mentor, the late Arthur Jack Snyder, a past president of ASGCA. Together, they collaborated for twenty years, completing more than seventy courses. Forrest established his own firm, Forrest Richardson & Associates, in 1988. The firm, based in Phoenix, Arizona, has completed new work, including The Hideout in Monticello, Utah; Phantom Horse Golf Club in Phoenix, Arizona; Olivas Links in Ventura, California; Coldwater Golf Club and Wigwam in Arizona; and The Links at Las Palomas in Sonora, Mexico. His historic renovations include the Arizona Biltmore's Adobe Course and Wailea Old Blue on Maui. He has authored three books on golf course design.

This is a lesson in site economics. I could probably fill a book with stories about my time in the Soviet Union, working with a team of planners, construction executives, and resort architects trying to figure out the master concept and plan for a 30,000-acre peninsula. I remember the crab leg dinner I ate in the sauna at Brezhnev's mansion (Brezhnev was not there). I can still smell the fumes from the enormous helicopter that ran on diesel fuel … and the cigarette smoke of its three pilots who sat down and lit up just a few feet away from the fuel tank.

Maybe my most enduring story—or lesson—is about the site we worked on: an amazing 30,000-acre peninsula jutting into the Sea of Japan and lapped by blue waters to the south and the calm ripples of a bay to the north. We were there, as our client pointed out, "to plan the Pebble Beach of Asia." And we eventually did.

Our approach was to create a destination that would draw the golfing population of Japan, which was a mere hour's plane ride away. This amazing land was in Asiatic Russia near the maritime submarine port of Vladivostok. The chief planner was Vernon Swaback, an acclaimed architect, visionary, and author who had worked with the legendary designer Frank Lloyd Wright. Swaback started his own practice in the desert of Arizona, where he has planned several large resorts and communities: each some-

thing to behold in the creativity and comfort they reflect.

Swaback pointed out how we needed more than golf at what became known as The Peninsula. "The destination will require activities which will keep guests at The Peninsula for longer stays," said Swaback, "especially when the weather is not conducive to golf."

As the plan unfolded, the team had sketched a fishing marina, a recreational boat marina, three resort lodges, a major spa, hunting grounds, and as many as 108 holes of golf spread over seven miles. The courses were clustered, some sharing a clubhouse while others stood alone as eighteen-hole layouts with individual themes. There were as many as twenty credible ocean holes among the courses. Two in particular, I remarked, would be nearly as special as anything Seventeen-Mile Drive in Monterey, California, had to offer.

It was a breathtaking and ambitious plan. Everybody was enthusiastic about taking it to the next step. But as the plan progressed it became clear to us that the absence of infrastructure was perhaps an insurmountable obstacle. The site would require a nearby airport, a desalination plant (for drinking and irrigation water), and the construction of a new road, if not for access by guests, at least for the purposes of delivering goods from Vladivostok, which was some three hours away by truck. All told, the bill—even before development—had the possibility of exceeding $2 billion.

Eventually, the Soviet Union became the Russian Federation. The Iron Curtain was lifted, and what little was left of the economy took an even greater beating. Not only would there be no help from the Russians, but the uncertainty of doing expensive business in such a tenuous political and economic climate was unappealing to investors.

Through planning and site evaluation, we determined exactly what any good planning team would conclude: the project was not viable. It was a painful realization, but maybe one day it will pay off. After all, the land is still there—and so are the plans!

The trip to Vladivostok, in the Soviet Union, involved nine Americans: a planner, two developers, two golf course management executives, a construction executive, two golf course architects, and an interpreter. Our charge was to investigate a large uninhabited peninsula, really an island, and determine the viability of turning it into a destination resort with multiple golf courses.

Before we left home, we asked the Russians to send us a copy of the topographical map of the land. The idea was for us to study the site and form general opinions before getting there. But no map arrived before we left.

When we arrived in Russia, one of the first questions asked was about the topo. "Topo is coming soon," was the reply. We believed this, and spent the next twenty-four hours adjusting to the time change a world away.

The next day arrived, but no topo. And then the second day. The third. And then a fourth. We had eaten plenty of Russian cuisine. We drank plenty of Russian "mystery juice," and sipped plenty of Russian vodka. Each of these was a precious commodity. The topo, apparently, was even more precious. So, too, was the ability to actually visit the site. Our hosts took us to virtually every corner of Vladivostok and the surrounding countryside, except the site itself.

The fact that we were in Russia trying to design such a major project and had neither visited the site nor been given topographical maps began to disturb us. While the developers met behind closed doors to discuss financial issues, the architectural and design contingency toured buildings, fisheries, and technical schools. When we inquired as to when we would visit the site, we were told the weather was not right for the helicopter. When we asked about the maps, we were told that they would soon be ready.

Our requests for maps were beginning to get old, for us and for the Russians. Finally, in the context of a financial discussion, one of the developers made a strong plea that we all really needed to get to the site and take a look at the topographical maps. This seemed to work, likely because developers tend to talk finances and finances mean business. So that evening we were informed that we would visit the site in the morning, by helicopter. The anticipation mounted.

We did take off in the morning, all nine members of the design team and an equal number of local officials, in a massive beast of a helicopter, which could transport forty-five soldiers. But, due to windy conditions, we could not land. We did manage a great flyover of the property, and it was absolutely breathtaking, but we still needed maps!

That night—the end of our fifth day in Russia— we conspired as to how to get maps. It was like a secret meeting of the nine Americans, plotting about who to ask next ... and wondering why it was so damned hard to get a map.

We cooked pasta for our hosts; we had brought it from the states complete with meat sauce. They apparently had never before enjoyed such a delicacy and were grateful for the cultural enlightenment. It must have worked: they told us that the next morning we would drive to the site, and they promised we'd have the maps.

This did, indeed, happen, and arriving at the site at last was a magical experience. Finally, we were on the site and not hovering in a military helicopter at 1,000 feet. Our motorcade made its way across dirt trails, and for the next several hours we absorbed the site and its tremendous potential. Toward the end of the afternoon we arrived at an old mansion, which had been used for bombing practice during World War II.

As we explored the ruins, we noticed a man in a trenchcoat unfolding a small map. At last! The topo! The topo, we would learn, was government property and as such it was closely guarded, which is why it took so long to get to us. In fact, it was stamped "Cherenko" (Secret). On the way back home a few days later I had the terrifying realization that I technically had a secret Russian document in my briefcase. I feared for a moment I might be detained by the Russians and accused of spying!

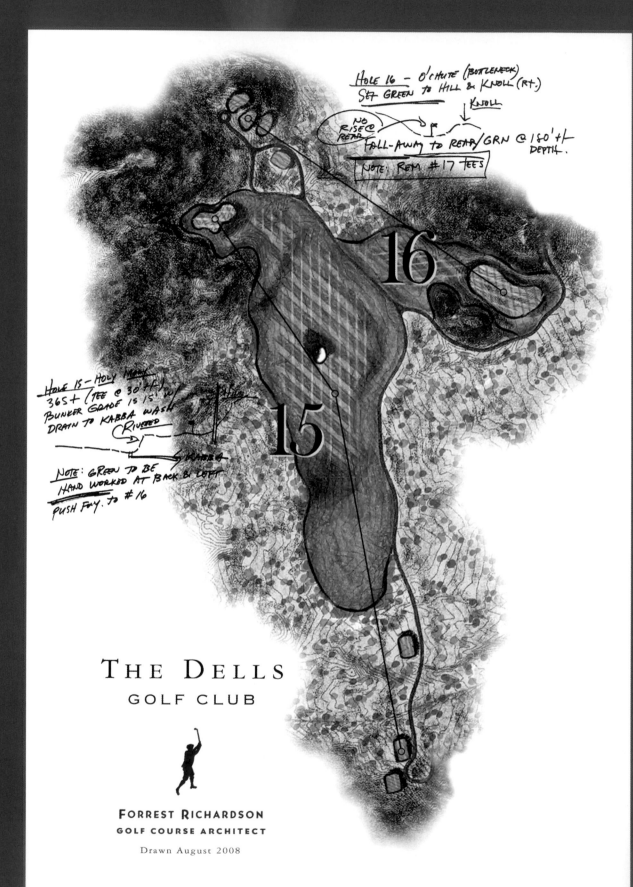

THE DELLS

GOLF CLUB

FORREST RICHARDSON
GOLF COURSE ARCHITECT

Drawn August 2008

CHAPTER 91
FORTUNE, FATE, OR JUST LUCK?
SOME VERY CLOSE CALLS

RICK ROBBINS

Rick Robbins is the director of golf course design for ETd, PA. He spent thirteen years with the design firm of Von Hagge and Devlin where, as lead designer, he played an important role in the design and master planning of Doral Country Club's silver course, The Woodlands Country Club in Houston, Admiral's Cove's east course in Jupiter, and Tucson National Country Club. He also served as vice president for Nicklaus/Sierra Development Corporation, and Nicklaus Design's senior design associate in the Hong Kong office. His work includes courses such as The Club at Mill Creek, The Tribute, Horseshoe Bay Golf Club, Royal Saint Patrick's, and a renovation of the historic Pine Lakes International in Myrtle Beach.

While serving as construction and design consultant for Nicklaus/Sierra Development Corporation, I worked with Jack Nicklaus on implementation of several projects. My job was to coordinate getting the course that Jack designed built on time and within the set budget. One of those projects was English Turn, just outside New Orleans.

One day, Jack was on a site visit to look at construction progress. There were five or six people on the tour of the course, and Jack wanted to ride standing in the back of the pickup truck so he could better see. I was riding on the passenger side, directing the driver where to go. We had just visited a green site and were ready to go to the next hole, when I climbed in the truck, grabbed the door handle, and was just getting ready to slam it when by some great stroke of good luck, I saw that Jack had his hand inside the door frame and I was within a few inches of smashing his right hand in the door! I stopped just in time!

"Jack, you came very close to making me quite famous." I still get the shakes thinking about how close that was to ending or setting back his competitive career. I expect Jack never tried to hold on to the side of a truck that way again.

I have been lucky in the way fate has treated me. In October of 1999 I was getting ready to design a new course with Payne Stewart in Asheville, North Carolina. I had spoken with Van Arden, Payne's agent, the week before Payne was to compete in the Tour Championship at Houston. Van had asked me to come to Orlando so we could fly with Payne on his private plane to Houston to have dinner with him on that Monday night and discuss the design project.

I had my office check the flights and found that to fly to Orlando one-way, then fly with Payne on his plane to Houston, and then fly one-way back to Raleigh, North Carolina, would be difficult to schedule and very expensive. I called Van and told him I would just book a round-trip ticket on Continental and fly on my own to meet them in Houston.

It was that quirk of logistical luck and a too-expensive airline rate that caused me to unwittingly avoid being on board Payne's private flight to Houston—the ill-fated, fatal flight, which suffered a technical malfunction, crashed, and took the lives of Van Arden, Bruce Borland, Robert Fraley, Michael Kling, and Stephanie Bellegarrigue. God bless them and their families.

Fate was looking out for me again on my first trip to Thailand. I planned to walk the untamed property and make my way through the landscape of dense grass and tree cover in order to get a feel for what would be a twenty-seven-hole routing. I asked the developer before we started out if there was anything I should know about the local fauna before I left. He told me there was nothing there to worry about and, on that particular walk, he was correct. I trudged and trounced though miles of uncharted, wild terrain.

However, on the first day we started constructing the course, a D-8 rolled over a boulder where the ninth green was to be built and uncovered a twenty-one-foot-long python! It took three experienced Thai workers to load the snake into the back of a utility truck. Imagine if I'd run across that python while wading through the long grass! I'm sure that snake would have taken his time ingesting me!

We had just visited a green site and were ready to go to the next hole, when I climbed in the truck, grabbed the door handle, and was just getting ready to slam it when by some great stroke of good luck, I saw that Jack had his hand inside the door frame and I was within a few inches of smashing his right hand in the door! I stopped just in time!

CHAPTER 92
SANDBOX TECHNOLOGY—
FEELING MY WAY THROUGH IT

TED ROBINSON SR.

Theodore (Ted) G. Robinson, a past president of the American Society of Golf Course Architects, died in March of 2008 at his home in Laguna Beach, California, after a ten-month battle with pancreatic cancer. He was eighty-four. Robinson served as ASGCA president from 1983 to 1984. With an architectural career spanning over five decades, Robinson is credited with over 160 projects that bear his influence, including courses in the Western United States, Hawaii, Mexico, Japan, Korea, and Indonesia. In 1954, Robinson established his own practice concentrated in golf course design, land planning, and subdivision and park design. Robinson spent the majority of his career working independently while wife Bobbi managed the office, until 1991 when his son, Ted Jr., joined the practice. Dubbed the "King of Waterscapes," Robinson endorsed the use of water as a defining hazard for course designs. Robinson was also widely recognized for his golf-oriented master planned community, Mesa Verde, in Costa Mesa, as well as twenty-six separate golf course architecture projects in the Palm Springs and Palm Desert area alone, including Sunrise, Monterey, Palm Valley, The Lakes, Indian Wells, Ironwood, Tahquitz Creek and Desert Springs. One of Robinson's most beloved projects was Sahalee Country Club in Redmond, Washington, which hosted the PGA Tour Championship in 1998. Other notable courses include Tijeras Creek and Tustin Ranch in Orange County, California; the Experience in Koele on the island of Lanai, Hawaii; and Robinson Ranch in Santa Clarita, California, a project designed and developed jointly with his son and named in his honor.

In the early 1970s, I was introduced to a Japanese man named Omori. He was looking to hire an American golf course architect. After an extensive interview, he invited my wife and I to Japan for several days to see his existing golf course and meet about what I thought was his proposed course. I had never been to Japan and welcomed the opportunity to go as his guest.

Upon arrival in Tokyo, we were picked up by Mr. Omori and his interpreter. After about an hour of travel, we ended up in an area of beautiful open country south of Mount Fuji. We were headed toward his country club and what I assumed to be the site of his proposed course. As we got closer to the club the roads became narrower, making it difficult to pass oncoming traffic. We drove to the clubhouse and

could see a beautiful golf course full of players on the left side, and on the right side, a mountainous parcel of land with about fifty pieces of grading equipment attacking the hills.

"What are the workers doing?" I asked Mr. Omori.

"They are grading my new golf course," he replied.

I was puzzled.

"If the course is under construction, why am I here?"

Mr. Omori quickly replied, "You design."

I then became extremely confused. Here I was in a foreign country, without a contract or any type of agreement, and Mr. Omori was ready for me to go to work!

Later that day, I met with Mr. Omori to find out what maps they had. The only map available was a mass grading plan. Armed with this bit of information, I walked the site and came up with a rough routing plan, but was unsure what to do next. I could look out the window of the clubhouse and see the lights of the tractors as they worked twenty-four hours a day. The subcontractors did not understand English, so how would they know what I might have them do?

I had an idea. I could build a sand model showing how a particular hole needed to look.

The next morning they brought me a large, flat, four-foot by six-foot box filled with sand, and I went to work getting my hands dirty. That evening Mr. Omori brought his engineers and tractor operators into the boardroom to look at the model I'd shaped by hand. I couldn't understand a word, but I got the impression they understood what the hole should look like. By the next morning, they had the entire fairway graded the way I had modeled it. After breakfast, I watched as they brought in seventeen more boxes and I spent the next couple of days playing in the sand. The entire course was designed in that fashion!

From the time construction began to the time the course opened for play, only five months passed. They did all of it by working twenty-four hours a day, seven days a week. Six hundred Japanese women walked down each fairway; the first row picked up rocks and smoothed the surface, and a second row followed shoulder to shoulder laying sod.

The literally handmade club, Lakewood Golf Club, has become very successful with memberships selling at over $1 million.

So much for drawings and computer models!

From the time construction began to the time the course opened for play, only five months passed. They did all of it by working twenty-four hours a day, seven days a week.

CHAPTER 93
COSTA RICAN CORNER CUTTING

TED ROBINSON JR.

Since joining the Laguna Beach, California–based family firm in 1991, Ted Robinson Jr. has been principally involved with the design of such golf courses as Rancamaya Golf Club in Bogor, Indonesia; Pinx Golf Club on Cheju Island, Korea; The Phoenician in Scottsdale, Arizona; Pelican Lakes in Windsor, Colorado; Tahquitz Creek Golf Course in Palm Springs, California; and, in collaboration with his father, Robinson Ranch, a thirty-six-hole facility in Santa Clara named in honor of Ted Sr. In addition, Robinson designed the Marriott Los Suenos Resort in Bahia Herradura, Costa Rica; Arrowood Golf Club in Oceanside, California; and Tuscany Hills Golf Club in Las Vegas, Nevada. Prior to joining his father, Ted spent fourteen years in real estate construction financing, the last six as senior vice president and regional manager for Wells Fargo Bank in Los Angeles.

On my first visit to Costa Rica, in the 1990s, my guide stopped briefly at a bridge leading to the project so that I might view the crocodiles sunning on the banks of the river below. There were no guardrails. With a very real risk of vertigo, maintaining one's balance was the only sure way to avoid becoming lunch. Modern golf was new to the country and the untamed natural beauty of the rainforest area was equally new to me. And so were local business practices.

My contacts were good-natured and well-educated individuals whose company I thoroughly enjoyed. The design and initial clearing of the site proceeded normally until Hurricane Mitch dropped five feet of water on the site in less than forty-eight hours. After re-examining and upsizing the drainage system, I arrived one afternoon to see huge trenches dug to accommodate even larger concrete pipe instead of the PVC specified. When I noted the change, the project manager good-naturedly shook his finger and said, "You Americans, always choosing the most expensive way. I was able to buy bigger pipe from my cousin that was ten cents a foot cheaper." Alas, the problems with using thirty-inch concrete pipe are the junction boxes and the manholes required to service them; not a significant concern in areas out of play, but tough to hide in the middle of landing areas!

Importing high-quality bunker sand from Nicaragua was included as part of the original budget, but when a cousin's crushed white marble proved cheaper, we ended up with brilliantly white sand traps ... as hard as concrete!

The most interesting experience, however, involved the grass chosen for the greens. At the time, the only in-country choice was 328 Bermuda grass. We had gained approval to import higher quality TifEagle, but when fifty crates of it arrived at the airport, paperwork held its release until it had rotted. And, yes, you guessed it: another cousin came to the rescue with 328!

"Ah, you Americans."

The Experience at Koele, at the Four Seasons Lana'i, in Hawaii, features dramatic shots such as this 390-yard, par-four 17th tee shot.

CHAPTER 94
FACING DOWN "THE DONALD" TRUMP

DREW ROGERS

Drew Rogers is a partner and senior design associate with Arthur Hills/Steve Forrest and Associates. He joined the firm in 1992 and his work to date has resulted in the creation of the River Course at the Lowes Island Club in Potomac Falls, Virginia; The Sunset Course at Mirasol Golf and Country Club in Palm Beach Gardens, Florida (site of the 2003 PGA Honda Classic); Oitavos Dunes in Cascais, Portugal (site of the 2005 European PGA Tour Portuguese Open); The Club at Olde Stone in Alvaton, Kentucky; and Newport National Golf Club in Newport, Rhode Island.

We were presented information in 1997, at Arthur Hills/Steve Forrest and Associates, which suggested that Donald Trump was getting into the golf business. Our team was quick to act, and by pulling a few strings, we arranged a face-to-face meeting for Arthur and "The Donald" in New York City.

When Arthur returned from that meeting, he had good news.

"Mr. Trump says our firm will certainly be given a shot at the job—all we have to do is create the best plan," Arthur announced.

Arthur visited the site several times, and then I spent about three solid days on site finding strategic green locations and tee sites while tweaking the routing.

The time and energy spent was worth it, because, in the end, Mr. Trump informed us that we managed to create that "best plan," and we got the contract!

All the while, I had never encountered the great entrepreneur, but had worked hard at keeping things on a straight and narrow for this perceptively demanding client.

Several months later, I was summoned to attend a design team meeting at Trump Tower in Manhattan. I had prepared thoroughly for the meeting and was excited, but the meeting was handled by several of Donald's key real estate assistants and there seemed to be more legal consultants in the room than the rest of us combined!

The meeting was just about to be adjourned when the door to the boardroom swung open ... and in came Donald Trump.

"How are things going?" Trump asked. "Give me a status report."

After hearing the report, Trump spoke with total conviction. "This project is very, very important to me. I want this golf course to be the best in the world. Unmatched, legendary," he insisted. "Where is my golf course architect?"

It took me a moment to realize that he was asking for me! I apologetically volunteered my identity and was then ushered away into Mr. Trump's office. He had to take a call first, so that gave me a chance to catch my breath, but all the while I was thinking, "Oh my God, what am I doing here? How did I get here in front of Donald Trump?"

Mr. Trump was quick with his call, and then he dove right into the meat of the matter and began making critical comments about the routing plan. Now we were talking my territory: golf architecture. I began to think, "Hey, I can do this. He's talking my language now!" Donald Trump had just come into my "boardroom."

For the next ninety minutes, Trump and I continued to share ideas and challenge one another just as though we had been working together for years. He had some good ideas and some that were not so good. It was during those moments I had to swallow hard. How do I tell Mr. Trump his idea is not suitable or possible? I stood my ground, though. He listened well, and as long as a good case could be made to the contrary, he would go with my suggestions opposite his initial instinct. That impressed me.

When we finished, it was very amicable and he thanked me for all the hard work and wished me

Oitavos Dunes Golf Club, in scenic Estoril outside Lisbon, has hosted the Portuguese Open near Europe's westernmost point.

well on my journey back to Detroit. Then it occurred to me—this extra session had caused me to miss my scheduled flight back! But what the heck, I had just gone toe to toe with The Donald and lived to tell the story. It was a real confidence builder for me in dealing with tough customers. Believe it or not, he was probably not my toughest!

As a golf course architect, other than Donald Trump's office, I've had the great opportunity to travel around the world to some pretty out-of-the-way places: some hardly inhabited and some just plain rugged and dangerous. Unlike some of my colleagues, I had been pretty fortunate to avoid the deadly creatures some architects had encountered, especially on initial site visits. I'd not come across any venomous snakes, alligators, bears, cougars ... or anything else for that matter. But, on a recent trip to Portugal, that lucky streak, for me, came to an end.

As we were touring a new site via jeep, our guide pointed out a wild boar outside the vehicle. I was excited because I'd never encountered anything like that, and I was comforted by the fact that I was safely inside the vehicle. So we chatted about this boar briefly and then drove onward.

We then reached a point where our guide urged us to get out of the vehicle to look at a hillside. We did, and soon I noticed another small boar coming down the hill toward us. The guide really did not get excited, but I was certainly edging toward the vehicle. Then, as if a silent message was sent to wooded area above, approximately thirty boars came charging down the hill toward us! I ran like crazy, like others in our group, scrambling to leap back into the vehicle for protection. But we noticed our guide walking inexplicably into the herd!

Only later did I find out he'd been feeding these wild pigs for months, which not only explained why he wasn't worried, but also why the wild boars came charging.

In addition to fascinating wildlife, over the years I have encountered some pretty interesting, and sometimes wild, landowners. I was near Pinehurst, North Carolina, working on a renovation project. The golf course was bordered by large, wooded, estate-type lots and homes. It was a very well-established and mature gated golf course community of reputation—the type where you expect a certain cachet, rank, and decorum among the residents.

We were out marking trees for removal. Marking and removing trees is always a dicey activity because nobody ever wants to see a tree taken down. Therefore we try to be inconspicuous in our efforts to mark the trees, and low-profile when we're actually removing them. There was a group of pines along the border of one of the holes just at the back of a real estate lot. Our surveys had been staked, so we were well aware of the property lines. I painted only a small dot on the back side of the base of a tree so nobody but our internal crew would be able to identify that this tree was marked to be removed.

But the construction crew just happened to have a chainsaw man at the ready, so we decided to get this one particular tree down so we could determine immediately whether more trees should be removed or just this one would suffice. As he fired up the chainsaw, we noticed an older lady coming down the hill from the house on the adjacent lot. That was a very normal occurrence, as residents often become curious about what is going on outside their doors—but this lady happened to be toting a twelve-gauge shotgun!

"I will take out every last one of you if you dare to cut down any of my trees!" she screeched.

We all backed away and allowed our club representative to take the lead and try to calm her down, but the lady was having none of his explanation.

"I have already called the sheriff," she told him.

Frankly, we were relieved that she had gone to the trouble of making this advance call to the authorities, because we sensed that might be the only way we were going to get out of this pickle!

The woman actually held us at gunpoint until the sheriff came!

When the sheriff arrived, he thankfully disarmed the lady and took her back to her house to talk to her. As soon as that shotgun was out of range, we went right ahead, fired up the chainsaw again, and cut the tree down!

CHAPTER 95
THE TIME I ALMOST QUIT ON ROBERT TRENT JONES

ROGER RULEWICH

Roger Rulewich, an ASGCA past president, designed Ballyowen Golf Club in Hamburg, New Jersey; Metedeconk National Golf Club in Jackson, New Jersey; Fox Hopyard Golf Club in East Haddam, Connecticut; Grande Dunes Golf Course in Myrtle Beach, South Carolina; and Saratoga National Golf Club in Saratoga Springs, New York. His notable remodeling work includes Yale Golf Club in New Haven, Connecticut; Half Moon Resort in Montego Bay, Jamaica; Tucker's Point Club in Bermuda; and Palmetto Dunes, The Jones Course on Hilton Head Island.

The learning process on my way to becoming an architect had many highs and lows with my mentor, Robert Trent Jones. The most traumatic, and at the same time one of the most enlightening, happened when our firm was competing for the design of two courses in the Canadian Rockies for the Province of Alberta.

Several other architects responded to the "Request for Proposals," a very comprehensive document requiring an exhaustive and detailed response to the concerns of the many government agencies. An area was already designated for the courses, but surprisingly, no layout or routing of holes was required for the proposals. This should have been a clue for me as to how the selection process would play out.

With Jones's approval I went to work on our proposal. I visited the area in the dead of winter, alone and on rented snowshoes, which was almost a very serious mistake when darkness and exhaustion in the thin air caught up with me!

As a result of my due diligence and research, I thought we went well-armed into the interview process with all the information I had so laboriously put together, including our proposed fees for design. I was later told it was the most thorough of the many proposals offered.

But, just before the interview, Jones had a change of heart. Instead of using my proposal, he ignored our presentation, doubled his fees, insisted on using his own people for some of the work, and then told them that they were planning to build the courses in the wrong place!

I was distraught and convinced that we had blown it.

Upon leaving, we came as close to parting professional company as we ever had in thirty-four years of working together. Believe me, it was an uncomfortable ride home!

To my amazement, the selection committee allowed us to revise our proposal and even agreed to consider a new site. Eventually, we were awarded the contract. We overcame many physical obstacles to build two very beautiful and challenging courses by weaving them along and over the river. They have been a great success ever since and represent some of Jones's best work.

For me, this experience was an unforgettable part of my learning process: Pride in one's reputation; the value of a famous name; being unafraid to challenge convention and put forth new ideas; and properly charging for your services.

From the lows of the beginnings of this project to the highs of our success in the selection process, not to mention the ultimate high of creating great golf, this was a milestone in my education as a golf course architect.

CHAPTER 96
AN EXPLOSIVE SITUATION
JOHN SANFORD

Juliette Falls Golf Club, in Ocala, Florida, has been compared to the vaunted Jupiter Hills Club.

With twenty years of experience in golf course design, Florida-based John Sanford has completed more than sixty new design and renovation projects. John has traveled the globe working in Asia, the Caribbean, the Middle East and throughout the United States. Designing courses on sites with diverse opportunities and constraints has given him unique experience and perspective. He designed The Links at Pointe West in Vero Beach, Juliette Falls Golf Club in Ocala, and The Links at Madison Green in Royal Palm Beach, Florida; Quarry Hills Golf Club in Quincy, Massachusetts; Jolie Ville Golf Resort in Sharm El Sheikh, Egypt; and Caguas Real Golf Resort in Caguas, Puerto Rico.

We were walking the beachside site of Sahl Hasheesh, which is Arabic for "easy grass," with the planner and engineers. It was a beautiful location on the Red Sea just south of Hurghada, Egypt, but it was 125 degrees and very dusty. One of the Egyptian engineers was telling us about the history of the property. Since there was a lagoon area with a fairly flat beach, the Israelis had often used amphibious vehicles to come ashore. In response, the Egyptians had scattered mines along the beach.

As we were walking along and learning this, I made the mistake of asking the planner an obvious question.

"Surely you've swept the mines from the beach, right?"

There was an uncomfortable pause followed by an even more uncomfortable answer: "No." The planner then explained that removing the mines would be the first phase of site work!

My instincts kicked in and I starting running toward the site vehicle about a half-mile down the beach! I don't know what made me think running would help me, but it was just an expression of my naturally fearful reaction.

The rest of the team was laughing at me when they got back to the truck. They calmed me down by taking me for some tea.

"There is no reason for you to be frightened," the engineer told me. "Your destiny is in the hands of Allah."

That, as you can imagine, was of little comfort to me.

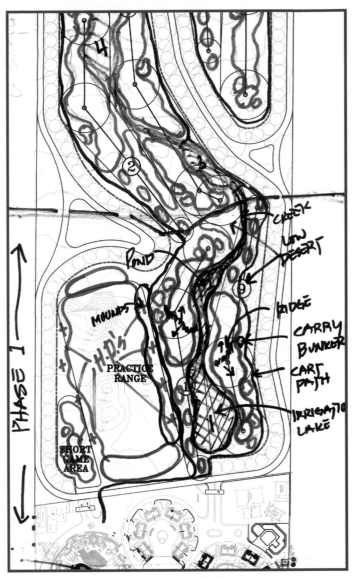

A sketch of Juliette Falls in progress.

"Surely you've swept the mines from the beach, right?"

There was an uncomfortable pause followed by an even more uncomfortable answer: "No."

CHAPTER 97
CLIMBING THE CADDY LADDER

GEORGE F. SARGENT JR.

Franklin, New Hampshire–based George Sargent Jr., a University of Massachusetts graduate, worked on home state courses such as the Stonebridge Country Club in Goffstown; Campbell's Scottish Highlands Golf Course in Salem; and the Lochmere Golf and Country Club. Other Sargent designs include the River Bend Country Club in West Bridgewater, Massachusetts, and Point Sebago Golf Resort in Casco, Maine.

I'd like to reflect for a moment on how lucky I am to be in this business, to be doing what I am doing, having come from such humble beginnings. I, like many others, started my career in the golf course industry as a caddy, at age thirteen, in my hometown of Franklin, New Hampshire.

At the club, all the caddies would sit silently on the caddy bench, and wait for the caddy master to pick them to go work. The trick, I quickly learned, to getting into the caddy master's good graces was to help out at the club. I would pick up trash, clean the locker room, sweep the walkway, and scrub toilets because these tasks were essential to becoming a good caddy ... or so we were told.

There was also a highly coveted, special bonus for the hardest-working caddies. There was a porch at the club that the golfers convened on, and the floor on the porch was wooden with large slots in it. If the caddy master really liked you, he would allow you to crawl underneath the porch and look for quarters that had fallen out of the golfers' pockets. You were only selected to do this, however, if the caddy master thought you were working hard enough.

Once I got the hang of caddying I loved it. I carried a bag around, got to learn about golf, was outside in the fresh air, and got to talk to a lot of interesting people. I thought it was the best job in the world and even wondered how I could go about making a living as a full-time caddy!

I became a golf architect, instead.

And can you believe that the club selected me to add nine holes to the course in 1999? My home course!

The old wooden porch is still there, slots and all. The only difference is that I no longer need permission to crawl underneath it to look for quarters.

CHAPTER 98
A TALE OF TWO COURSES

DAN SCHLEGEL

Edgewater, Maryland–based Dan Schlegel has worked on hundreds of national and international projects. Many clients have retained Dan's services to bring back lost design characteristics on courses designed by the Golden Age architects such as Donald Ross and William Flynn. His greatest experience is in the area of retrofitting existing facilities with new additions and other updates to expand their quality, profitability, and challenges. Some of his work includes Springwood Golf Club in York, Pennsylvania; the River Course in Pulaski County, Virginia; and in New Jersey, Mercer Oaks East Golf Course in West Windsor Township; Ballmor Golf Club in Egg Harbor; and Heron Glen Golf Course in Ringoes.

Two courses throughout my career really stick out in my mind. The first was in Korea, just north of Seoul. You can't go too far north of Seoul and still be in a safe area, but the dangers at our golf course project were a bit unexpected.

The site was called the Yoomyunzsan course. The course was covered in small trees and branches, and so the walking path around Yoomyunzsan had been hand-cut with machetes. Because the branches had been cut this way, they had pointed tops. Imagine walking through a course with small, pointed sticks jutting out of the ground. You had to be very careful not to trip, because if you fell, you would be in big trouble—impaled on one of the branches!

The other project I think about often was halfway around the world, in the continental United States, and it is my favorite course I ever worked on: Butte Country Club in Montana. It was absolutely beautiful.

In Montana, when you drive on the highway, you can see the horizon forever. The land is flat and you get the sense that the land is moving down, not up.

Butte Country Club was absolutely beautiful. Evel Knievel, the notorious motorcycle daredevil, was also a notorious golfer, and he lived on the fifteenth hole of the course.

Even though I've been to the other side of the world to work on a course, it is my preference to work in the most beautiful place in the world to me, the central flatlands of America.

CHAPTER 99
"ONLY ONE CHANGE," HE SAID

LEE SCHMIDT

A native of Carmel, Indiana, Lee Schmidt worked for Pete Dye for seven years as design associate on projects such as Kingsmill Country Club in Virginia and Casa de Campo in the Dominican Republic. Schmidt served as vice president of Landmark Land Company for twelve years heading the design and construction division while prominent California courses such as PGA West, La Quinta Hotel and Resort, and Mission Hills were built. Schmidt also spent seven years as senior design associate for Nicklaus Design. He is now a principal with Schmidt Curley Design and has thirty-five years of experience as superintendent, architect, and builder. His other works include Agile Country Club in Zhongshan City, China; Bali Hai and Siena Golf Club in Las Vegas; and, in Beaumont, California, PGA of Southern California Golf Club and Landmark Golf Club.

Early in my career I was working in the Dominican Republic for the famed architect Pete Dye as a site coordinator on the construction of the Links course at Casa de Campo in La Romana.

Some bulk grading and initial main drainage systems were being installed since the course was in the early stages of construction.

I had proposed to my girlfriend over the previous Christmas holidays and was making arrangements to travel back to Indiana at the end of May for ten days to get married. Pete volunteered to come to the Dominican Republic while I was gone and run the construction of the course.

What a great idea!

I made detailed lists of the various tasks to be accomplished and who should do them during my absence for Pete, since he is not known to be the most organized person.

After getting married, and then spending a short honeymoon in Florida, I returned to the Dominican Republic anxious to see the progress on the course. Pete met me at the hotel upon my return.

"Everything could not have gone better," Pete said. "What a great crew you have organized! The lists of tasks you left me were very detailed and helpful, too."

I then asked Pete, "Were there many changes?"

"Only one," he answered.

"Only one?"

"Yes," Pete said. "Only one; on the back nine. The more I walked the back nine while you were gone, the more I thought it would play better in reverse."

Yes, Pete made the change and the course was finished with this new routing direction!

Now when I lay out routings of new courses and review other staff member's routings, I continue to rely on Pete's reversal as a reminder to look at all options, even routing the course in reverse, before deciding on a final routing. Thanks, Pete, for the great advice!

I was a design associate with Nicklaus Design in the 1990s. It was always tense when Jack would come for a course site visit. I always wanted the visit to go smoothly with no glitches.

One morning, in Canada, I met Jack for breakfast in his hotel room. Jack and I discussed what he would be seeing that day and I updated him on the construction progress of the course.

We left the room and took the hotel elevator to the lobby to meet the owners and the other staff members. The elevator stopped on the way down and an elderly lady walked in and began staring at Jack. You could just see her mind racing the more she studied him.

"I know who you are," she finally said just as the elevator door opened. "You're Arnold Palmer!"

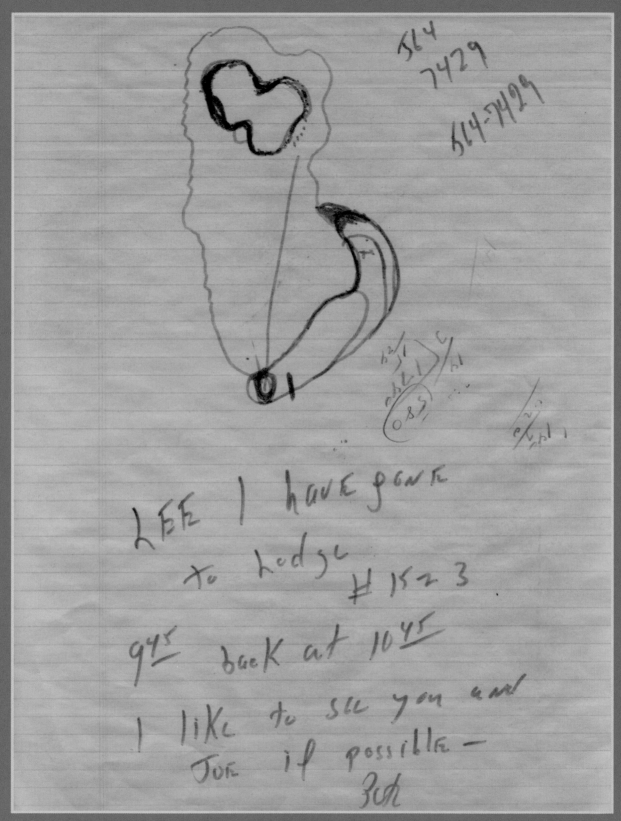

Rough sketch of PGA West 17th Alcatraz.

The look on Jack's face was priceless. He was very cordial, though, in correcting the lady.

"Ma'am, you have the right sport but wrong name," he told her gently.

My compliments to Jack on how well he handled this awkward situation, as well as the many others he encounters with his celebrity status. It may have set the tone for the day; the site visit was perfect.

CHAPTER 100
TELLING JACK NICKLAUS
"NO, THANK YOU"

CRAIG SCHREINER

Myrtle Beach–based Craig Schreiner, president of Schreiner Golf, Inc. (SGI), has designed golf course projects throughout North and Central America. He holds a BS in landscape architecture from Oregon State University and an AAS in turfgrass management from Ohio State University. He has designed such courses as Prairie Highlands Golf Course in Olathe, Kansas; The Signature of Solon in Solon, Ohio; Hawks View Golf Club in Lake Geneva, Wisconsin; and Beaver Creek Golf Course in Baton Rogue, Louisiana. The First Tee program has recognized Craig as its "resident architect," since he has collaborated with PGA Tour player Tom Watson on a facility outside Kansas City, Missouri and worked on the design and construction of First Tee Facilities Clark Park in Baton Rouge and Mud Run in Akron, Ohio.

It took fifteen years of preparation, but after all my schooling, I was finally ready to get out there and design some courses, so I was trying to get my name out by working with a head-hunter who really taught me how to interview and market myself to the different firms. I was knocked over by the response I got! I had offers from Tom Watson, Tom Fazio, and several other famous firms. I even had a very rare offer from Jack Nicklaus to come on as a senior associate.

The headhunter I was working with had taught me how to put on my poker face and not jump at the first offer, but rather, to really wait for the position that was right for me. But at the same time I was starving and my funds were beginning to be depleted, and I needed to make some sort of a decision soon.

During the time I was debating my different offers, I was at a golf event for the American Society of Golf Course Architects in Pebble Beach, California. During the first round of the three-day tournament, I made it to the most photographed hole in the world, Pebble Beach's scenic, oceanside par-three seventh hole.

I thought to myself, "Wow, wouldn't it be spectacular if I were to make a hole in one today on the most famous hole in the world?" So I grabbed my three-quarter wedge, aimed, and hit the ball solidly … and apparently perfectly, because it landed in the hole!

Later that evening, in the 19th Hole Lounge, I was enjoying the accolades, and thinking about my future. If all these different companies had an interest in hiring me, maybe I should go into business for myself? If everyone wanted me to work for them, I must really be ready to do this. If I could make an ace on the seventh hole, I could certainly start my own company, right? The ace gave me confidence. I considered it a "sign." I decided, right then and there, to tell Mr. Nicklaus, and all the others, "No, thank you," and start my own business instead.

My family about died when I told them I had declined the senior associate position with Jack Nicklaus. Everyone thought I was crazy.

I interviewed shortly after to build a course in Willoughby, Ohio. I was in the final three competing for the job, and ended up getting my first job.

I haven't stopped since. I am in business with myself, all because of a revelation on the golf course through a hole in one.

CHAPTER 101
BIG TROUBLE ON THE BIG ISLAND

SCOT SHERMAN

Scot Sherman, who earned degrees from Georgia Tech and Furman University, began his golf course architecture career working first with Perry Dye and later with Bobby Weed. He is currently based in Greenville, South Carolina. His portfolio includes, in Virginia, Cannon Ridge Golf Club in Fredericksburg and the Olde Farm Golf Club in Bristol. Sherman also designed the Golf Club at Fleming Island in Orange Park, Florida; The Weed nine at Hilton Head National; and the Golf Course at Glen Mills.

I was working with Perry Dye in 1994 on the design and construction of Big Island Country Club, on the Big Island of Hawaii, near Kona. My task was to lay out the lake and green for the seventeenth hole—a par-three very much like the infamous island green par-three seventeenth hole Pete Dye designed at Tournament Players Club at Sawgrass.

Since I learned to build golf holes on the ground and not in ponds, the only way I knew to accomplish such a task was by using a tape measure and flags as the starting point. So I set out early one morning and began to wade into an area of native grasses growing about eyeball high. I could see no further than ten feet in front of me.

My plan was to trample down the grass along the perimeter of the lake then go back to the elevated tee and view what I had done. I could then make changes from there. But during the first half-hour of trampling, I got the distinct feeling I was being watched. I would hear a bit of rustling grass, but could not see anyone or anything. The feeling unsettled me.

Suddenly I was attacked. Apparently I had gotten too close to my observer, and he decided to retaliate. I was rushed by a large, bellowing, wild boar!

The boar's first action was to ram my shins and flip me on my back; my first reaction was to begin screaming at the top of my lungs hoping that our Hawaiian crew would come to the rescue! After the initial tussle, the boar briefly stood over me, tusk-to-nose. As I screamed, he made his displeasure clear and trampled over my head into the bush.

My screaming was effective, though. When I emerged from the grass, I saw no less than ten Hawaiian men running toward me from other parts of the site. They were wielding machetes and rifles.

Apparently, my hollering was a familiar wild boar alarm and the crew wanted in on the action. I was completely hoarse from screaming, so I simply pointed in the direction of the monster's retreat and watched the men disappear into the grass. I headed in the opposite direction. I was most certainly done for the day!

That night, my wife and I were invited to a luau where we were reintroduced to the boar: all 225 pounds of him, cooked to a perfect medium-rare and sporting a fresh pineapple glaze!

CHAPTER 102
WHY SO MANY TEES?

BRIAN SILVA

Mount Washington Resort, Bretton Woods, New Hampshire,
and the appropriately named Mount Pleasant Course.

Brian Silva heads up Brian Silva Design. Brian's first original eighteen-hole design, the Captains Golf Club, in Brewster, Massachusetts, was named Best New Public Course by *Golf Digest* in 1985. His other works include Massachusetts golf clubs Waverly Oaks Golf Club in Plymouth, Black Rock Country Club in Hingham, and Red Tail Golf Club in Ayer, as well as Black Creek Golf Club in Chattanooga, Tennessee, a firm he formed after spending more than 20 years working with Geoffrey Cornish. Prior to joining Cornish, he earned his BSLA from the University of Massachusetts, taught agronomy at the UMass Stockbridge School of Agriculture and worked for the USGA Green Section.

I was in a new course job, working for two partners. As is often the case, one of the partners handled the finances and the other directed the day-to-day details of the job. The finance guy only occasionally turned up at the job site, and on this particular day, he'd come for one of his infrequent site visits.

The course was under construction, and we walked the holes. I led him through the routing, stopping every so often to explain the status and the strategic goal of each hole. We stopped at a par-three.

"This hole is a par-three," I told him. "It plays about two hundred yards from the back tee; one forty-five from the tee you can see just ahead; and one hundred five yards from the front tee."

The finance guy spoke up. "Why are there so many tees?" he asked.

"Well, from each individual tee, the hole requires a shot to carry over a wetland," I explained. "Better players will use the back tees and have to hit a longer shot to safely clear the wetland."

He stared at me, so I continued.

"Golfers have varying skill level, so those players of lesser caliber can still enjoy the challenge of the hole with a shorter, less challenging shot from one of the other tees."

He responded by asking, again, "Why so many tees?"

I hesitated for a moment, but then tried a different approach. I detailed the yardage carry from each tee and how the angle of each successive tee better lined up with the axis of the green. "You see, the closer you get to the green, the easier play from each tee is. There will be a wide variety of golfers playing your beautiful course."

"Why so many tees?" he asked, yet again.

I explained again.

"The hole is a par-three. People take divots. You need to move the markers about so people will have fresh grass to tee from and allow the damaged grass to recover. The three tees, in order, need to have adequate space to maintain turf growth. See?"

The finance guy looked like he was finally catching on. But he then asked: "Why don't you just put in a rubber mat?"

At this point, even I was at a loss for words.

As we started walking the path to the green, one of the shapers sidled up to me and whispered, "Do you think Robert Trent Jones started this way?"

A shot of the Red Tail Golf Club in Ft. Devins, Massachusetts.

CHAPTER 103
COLLEGE REUNION TURNED
HAPPY HOMECOMING

MIKE SMELEK

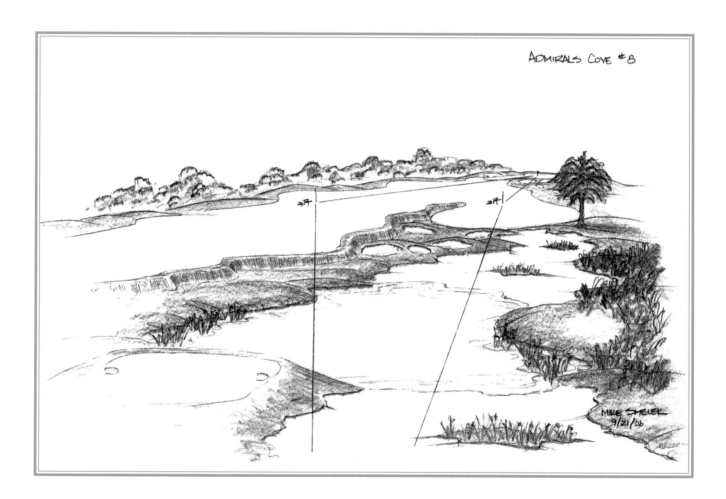

After graduating from the University of Idaho in 1980, Smelek moved to Texas and began his apprenticeship with Robert von Hagge. By 1995 he was a senior partner with von Hagge, Smelek, and Baril Golf Course Architects. His works include Torreon Golf Club in Show Low, Arizona; Los Lagos in Edinburg, Texas; Grey Hawk Golf Club in LaGrange, Ohio; and, in Mexico, Bosque Real in Huixquilucan and La Herradura Club de Golf in Monterrey.

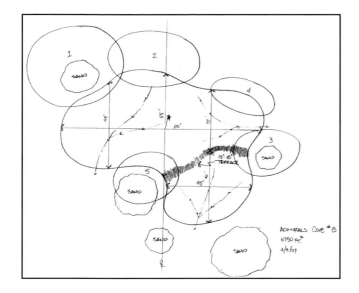

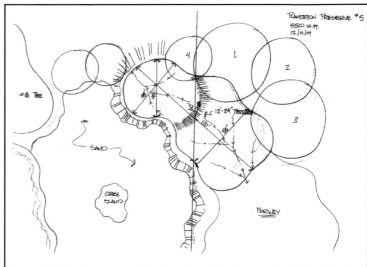

I designed my first golf course before I really knew that I wanted to pursue golf course architecture as a career. The idea of designing a course occurred to me when I had to choose a topic for my senior design thesis to complete my landscape architecture degree at the University of Idaho. I had played golf since the age of eleven and had a real passion for the game, so it seemed logical at the time to marry my two passions and attempt to design a golf course.

The property I chose for my project was an actual site being developed in Idaho as a small mountain resort and nine-hole golf course. I learned about the property from my girlfriend's brother, who would soon after become my brother-in-law. Since he was involved in the financing of the project, he helped acquire the necessary topographic mapping and programming for the project.

After finishing my thesis project, I proudly shared my golf course design with my brother-in-law to be and the developer. They were either very impressed—or knew very little about golf course design and saw the opportunity to get the course designed cheaply—because they hired me to design the course! I was suddenly a golf course architect for the summer!

I completed the drawings, sent them to the developer, and returned to school in the fall to complete my degree. Upon graduation I was fortunate enough to get the opportunity to officially begin my career with Robert von Hagge in Texas.

Several years after moving to Texas, my wife and I returned to Idaho for a summer vacation. We had the opportunity to play golf at that same, rather obscure little nine-hole mountain course I had designed for my college project.

Although by time I'd returned I had only been an apprentice golf course architect for a few years, it was immediately evident to me that my first course design was seriously lacking in both a sophisticated tactical examination and aesthetic composition.

I designed my first golf course before I really knew that I wanted to pursue golf course architecture as a career.

But when we reached the eighth hole, I was puzzled. I was sure I clearly remembered designing the hole as a 530-yard, dogleg right, par-five. But as we stood on the tee, with trees lining both sides of the fairway, it appeared that the blind tee shot was only 140 yards or so long. Not knowing how the hole had been changed, we hit our nine-irons out into the fairway, but when we reached the landing zone we discovered the rest of the par-five! The green was still some 440 yards away. My original par-five design had been compromised and was now essentially a par-five-and-a-half. Apparently the developer wanted to preserve the entire small grove of trees to the right of the tees and, on his own, adjusted the hole accordingly (but nonsensically).

It was a valuable lesson to learn very early in my career: don't ever just send plans. But if you must, send them anonymously!

195

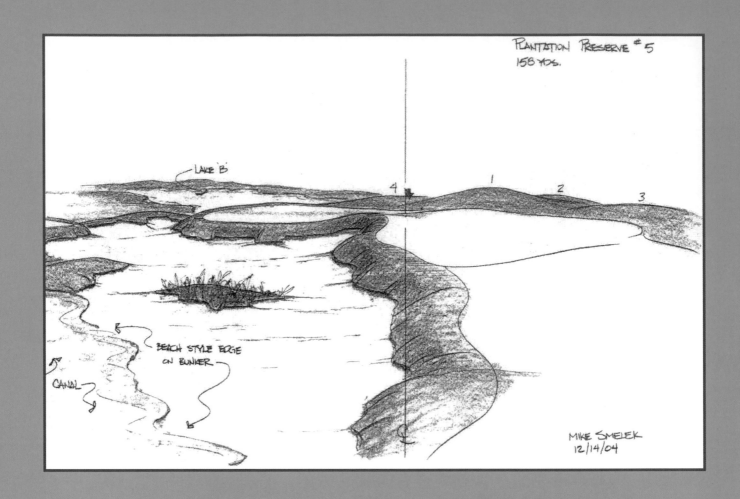

PLANTATION PRESERVE #5
158 YDS.

LAKE "B"

CANAL

BEACH STYLE EDGE
ON BUNKER

MIKE SMELEK
12/14/04

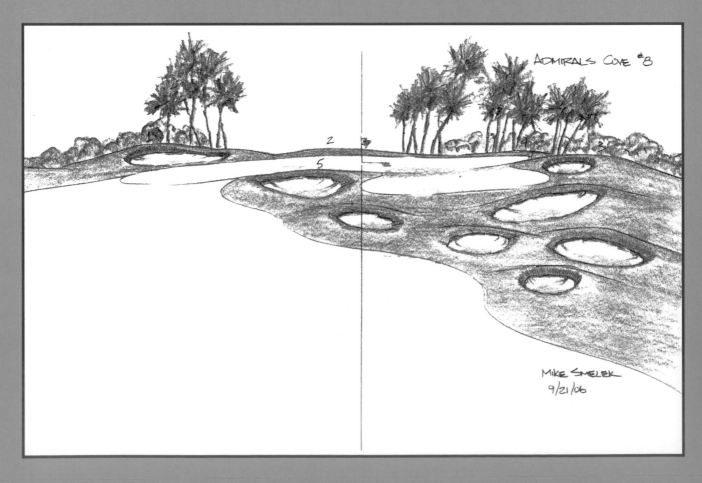

ADMIRALS COVE #8

MIKE SMELEK
9/21/06

CHAPTER 104
SNAKEBITTEN, BUT YOU PROBABLY WON'T DIE

PHIL SMITH

Phil Smith is the senior design associate for Scottsdale, Arizona–based Weiskopf Design. Golf courses to his credit include the Tournament Players Club at Craig Ranch in McKinney, Texas; Silverleaf in Scottsdale, Arizona; Seven Canyons in Sedona, Arizona; the Club at Flying Horse in Colorado Springs, Colorado; and Hualalai in Kona, Hawaii.

I am the senior design associate for Tom Weiskopf and have been with him for nine years. However, I cut my teeth in this business with Jack Nicklaus and worked for him ten years prior to joining up with Tom.

After doing a lot of drafting for my first few years with the company, my project assignment in the field with Nicklaus was to oversee the design of the Apache Course at Desert Mountain in Scottsdale, Arizona. Desert Mountain was developed by Lyle Anderson and is a wonderful development that has six golf courses now and has been the host of the Champions Tour's Tradition Tournament for years. Apache was the fourth course to be built at Desert Mountain.

I moved to the Valley of the Sun in August, 1992 to take on the project under the supervision of senior designer Jim Lipe. The centerlines for each hole had been staked and we were awaiting the arrival of Jack Nicklaus so he could tour the corridors and develop his strategy plan for the course.

Anyone who has been to North Scottsdale knows that the desert is not really a desert landscape in the truest sense. Although it gets very hot, it is a very lush desert and has some spectacular plant and animal life.

The site tour with Jack started just fine and we zipped through the first couple of holes with not much problem. We walked in a single-file formation, weaving through and between the cactus, rock, and desert plants. Lipe was leading the way; I followed and Nicklaus was right behind me. Trailing behind Jack were Lyle Anderson and about twenty other consultants, photographers, and onlookers.

Lipe and I were casually talking as we made our way from the proposed tee complex site toward the green. He stepped over a small, twenty-four-inch-tall turpentine shrub just in front of me. Turpentine shrubs grow to be about two to three feet wide, with no thorns or spines, so they are quite easy to step over and usually allow the path of least resistance when trudging through the desert. I followed Lipe's steps very carefully because I didn't want to fall and embarrass myself in front of Nicklaus and all the others. When I stepped over the same turpentine shrub Lipe had, I must have short-stepped just ever so slightly because I could hear the crunch of the shrub under my foot. But then I felt and heard something quite different. It felt as if I was stepping on a giant marshmallow. I then heard a loud hissing and the ground shifted wildly under my foot! It took only a split-second for me to jump away and scamper down into a nearby dry wash bed. Lipe had run ahead after hearing a rattle, while Nicklaus and the rest of the crew retreated backward. A rattlesnake scurried in their direction from underneath the shrub I'd stepped on!

We all marveled at the long snake as it slithered past. No one could quite tell if it was a Mojave or western diamondback rattler, and as they all looked at the snake and tried to decide, I found myself trying to catch my breath.

Carlos Velasquez, the lead shaper for the golf course contractor, came up from behind me to see how I was.

"I think it spit on you," he said, looking at my feet.

My heart just sank when I looked down. On my right pant leg were two blobs of liquid, each about the size of a nickel. I gently pulled up my pant leg and there they were: two small pinholes, just above the ankle, with blood trickling down each.

The next few minutes were a blur. Anderson and Nicklaus came over to inquire about my condition. Someone got on the radio to get a truck over to transport me to the hospital and requested Wally Camp, the local wildlife expert, to drive me.

We sat there waiting for the truck to arrive and I can still remember some of the conversations. One group was snapping photos—some of the snake and some of me. I wasn't too scared yet—the lethal reality hadn't sunken in because the wound didn't hurt all that bad. I felt just a slight burn.

Wally finally arrived with the truck and drove me to an emergency center in Cave Creek. The drive took fifteen minutes, and Wally talked to me on the way, trying to calm me and keep my heart rate down.

"You probably won't die," he said.

That was some bedside manner, eh?

He then explained that the rattlesnake's venom is meant to react with your body tissue and slowly eat away at the muscle, flesh, and bone until it is easy for the snake to digest! Doctors at the emergency center examined me and determined that the snake probably had ejected most of the venom from its fangs before sinking them into my leg. In a stunning bit of luck, most of the venom ended up on the outside of my pants instead of in my veins. The doctors gave me an injection for infection and some antibiotics and kept me under supervision for six hours before releasing me.

I know I would never have forgotten my first site visit with Jack Nicklaus ... but the snake made my first site visit with Jack Nicklaus memorable for Nicklaus, too!

Desert Mountain was developed by Lyle Anderson and is a wonderful development that has six golf courses now and has been the host of the Champions Tour's Tradition Tournament for years.

CHAPTER 105
MOO-VING EXPERIENCE
STEVE SMYERS

S teve Smyers is president of Steve Smyers Golf Course Design of Lakeland, Florida. He played on the 1973 University of Florida NCAA National Championship golf team, and designed, among others, Wolf Run Golf Club in Zionsville, Indiana; Old Memorial in Tampa, Florida; Chart Hills Golf Club in Kent, England; Southern Dunes in Haines City, Florida; and Four Streams in Beallsville, Maryland. Smyers redesigned Tiger Woods's home course, Isleworth, in Orlando, and Royal Harare Golf Club in Harare, Zimbabwe.

After walking a site for majority of a day, I returned to my rented Jeep to find approximately fifty head of cattle surrounding the vehicle. As I approached, the cattle started to charge me!

I quickly turned, ran up a small incline, picked up a stick, held it over my head and started screaming at the small herd!

To my surprise, cows stopped in their tracks, which allowed me to scamper off and seek help from a local rancher. The rancher took me to my vehicle.

"You did the right thing," he told me. "You stop charging cattle by holding up your arm." The cattle won in the end, though: I ended up missing my flight, which of course, was the last one of the day.

CHAPTER 106
JACK NICKLAUS DOESN'T HAVE
TO PUT UP WITH THIS!

JOHN STEIDEL

Kennewick, Washington–based John Steidel has designed home state courses Apple Tree Golf Club in Yakima, Eaglemont Golf Club in Mount Vernon, Lynnwood Municipal Golf Club in Lynnwood, and Riverbend Golf Club in Kent. He also created the Wildhorse Resort Golf Course, in Pendleton, Oregon.

In the summer of 1982 I was inspecting the construction of my new, nine-hole Marian Hills Golf Course in Malta, Montana (population 2,367). It was being built for and by rancher Mark Niebur and his family, along with a friend who had a scraper and one guy who helped install irrigation.

In those days I would go anywhere and do anything to do or get work. Malta is about a four-hour drive northwest of Great Falls on U.S. Highway 2, which is referred to locally as being along "the Highline." I often reached this project by taking Amtrak's Empire Builder from my office in Tri-Cities, Washington, to Malta: a not-so-convenient, overnight, fourteen-hour trip each way. The eastbound train dropped me off at 1 p.m.; twenty-four hours later I would catch the westbound train home. One consolation was enjoying breakfast and dinner while riding through the Rockies and crossing the continental divide just south of Glacier National Park.

That summer, seventy-five miles to the west, some golfers in Chinook, Montana (population 1,660), heard Malta was getting a golf course. Somehow they contacted me, so I agreed to come over to meet with them after one of my Malta inspections. They wanted to talk about dramatically upgrading their nine-hole course, which was without irrigation and had oiled-sand greens.

On the day I was supposed to leave Malta and travel to Chinook it was hot: nearly 100 degrees. I had decided to take the bus over to Chinook, so my Malta clients dropped me and my bags off, just before noon, at the Missouri Valley Stage Lines bus pickup spot: Mustang Lanes. It was a six-lane bowling alley where it seemed like smoking was mandatory.

"Your bus is late," I was told by the counter attendant. He didn't say how late, so I waited, but it was a hell of a choice: should I wait inside a stuffy, smoky bowling alley with no air conditioning, or sit outside where it probably was 100 degrees in the shade?

I went back and forth.

One o'clock became two o'clock, so I started to worry about missing my 5:30 meeting, but around 2:30 the other would-be passengers and I were told the bus was almost here and that we should wait outside.

Then, all of a sudden, there it was: the bus, which was actually two late model sedans, one of which was pulling a U-Haul trailer. Although I was hot, sweaty and uncomfortable, at least I was on my way and it seemed like I was going to be on time.

After an hour of driving through the nothingness that is most of that part of Montana, we stopped, without discussion, in Harlem, Montana.

After our fifteen-minute stop, we drove fifteen more miles west to Chinook, where I was dropped off on what seemed like the edge of town—though that was hard to ascertain. It was now thirty minutes before my meeting and there I stood, hot and sweaty on the side of US 2, lugging my briefcase, suitcase, and slide projector containing my presentation. I was wearing slacks, a short-sleeved shirt and tie, and had my sport coat under my arm. I probably looked suspiciously like a missionary or Bible salesman, and most definitely an out-of-towner.

Fortunately, I came across a car dealership, which was the first good thing to happen that afternoon. I ducked into the showroom and asked one of the salesmen where the golf course was located. One of the guys at the dealership told me it was "Men's Night," and since he was just leaving for the course, he would give me a ride there.

The golf course was a bit out of town near a place called Milk River. I would not have found it myself, and certainly would never have reached it on foot. It was a pretty site, though, with a small, very modest clubhouse on a hill. Only the trees were green—the rest of the course was brown since there was no irrigation. The course wasn't much, but was worth the $40 per year they charged the members.

Men's Night was nine holes of league play followed by beer and burgers afterward. I was to be their entertainment.

As I tried to set up my presentation and regain some composure, fifty to sixty golfers left the clubhouse area for what was to be a shotgun start in the truest sense of the term. Most of the golfers just drove their pickups with clubs and more than a few loaded gun racks across the course to their appointed tees, where they awaited a shotgun blast from someone near the clubhouse to signal the start of the round!

After the beer and burgers I finally got to make my presentation. The members seemed to be impressed by the greenness of my courses, and the fact that I'd hung sheets to darken the room and create a screen for my slide projector.

I did some preliminary design work for them that fall and winter, and after eight tries I came up with a pretty decent layout for them. My cost estimate was minimal. It included green sand that was to be purchased for $1 per yard and trucked to the course for free on weekends by the National Guard. But in 1983, all the golfers of Chinook together couldn't put together enough money for my minimal cost estimate for their golf course.

I didn't hear from anyone in Chinook again for seventeen years, until one of my old contacts there called to get some information. He said the club officers might be calling me, but they never did.

I did hear, though, that sometime in the past eight years the golfers of Chinook, Montana, got their grass golf course, but I wasn't part of it. I've never called or been back to Chinook, and I don't know if they used my layout or not. I don't even know if the course is on the same site, but I'm glad they got their course.

JOHN STEIDEL
GOLF COURSE ARCHITECT
P. O. BOX 6566 - KENNEWICK, WA 99336
PHONE: 509/582-6706 FAX: 509/586-7363

GLENDALE COUNTRY CLUB
BELLEVUE, WASHINGTON

Proposed
#18 GREEN
Perspective View
(From Approach)
July 1992

CHAPTER 107
EVEN BLEARY EYES CAN
YIELD A FRESH LOOK

BRIT STENSON

Cleveland, Ohio–based Brit Stenson has collaborated with a number of professional golfers who have served as design consultants, including Vijay Singh, Mark O'Meara, Curtis Strange, Nick Faldo, and many others at the behest of IMG, the world's premier and most diversified sports, entertainment, and media company, founded by Arnold Palmer and the late Mark McCormack. Courses to his credit are the Mark O'Meara Course at Grandview Golf Club and The Rock in Ontario, Canada; Tuhaye in Park City, Utah; and in China, Hang Gang Golf and Zhuhai Golden Gulf Golf.

Two giants of the golf business, IMG founder Mark McCormack and Sol Kerzner, the international resort developer from South Africa, had a conversation at the 1998 Wimbledon tennis tournament in London.

"I'm having some trouble getting my golf course in Mauritius designed," Kerzner told McCormack. Apparently the site, on a tiny island called Ile aux Cerfs, which was actually off the coast of Mauritius, was great, but the course designer Kerzner was using for the project wasn't coming up with an approvable plan.

"Sol, you should have IMG's designer take a look at it," McCormack advised Kerzner.

That meant the very next day, I was on my way to Mauritius—once I'd located it on the map. It is not easy to get to the middle of the Indian Ocean! I took the red-eye flight to London's Heathrow Airport, followed by a second red-eye to Mauritius and Ile aux Cerfs, where I arrived, bleary-eyed, at 6 a.m. I wasn't sure what day it was.

Mark and Sol had worked out a scenario whereby I was to look at the maps, visit the site, fly back to Cleveland, work up a plan, and present it to Kerzner the following Monday at his home outside London. I learned to keep my passport ready and tried not to fret about the prospect of four red-eye flights in seven days.

A review of the proposed plan alternatives revealed that the current designer was insisting on creating two cape holes by incorporating a beautiful sand beach. The trouble was that the beach was also used daily by local beachcombers, picnickers, and fishermen. Fortunately for me, that same insistent designer, who had personally been to the site twice, had almost entirely ignored the island's other coastline—which was mostly lava rock surrounded by mangroves instead of beaches. I had a pretty strong hunch, confirmed by a long, scratchy walk through the brambles, that a very good golf course was possible by shifting our emphasis to the rocky coast instead. After a long-awaited great night's sleep, I spent some more time with the maps and the project team, making sure I knew all the issues facing the development, and made a second site visit to confirm my initial impressions.

Back in Cleveland, I put together a short presentation during the next few days. Then I repacked my bag and flew to London as planned. Kerzner approved my concept on the spot. He then decided that IMG client Bernhard Langer, the German-born Masters champion, should be the signature architect.

Getting the plans fully approved by the local authorities in Mauritius was another matter: it required almost three years of perseverance, patience, and tweaks to the plan. The story has a happy ending, though—the course was eventually finished pretty close to the way we'd drawn it up. Le Touessrok now provides a unique and memorable golf experience for people to venture to Kezner's golf course on Ile aux Cerfs. In 2005, Golf World International ranked Le Touessrok number ten on its list of the World's Best Courses.

CHAPTER 108
MY FIELD OF DREAMS MOMENT
JASON STRAKA

Sunset over the gorgeous 3rd hole at Georgian Bay in Ontario, Canada.

Jason Straka joined Hurdzan/Fry Design in October of 1995. Straka's primary university work at Cornell was on the development of Widow's Walk Golf Course in Scituate Massachusetts, which is widely recognized as the United States' first environmental demonstration and research golf course and winner of *Golf Digest*'s prestigious Environmental Leaders in Golf award. Straka has also worked on Le Diable Golf Club in Tremblant, Quebec; Troy Burne Golf Course, in Hudson, Wisconsin, which he co-designed with Tom Lehman; and, with Fuzzy Zoeller, Dornoch Golf Club in Delaware, Ohio.

I was very fortunate that my father introduced me to the game of golf at a very young age. I grew up spending a lot of quality time with him walking the links, listening to the cadence of clubs clinking together, and enjoying nature. The personal time with him would shape me as a person and forever provide lifelong memories and lessons that I hope to pass along to my children.

When the Georgian Bay club opened, my father attended the grand opening and was the guest of honor. I was able to play a spectacular par-three with him, and I dedicated my work to him in front of the membership.

Interestingly, the owner of the course dedicated one of the main streets in the club in honor of my son by naming it after him. So father, son, and grandson will forever be linked at Georgian Bay to remind everyone of the special bonds between fathers and their children.

It is instances like this that make my chosen profession of golf course architecture such a rewarding experience for me.

CHAPTER 109
ANY PORT IN A STORM

BRYCE SWANSON

Bryce Swanson is senior designer for Rees Jones, Inc. He graduated from Iowa State University in 1995 with a bachelor of landscape architecture degree. His notable projects include Royal Montreal Golf Club's Blue Course in Ile Bizard, Quebec, Canada; Daniel Island Golf Club's Ralston Creek Course in Charleston, South Carolina; and Atlanta Athletic Club's Highlands and Riverside courses in Duluth, Georgia.

Oh, the great travel of being a golf course architect!

One day I was flying thru Miami airport and needed to connect to the last flight of the day going to Nassau, Bahamas. It was the Friday night of a holiday weekend in the winter, and I had a client meeting the next morning in Nassau. I missed the connecting flight by five minutes, so I was stuck in Miami for the night.

After trying to get a room at the hotel in the airport and calling eight others, I decided it was better to try in person. I was directing the taxi driver from hotel to hotel. It was a good thing my taxi driver was willing to help me, because we tried another few spots and had no luck. It was looking like a night in the airport until the taxi driver asked if I wouldn't mind her suggesting a motel. She said she knew of a spot I might like, and took me there. Indeed, there was a vacancy.

The TV remote was anchored to the table and the headboard had a car stereo built into it, but at least it was a bed to sleep in!

Oh, the great travel of being a golf course architect!

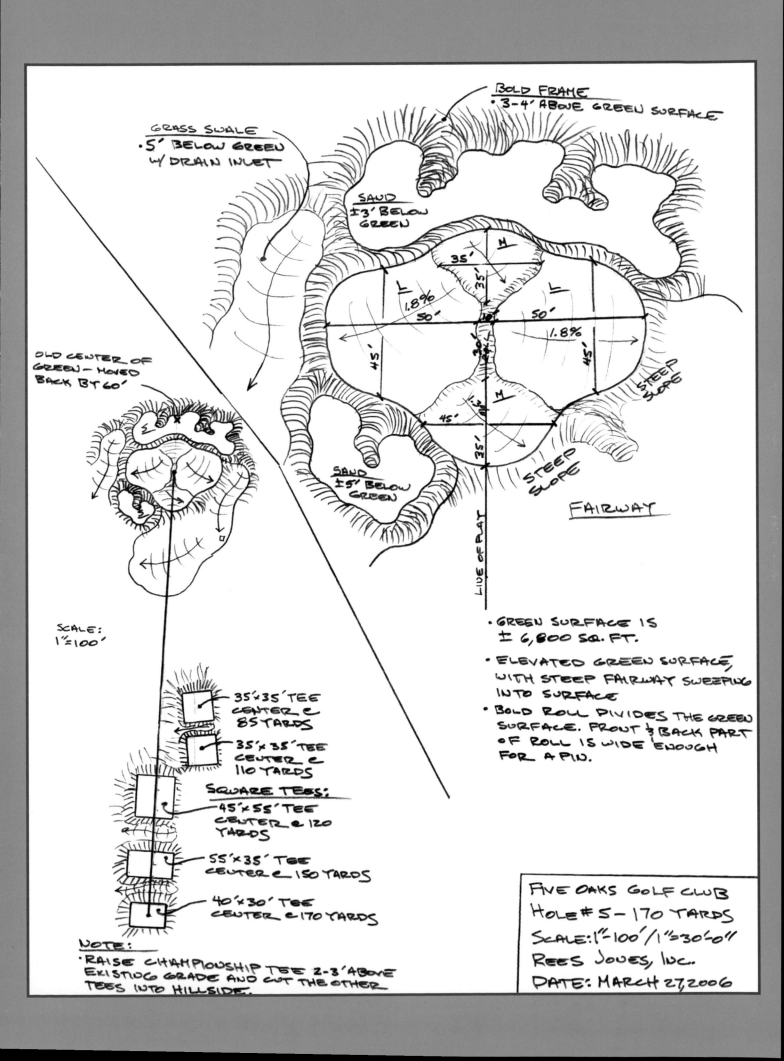

GRASS SWALE
• 5' BELOW GREEN
  W/ DRAIN INLET

BOLD FRAME
• 3-4' ABOVE GREEN SURFACE

SAND
±3' BELOW
GREEN

35'
35'
M
L
1.8%
50'
L
50'
1.8%
45'
45'
STEEP SLOPE
STEEP SLOPE
M
45'
45'
35'

SAND
±5' BELOW
GREEN

LINE OF PLAT

FAIRWAY

OLD CENTER OF
GREEN - MOVED
BACK BY 60'

SCALE:
1"=100'

35'x35' TEE
CENTER @
85 YARDS

35'x35' TEE
CENTER @
110 YARDS

SQUARE TEES:
45'x55' TEE
CENTER @ 120
YARDS

55'x35' TEE
CENTER @ 150 YARDS

40'x30' TEE
CENTER @ 170 YARDS

NOTE:
• RAISE CHAMPIONSHIP TEE 2-3' ABOVE
EXISTING GRADE AND CUT THE OTHER
TEES INTO HILLSIDE.

• GREEN SURFACE IS
± 6,800 SQ. FT.

• ELEVATED GREEN SURFACE,
WITH STEEP FAIRWAY SWEEPING
INTO SURFACE

• BOLD ROLL DIVIDES THE GREEN
SURFACE. FRONT & BACK PART
OF ROLL IS WIDE ENOUGH
FOR A PIN.

FIVE OAKS GOLF CLUB
HOLE #5 - 170 YARDS
SCALE: 1"=100'/1"=30'-0"
REES JONES, INC.
DATE: MARCH 27, 2006

CHAPTER 110
ARE WE SPEAKING THE SAME LANGUAGE?

ROBERT WALKER

Bob Walker played on the golf team at Texas A&M at Commerce (then known as East Texas State University), and then performed golf course construction inspection and quality control for Club Corporation of America. In 1974, he became a design associate with the Arnold Palmer Design Company, where he was involved in the design of more than seventy-five golf course projects spanning twenty-three states and seven foreign countries, including the Legend Course at Shanty Creek in Bellaire, Michigan; the Fossil Creek Golf Club in Fort Worth, Texas; and the Chung Shan Golf Club near Canton, the first golf course built in the People's Republic of China. In 1986 he formed Robert C. Walker, Inc. and designed, among others, in Georgia, Stonebridge Golf & Country Club in Albany and Arrowhead Pointe Golf Club in Elberton; and in Florida, Regatta Bay in Destin, Glen Kernan Country Club in Jacksonville, and St. John's Golf Club in St. Augustine. Walker also created River Run Country Club in Davidson, North Carolina.

During my employment with the Palmer organization, we added a nine-hole golf course to an existing eighteen-hole facility near Savannah, Georgia. The finishing hole of this nine-hole course was designed to be a short par-five, reachable with two well-executed shots.

When we presented our plan to the owner's representative, he immediately had a problem. Because the ninth and the eighteenth holes of the existing golf course were long par-fours, the owner's representative argued that the finishing hole on the new nine-hole course should also be a par-four.

"If a group finishing on the new nine-hole course is playing against another group that may be completing play on one of the existing finishing holes," he explained, "that group would have an unfair advantage because it would be easier for them to make a birdie on a short par-five than it would be for their opponents to make a birdie on a long par-four."

As hard as we tried to convince him that groups competing against each other would all be playing the same holes, we were unsuccessful.

The customer may not always be right, but he's still the customer.

The new ninth hole was redesigned as a par-four.

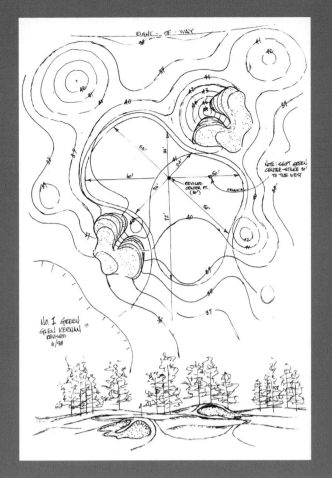

No. 1 Green
Glen Kernan
Revised
6/98

PLAN "A"
VIEW OF CLUBHOUSE
APPROACHING No. 9 GREEN

Glen Kernan Golf Course in Jacksonville, Florida.

CHAPTER 111
INTERSTATE FAIRWAY
BOBBY WEED

Bobby Weed began his career with an apprenticeship under Pete Dye. Weed was hired by the PGA Tour in 1983 and became the in-house architect in 1987. In that post, he was responsible for the design of many of the best known Tournament Players Club venues, which continue to host prominent PGA Tour events. He collaborated with World Golf Hall of Fame members Sam Snead, Gene Sarazen, Arnold Palmer, Jack Nicklaus, Raymond Floyd, and Chi Chi Rodriguez. In 1994, he founded Bobby Weed Golf Design in Ponte Vedra Beach, Florida. The firm designed Spanish Oaks Golf Club in Austin, Texas; Stoneridge Golf Club in St. Paul, Minnesota; the Olde Farm Golf Club in Bristol, Virginia; Glen Mills Golf Club in Philadelphia; and the Slammer and Squire at the World Golf Village, in St. Augustine, Florida.

I was helping Pete Dye build Long Cove Club on Hilton Head Island in 1980 and '81. We were using a local road contractor to excavate the lagoons and build the roads. They were also doing some heavy earthwork for us on an as-needed basis. Since we were responsible to design and build the project, Pete and I were directing all of the equipment on an hourly basis using the road contractor's equipment and operators. One morning, Pete and I were sticking pin flags (little wire flags) in the ground to mark out a long, linear bunker along the tenth hole, between the lagoon and fairway. We spent a considerable amount of time laying out the flags in the dirt and had a nice, slow-flowing line paralleling the fairway from tee to green.

We had an older, leather-skinned operator running a Cat D6 straight-blade 'dozer. Pete motioned him over and rattled off specific instructions for him to follow the flags and to cut three feet out between the flags.

"Hog it out and work it over to one side of the flags to give us a four- to five-foot elevation change from one end to the other," Pete told him.

We then left to attend to other construction activities elsewhere on the golf course.

When we returned a few hours later to check on the progress of the operator, we pulled up and motioned toward the dozer driver. He shut down the dozer, eased out of his seat, stood on the tracks, and hitched up his pants. The he spit a little tobacco out the side of his mouth, wiped his hand across his mouth and cheek, and cleared his throat before talking to Pete.

"Look here, Pardner," he said. "Is this here going to be two lanes or four?"

Pete dropped to his knees, grabbed a couple handfuls of sand, tossed them aside, and said, "It looks great. Just keep pushing, ol' buddy!"

CHAPTER 112
SEPARATION ANXIETY

STEVE WEISSER

Montclair, New Jersey–based Steve Weisser obtained his bachelor of science degree in landscape architecture from Texas A&M University in 1989 and, after working abroad for two years, joined Rees Jones, Inc. Among his projects of note are Quintero Golf and Country Club in Peoria, Arizona; the Golf Club at Briar's Creek in St. John's Island, South Carolina; Club de Golf Santander in Boadilla de Monte, Madrid, Spain; Lake of Isles Resort's south course in North Stonington, Connecticut; and the Golf Club of Cape Cod in Falmouth, Massachusetts.

The new construction site is where to find the most rewarding and most stressful part of the design process. Until then, all design ideas are theoretical and disposable. The site is where that work comes to fruition and the golf course belongs to the designer and the construction team.

It's where the infinite variety that is the Earth makes each design unique.

It's where the course is made and will likely remain—where ideas are realized and lessons are learned.

It is a strangely bittersweet process. As each area is shaped, the golf course begins to appear, and as it is refined, the finished product becomes apparent. One by one, each hole is completed and covered with turf. Soon the course becomes playable. The golf course has left the hands of the designer and becomes the domain of the superintendent and, in turn, the golfer. The architect's thoughts and designs move on to the next piece of earth.

The new construction site is where to find the most rewarding and most stressful part of the design process.

CHAPTER 113
TOO CLOSE FOR COMFORT

DAVID WHELCHEL

David Whelchel has worked with Hurdzan/Fry Golf Course Design since 1990 and serves as senior project design manager and assistant to Dr. Hurdzan and Mr. Fry. He was the University of Arkansas men's golf coach before becoming involved with golf course construction and design. Whelchel was lead designer for the Little Bennett Golf Club in Hyattstown, Maryland; the Meadows Golf Club for Grand Valley State University in Grand Rapids, Michigan; and Gibson Bay Golf Course in Richmond, Kentucky. He also assisted Dr. Hurdzan on the design of Lassing Pointe Golf Club in Union, Kentucky, and assisted Mr. Fry on the design of the Fieldstone Golf Club in Wilmington, Delaware. He was lead designer for Tallwoods Golf & Country Club, north of Sydney, Australia in the resort town of Forster-Tuncurry. Whelchel is currently lead designer for a new eighteen holes at I Roveri Golf Club in Torino, Italy, which is scheduled to open in 2009.

We were preparing to start work on an absolutely beautiful piece of land just north of Mexico City. The project had been commissioned by two wealthy Mexican businessmen who had bought the land. During the design process, we encountered a unique problem: there were squatters inhabiting the site at the time we were trying to build the course.

The squatters were living in very bad conditions. They had no running water, they were sleeping in shacks, and most only owned maybe a cow and a few chickens.

The Mexican businessmen who bought the land had agreed, in the purchase contract, to build houses for the squatters with running water and plumbing and create a school. Everyone involved would be getting a good deal: we would build our golf course, and the squatters would get improved conditions. Unfortunately, the squatters did not want to give up their land. Due to the questionable safety of the area, we were escorted by a bodyguard, Sergio, whenever we made visits to the site. There were about ten members of our design and construction team on foot surveying the site when, as we were examining the spot for the third green, Sergio signaled for our team's attention. He pointed frantically. In the dis-

tance, about a half a mile away, we could see a group of about a hundred Mexicans, some even on horses, headed our way. They were carrying pitchforks and machetes. Clearly, we were not wanted on their land!

Sergio led our group to some bushes for us to hide behind. I could tell some of the members of our group were getting quite nervous. We immediately radioed for the helicopter, but we were quietly aware of the ominous fact that only five people could fit in the chopper at one time.

The helicopter landed and rescued as many people as could reasonably fit on board, so the first bunch was flown away safely. We knew it would be about ten minutes before the chopper would drop them off and come back to pick the rest of us up. I stayed behind because I wasn't too worried about the situation. I figured we were with Sergio, who was armed, and I knew he'd shoot if he had to.

Sergio, another engineer, and I waited for about seven minutes. By that time the angry mob of squatters was about three hundred meters away. We could see them in their white outfits and hats, and boy, did they look angry. Thankfully, at the same time, we heard the helicopter coming. Unfortunately, the squatters were close enough that they, too, heard the helicopter coming, and when it hovered near the ground for us to jump in, the mob started charging toward us. We climbed into the helicopter but I couldn't get the door shut.

"Just hold it shut!" the pilot yelled as we took off.

The mob was right there, swiping and grasping at us. I thought the blades of the helicopter were going to chop someone's head off! Thankfully, we all made it back to the main site safely, but needless to say, the project died after that.

The 12th hole at Fieldstone Golf Club in Wilmington, Delaware.

CHAPTER 114
PECAN PIE

CHRISTOPHER WILCZYNSKI

Wolfdancer Golf Club, in Lost Pines, Texas, offers a unique par-six hole, playing 603 yards.

Christopher Wilczynski, a Michigan State University landscape architecture graduate, is a senior design partner with Arthur Hills/Steve Forrest and Associates. He has worked on such courses as the Red Hawk Golf Club in East Tawas, Michigan; the Heritage Eagle Bend in Aurora, Colorado; the CrossCreek Golf Club in Temecula, California; the Heritage Ranch in Fairview, Texas; and the Black Golf Club in Yorba Linda, California.

I started working for Arthur Hills in 1987 as an intern. Over the years I have learned a lot from Art. He taught me to be very client oriented—making sure the client is getting what they want and getting a good value. Arthur taught me to be very business savvy.

Fresh out of college, all I had was my design school background. He shaped me and showed me how to make a design better, to make sure the contractors were turning a profit as well, and how to do it all with a smart business sense. He also showed me how to enjoy some of life's simple pleasures, too.

We were doing a course in San Antonio, Texas in 2001—adding nine holes to the Hyatt Hill Country Resort for our longtime client, Woodline Development. We were going to spend a day in San Antonio and then head to Austin the next day to start work on a new project there. We had dinner that night at a famous steakhouse, and we were all climbing into the car, headed to Austin, when Art turned around and ran back inside the restaurant.

We assumed he'd either forgotten something or was going to use the restroom before getting on the road. Whatever Art's reason, he ran back inside with such urgency, we didn't question it.

He returned a few minutes later with a gigantic pecan pie and four forks!

The next day in Austin, during our design meeting, we had our midmorning break. I went out to the car to grab some paperwork, and there was Art, eating the leftover pecan pie. I didn't bother asking for a bite!

Over the years I have learned a lot from Art. He taught me to be very client oriented—making sure the client is getting what they want and getting a good value.

CHAPTER 115
DANGER OR INTRIGUE?
INSPIRATION ON THE ROAD

KEN WILLIAMS

Catawba Island Club's 423-yard, par-four 8th hole, in Port Clinton, Ohio, near Lake Erie.

Ken Williams is a senior design associate with the acclaimed Toledo, Ohio–based golf architecture firm Arthur Hills/Steve Forrest and Associates. His previous work with MacCurrach Golf Construction included development of both the World Golf Village in St. Augustine, Florida and the Legends Course at LPGA International in Daytona Beach. His new courses with Arthur Hills include Bolingbrook Golf Club near Chicago; Catawba Island Club in Port Clinton, Ohio; Pheasant Run in Canton, Michigan; and renovations of the historic Bayshore Golf Club, now known as Miami Beach Golf Club.

Shortly before flying to Moscow for a construction visit, I received an email from the Russian project manager. I sometimes got requests from our clients, and this time he requested that I bring twenty pairs of sunglasses! The Russian operators had liked the pair that our American shaper wore. They were a cheap $9.99 pair from Wal-Mart, but those cheap sunglasses would have cost five times as much in Russia. Wal-Mart didn't stock twenty of any particular item at one store, so after visiting five northern Ohio Wal-Mart stores to find them, I called the project manager in Russia and told him I had twenty pairs of the particular sunglasses for him. While I had him on the phone, I inquired about the availability of a paint gun—a simple mechanism that allows someone to use inverted spray-paint cans to make markings on the ground. He told me that although they had the paint cans in Russia, the marking wands I wanted were extremely difficult to come by. He said I'd have to bring my own.

I began to consider the volume of foreign merchandise that I was going to attempt to take into Russia, so I thought it might be best to contact FedEx and ship the items. FedEx politely (and politically) informed me they do not encourage their customers to ship anything of value to Russia due to difficult customs practices and a high rate of customs theft. I was on my own.

So, carrying everything, I made my way though Moscow's Sheremetyevo International Airport trying very hard, like 007, not to look at the customs agents or act suspicious while carrying twenty pairs of sunglasses and a paint gun. Of course, a customs agent singled me out and insisted I put my bag through his X-ray machine.

"What is it you are you doing in the country?" the agent asked me.

Apparently, the thought of golf in Russia still befuddles some Russians, because when I answered him, he was distracted enough by our broken conversation and his attempt to determine whether I was a golf course architect, smuggler, or international spy that he neglected to actually look at the X-ray machine. After determining that I posed no threat to the Russian government, he let me continue on my way.

The most difficult thing about working in Russia, as it likely is in many economically emerging countries, is the scarcity of common conveniences, tools, and devices. For instance, we were marking the cart path routing with my smuggled paint gun, and I requested that wood stakes to be placed along the line that had been marked. The stakes would ensure that the route remained marked after our departure or following rain. The project manager said something in Russian to one of the workers who then promptly ran off into the woods with an axe. The worker returned a few minutes later with several birch saplings under his arm and proceeded to chop the saplings into twenty-inch sections, which became our marking stakes.

Returning from Moscow was not always easy. I was delayed in France at Charles de Gaulle Airport because the jet bridge would not work. After waiting thirty minutes on the plane, we were eventually herded onto a bus only to make a U-turn because the traffic controllers would not let us cross an interior airport traffic road. So with only maybe thirty minutes to catch my flight to Detroit once I finally reached a terminal, I began to run through the airport. I had decided to make the return trip home without wearing a belt in order to make my requisite passes through the metal detectors easier. This strategy to simplify my travel turned out to be a tactical error, as I discovered while running through the terminal. It is an understatement to say the food in Russia was not good, and, as such, I had dropped a few pounds—a slimming that was needed, but not timely, because as I ran through the airport, my ill-fitting, beltless pants were falling down to show Europe's second-busiest airport my particular brand of underwear!

Once I was finally aboard the plane and relaxing, my calm was interrupted by a chemically imbalanced twentysomething who decided to threaten to take down the plane by trying to open the emergency exit door! The misguided perpetrator (it is physically impossible to open an emergency door at that altitude) was quickly restrained, but the pilot's voice filled the cabin.

"We will be diverting the flight due to a security situation that cannot be ignored," he said.

My travel nightmare continued when I departed the plane in Detroit after spending almost thirteen hours, including the security-related delay, in a pressure-controlled tube. After presenting my passport, I stood in front of the immigration officer waiting to hear the sound of the passport being stamped and the words, "Welcome to the United States."

Instead, after he looked at my passport and itinerary, the conversation was intense.

"How long have you been out of the country?" the officer asked.

"One week."

"Sir, I am going to have to ask you to step over to lane thirty-six, the special inspection line."

Henceforth, every time I returned to the United States, my travel was delayed because I was sent to the special inspection lane. After the fifth special inspection, I figured it could not be a coincidence, so I asked the officer, "Why me?" It turned out that someone else by the name of Ken Williams had done something really bad, so the name was put on a watch list.

Apparently, the thought of golf in Russia still befuddles some Russians, because when I answered him, he was distracted enough by our broken conversation and his attempt to determine whether I was a golf course architect, smuggler, or international spy that he neglected to actually look at the X-ray machine.

CHAPTER 116
ODE TO ED SEAY

RAY WILTSE

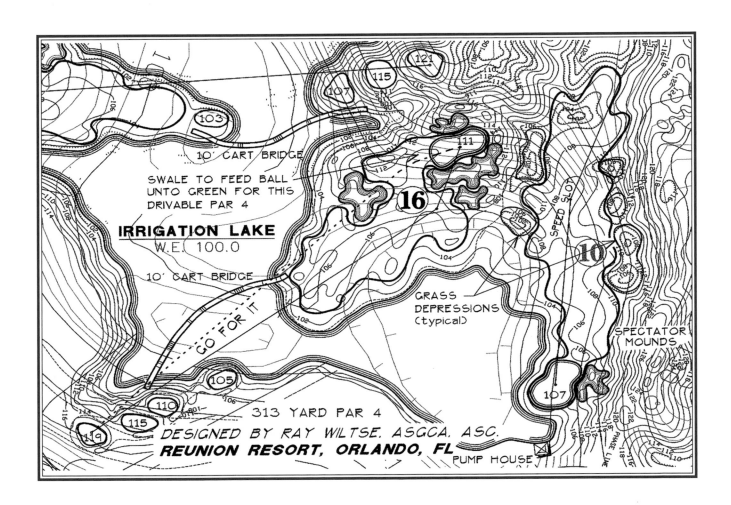

Ray Wiltse's experience includes more than seventy-five golf course projects worldwide, and traces his golf course architecture exposure back to his grandfather Duncan McLean, who was from Scotland and was a student of golf history. After a fifteen-year career with Arnold Palmer Design Company, Wiltse now heads the Wiltse Golf Design Group, based in Ponte Vedra Beach, Florida. Projects over the years have included destination resorts, equestrian facilities, eco-trails, marinas, golf academies, short game areas, beach parks, executive courses, and championship courses, including, in Michigan, Kings Challenge in Cedar and Ravines Golf Club in Saugatuck. His work also includes Belmont Country Club in Leesburg, Virginia; King's Walk in Grand Forks, North Dakota; and Orlando's Reunion Resort.

When I worked for Arnold Palmer Design as a project architect, I received a phone call early one autumn day from a client requesting a site inspection of the course we had designed, which was under construction. The course was King's Challege on Lake Michigan, near Traverse City.

The client asked that I bring Ed Seay, who was Mr. Palmer's partner and a past president of the American Society of Golf Course Architects. The client had the entire construction crew working for the previous two days putting lime in all the bunkers to simulate sand. This is a helpful technique used to get a good look at how the bunkers, when they are finished, will look to the golfer.

While Ed and I were flying up to Michigan, a lake-effect snowstorm hit the site. By the time we reached the site, the course looked like a ski resort.

As we walked the snowy course, the owner seemed very nervous, but Ed didn't say a word. As we were leaving the course, though, Ed turned to the owner and said, "Next time use green paint in the bunkers!"

While Ed and I were flying up to Michigan, a lake-effect snowstorm hit the site. By the time we reached the site, the course looked like a ski resort.

CHAPTER 117
HACHI! A JAPANESE
COWBOY IN ARIZONA

SHANE WITCOMBE

Shane Witcombe is a design associate with Greg Norman Golf Course Design. First established in 1987, Greg Norman Golf Course Design is headquartered in Jupiter, Florida, with sister facilities and personnel in Sydney, and has opened sixty-one courses worldwide with an additional sixty projects in various stages of development. Witcombe has designed Surprise, Arizona courses Desert Springs Golf Club and the north and south courses at Granite Falls. He's also created the White Wing Golf Club in Georgetown, Texas, and the Lincoln Hills Club, in Lincoln, California.

I was able to let golf foster a new friendship a few years ago in Phoenix while working for fellow ASGCA member Greg Nash. Greg had an opportunity to co-design a golf course in the Philippines with Japanese golf designer Shiro Tashiro. Mr. Tashiro was excited to learn about our target-style golf courses of the desert Southwest, so he booked a trip to Phoenix with his translator.

The first day of his trip was spent in our office going over the new project. Shiro was excited to look through our plans. Although he spoke almost no English, he would inquisitively ask, "Green?" or "Trap?" followed by, "Oooooh!" and the snap of his camera.

He soon proudly displayed a set of his grading plans, which gave us a chance to learn more of his ornamental style of design. Most of the meeting, however, was spent with the interpreter relating how badly Shiro wanted to play golf!

The day after our meeting, Shiro and I took off for Los Caballeros Golf Club in Wickenburg. I anticipated a rather quiet trip to the golf course considering our language barrier; I was wrong. Shiro laughed and giggled and snapped photos the entire way, even after we started our round.

At the sixteenth hole we had to pause briefly to let a dozen horseback riders play through, because the golf course is part of a resort and ranch where the guests, wearing cowboy hats, bandanas, and chaps, ride the desert trails adjacent to and through the golf course. Shiro couldn't believe his eyes.

"Cowboys?! Cowboys?!" he yelled, raising his hands with mock six-shooters firing air bullets into the sky. He grabbed his camera and took off down the hill to take photos.

That was by far one of my most enlightening days on the golf course. The game of golf certainly shatters the language barrier. We were able to communicate through our passion for the game and our thirst for discovery. I truly treasure the friendship that was formed that day on the course.

CHAPTER 118
WHEN NATURE CALLED

BRIAN YODER

Brian Yoder grew up playing the the Inverness Club, the historic Donald Ross course in Toledo, Ohio. He attended Ohio State University. He was nearing graduation with a degree in turfgrass management when he decided that there were just too many hurdles to overcome as a golf course superintendent, such as members, committees and Mother Nature. He decided to go back to school earn a degree in landscape architecture after conversations with Tom and George Fazio. Yoder began working for Arthur Hills in 1990, and has collaborated on Bay Harbor Golf Club near Petoskey, Michigan; Longaberger Golf Club in Hanover, Ohio; The Creek Course at Fiddler's Creek in Naples, Florida; Chaska Town Course in Chaska, Minnesota; and Palencia in St. Augustine.

My day began as usual with my early-morning departure from my Mexican hotel. I made my way down to the beach to board the fishing boat that took me across the beautiful Bay of La Paz to our sandy, dune-laden golf site on El Magote.

Considering our golf course site was typically dry as a bone 364 days out of the year, one tended to get quite thirsty walking around in the desert-like conditions. So when I finished my daylong site visit I boarded my Panga and returned to the mainland.

Later that night, I got cleaned up and met one of my amigos at a local cantina for dinner and drinks: freshly caught fish and mucho bottles of cold cervezas.

After dinner we decided to drop by one of the local bars located behind the Malecón strip to continue our thirst-quenching venture. We threw back a few more cervezas and, when it was time to head back to my hotel, the most bizarre day of my life started!

I was walking back to my hotel just after midnight when I decided to cut through the vacant lot of an old building being prepped for demolition. After all the beers, nature called, rather insistently. I looked around and didn't see anyone so I relieved myself. But just as I finished, I noticed a figure approaching me and yelling something in Spanish. Fearing the worst, I started running toward my hotel.

Looking back, out of the corner of my eye I saw that the figure was a man in a dark cap, khaki pants,

boots, and a white shirt with the word "Policía" emblazoned on it. I felt it prudent, out of respect for the law, to stop running and see what the police officer wanted.

The cop approached me and then grabbed me by the back of my belt. He pulled me by my britches back toward the scene of the crime. While the policeman did this, I became scared to death that he was going to arrest me and haul me off to a Mexican jail! I was having flashbacks of the old movie *Midnight Express*, in which an American was thrown in prison for years.

When we reached the wall of the old building, he pointed at the puddle, and I acknowledged that the wet spot was mine.

I was just about sure he was going to take me to jail ... until he asked me to give him money. In my naiveté, I hadn't realized that bribery in Mexico was the norm.

"How much?" I asked him.

"Two hundred pesos," he answered.

Since that was roughly twenty U.S. dollars, I told the policeman I didn't have any cash on me, but explained that I could go to the ATM machine at the bank, which was only a couple of blocks from the old building.

He escorted me to the bank, still by the seat of my pants, and we both entered the small ATM area connected to the main lobby entrance of the bank. I inserted my debit card and entered my PIN number to start the transaction, but the officer reached around me and pushed the cancellation button.

"What are you doing?" I asked.

He only pointed to the keypad and nodded for me to continue.

I reentered the card and, as I typed in my PIN number. He let me continue this time, and two hundred pesos came out of the ATM machine. I gladly turned over the money to him. To me, the equivalent of $20 was well worth it to avoid jail and make the officer go away.

But he didn't go away.

"Do you have any drugs?" he asked me.

"No! No drugs."

"Drugs?"

"No drugs," I insisted.

The policeman then pushed me up against a car and motioned for me to assume the position. He then started going through all my pockets, examined my cell phone, looked inside my shoes, and finally rifled through my wallet! At last, he handed everything back to me and motioned for me to move along.

I felt very lucky that I was able to pay this guy off for only twenty bucks and that he didn't throw me in the jail.

Later that morning there was a knock on my hotel room door.

Standing in the corridor was a man wearing a hotel shirt. He was holding my debit card.

"Are you Brian Yoder?"

I nodded.

"This card was found on the street in front of the hotel," he said, and handed me the debit card.

The last time I'd seen my card was when I used it to pay off the cop. I was sure I remembered sticking it back in my wallet.

I thanked the hotel man for returning the card. Finally, some good luck.

I closed the door and got dressed for my site visit. I packed up all my belongings and headed back to the site.

After the site visit I was getting ready to depart La Paz and drive to Cabo and catch a flight back to the U.S. I figured I'd better get some cash for the road, so I went back to the bank to withdraw some travel money. I inserted my card, entered my PIN, and requested a small amount, but was denied. I tried it several more times but had the same result: denied, denied, denied. I immediately called my credit card company to find out what the problem was.

"Mr. Yoder, you're over your limit on cash withdrawals," the customer service representative told me. "My computer shows you used your card ten times between one o'clock and three o'clock a.m. The exact total you withdrew was $2,617.35."

I called my friends at the real estate office immediately, and they contacted their friends at the Justice Department and related my story. The Justice Department officials told my amigos to have me write down exactly what happened and to send it to them when I got back to the states. My amigos then lent me enough cash to get home. I was very grateful for that.

When I got back home I was on the phone for hours and hours with my credit card company and my bank explaining to their fraud departments what had happened.

I went round and round between my bank and the credit card company for a solid month before we figured out that it was the bank's responsibility. It came down to the fact that it was indeed bank fraud and that there was no way the bank should have allowed more than $300 to be withdrawn in a twenty-four-hour period. I was covered! Thank God!

The bank sent me ten separate claim forms, one for each withdrawal. I filled out each form and attached my signed Spanish affidavit from the La Paz Policía. I mailed them all in to the bank's fraud department for their review and on December fifteenth or thereabouts, the bank sent me a letter saying they would cover it and the monies would be redeposited back into my account.

I am still working on our golf course project in La Paz and frequently go down the same street where my "crime" took place. The funny thing is, the building I peed on has since been razed, all except for the historical exterior façade, which was saved!

Bay Harbor Golf Club's Quarry holes were cut through a former industrial site in Petoskey, Michigan. The 495-yard, par-five 5th hole is in the center of a quarry.

ACKNOWLEDGMENTS

Steve Forrest, ASGCA *for coming up with the idea for this book and introducing me to ASGCA and its members*

Don Knott, ASGCA chairman of the ASGCA Foundation, *who embraced the concept and approved funding for the writing and editing of the book*

Greg Muirhead, ASGCA; Bruce Charlton, ASGCA; Doug Carrick, ASGCA, and Erik Larsen, ASGCA, of the ASGCA Executive Committee *for approval and support of this project*

Chad Ritterbusch, Aileen Smith, and Therese Swenson, ASGCA staff

Jennifer Semetko and Paul Keehn

All ASGCA members *who allowed me to probe their memories and come up with the great stories that make up this book, and who submitted their photographs and drawings to enhance those stories*

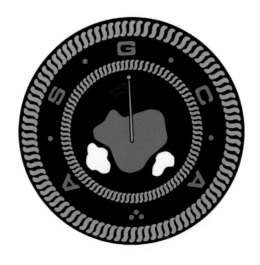

ABOUT THE AUTHOR

Michael Patrick Shiels is an American radio personality and author. He is the host of *Michigan's Big Show* and is also known for authoring books with Donald Trump, Larry King, Arthur Hills, and Ben Wright. Shiels has written for newspapers and magazines on golf and travel. His articles have appeared in publications including *PGA Magazine*, *Travel + Leisure Golf*, *Golf magazine*, and *DeltaVacations*.

Michael Patrick Shiels interviews Arnold Palmer
at the 2008 Senior Skins Game on Maui.

ABOUT ASGCA

When the American Society of Golf Course Architect's (ASGCA) then-president Steve Forrest, ASGCA, announced at the group's sixty-first Annual Meeting in Atlanta that he hoped to shepherd through a book of stories of each member's most memorable day, he almost immediately listened to a dozen or so candidates for inclusion. ASGCA members love a great story and enjoy nothing more than gathering at the Annual Meeting and swapping the latest yarns.

But, the group is much more than a bunch of convivial storytellers. It's a professional membership association made up of the most qualified, experienced golf course architects in the world. From its beginning in 1947 when fourteen golf course architects—including Donald Ross and Robert Trent Jones—held their first meeting in Pinehurst, North Carolina, ASGCA has sought to raise awareness of the profession and advance new design concepts and construction techniques by gathering and sharing ideas. Each member has designed and brought to opening at least five eighteen-hole equivalents, though most average in the dozens of layouts. The application process is detailed, peer-reviewed, and typically takes two years to complete, resulting in members with the most respected professional standing.

Today, ASGCA is one of the members of the Allied Associations of Golf, which is dedicated to growing and preserving the game worldwide.

—Bruce Charlton, ASGCA
2008-2009 President,
American Society of Golf Course Architects

The Founding Fathers of ASGCA, 1947.

American Society of Golf Course Architects
125 N. Executive Drive, Suite 106
Brookfield, WI 53005

(262) 786–5960 • www.asgca.org